DEPRIVATION, ITS SOCIAL ROOTS AND PSYCHOLOGICAL CONSEQUENCES

DURGANAND SINHA (M.Sc., Cambridge University) is Professor and Head of the Department of Psychology, and Chairman of the U.G.C. Centre of Special Assistance, Allahabad University. He is the author of six books including *Indian Villages in Transition, Motivation and Rural Development, Academic Achievers and Non-Achievers,* and *The Mughal Syndrome*.

RAMA CHARAN TRIPATHI (Ph.D., University of Michigan) is Professor at the Department of Psychology, Allahabad University. He is the author of *Environment and Structure of Organizations*.

GIRISHWAR MISRA (Ph.D., University of Gorakhpur) is Reader at the Department of Psychology, Allahabad University. He has co-authored *Psychological consequences of Prolonged Deprivation* with Professor L.B. Tripathi.

DEPRIVATION

Its Social Roots
and
Psychological Consequences

Edited by

DURGANAND SINHA
R.C. TRIPATHI
GIRISHWAR MISRA

CONCEPT PUBLISHING COMPANY, NEW DELHI-110 059

First published in 1982 with the grant from the UGC Centre for Speciaı Assistance, Department of Psychology, Allahabad University.

ISBN 81-7022-162-5

First Published 1982

First Reprint 1995

Published and Printed by
Ashok K. Mittal
Concept Publishing Company
A/15-16, Commercial Block, Mohan Garden
New Delhi-110 059 (India)

PREFACE

Socio-psychological and economic disadvantage has emerged as a focal theme in recent years for Western social scientists. The conceptualisation of deprivation and the study of its socio-psychological consequences have not been systematically attempted in our Indian social context where widespread poverty and socio-cultural inequalities are rampant. The Department of Psychology, Allahabad University, under the auspices of the U.G.C. Centre for Special Assistance on Psychological Studies of Social Change and National Development organized a symposium from November 20—22, 1977 focusing on the problems attendant upon conceptualisation and measurement of deprivation, studies on its socio-psychological correlates and intervention strategies for combating the disadvantages. Eminent psychologists, sociologists and political scientists contributed papers to this interdisciplinary symposium. The present volume constitutes a selection of some 12 papers presented during the symposium and 2 supplemented to it later on.

The book is divided into three sections. The first section comprises papers on problems of conceptualisation and measurement, the second on studies on socio-psychological consequences of deprivation, and the last one on intervention strategies. It is hoped that this publication would serve the need of social scientists interested in the area of deprivation studies and stimulate further studies in the Indian socio-cultural context.

The holding of the symposium was made possible by the generous grant made available to this Department by the U.G.C. This publication has also been possible with the grant available to the Department under the U.G.C. Special Assistance Scheme.

Many individuals have contributed to the preparation

of this manuscript. There are too many to be mentioned individually. However, the assistance rendered by Yoganand Sinha, Lydia Anthony, Anjali Singh, Ambalika Kashyap, B.K. Tiwari, R.P. Singh, and Anjali Srivastava is gratefully acknowledged. M.Y. Siddiqui, Stenographer in the Department and A.K. Srivastava deserve special thanks for the patience with which they prepared drafts and the final copy of the manuscript. Rajendra Kumar, our office-head looked after the production of the manuscript. The Department is particularly beholden to the contributors and participants of the symposium without whose cooperation this publication would not have been possible.

Department of Psychology
University of Allahabad
Allahabad-211002.

DURGANAND SINHA
R.C. TRIPATHI
GIRISHWAR MISRA

1 August 1981

CONTENTS

LIST OF CONTRIBUTORS

S. Anandalakshmy
Department of Child Development, Lady Irwin College, New Delhi

E. Annamalai
Central Institute of Indian Languages, Manas Gangotri, Mysore

B.B. Chatterjee
Psychology Department, Utkal University, Bhubaneshwar, Orissa

J.P. Das
Centre for the Study of Mental Retardation, University of Alberta, Edmonton, Canada

Girishwar Misra
Psychology Department, Allahabad University, Allahabad, U.P.

Namita Pande
Psychology Department, Allahabad University, Allahabad, U.P.

Radhanath Rath
Psychology Department, Utkal University, Bhubaneshwar, Orissa

Ramashray Roy
Centre for the Study of Developing Societies, Delhi

Shantilata Sahu
Psychology Department, Utkal University, Bhubaneshwar, Orissa

Durganand Sinha
Psychology Department, Allahabad University, Allahabad, U.P.

Priyani Soysa
Faculty of Medicine, University of Sri Lanka, Colombo, Sri Lanka

L.B. Tripathi
Psychology Department, Gorakhpur University, Gorakhpur, U.P.

R.C. Tripathi
Psychology Department, Allahabad University, Allahabad, U.P.

LIST OF TABLES

SECTION ONE

CONCEPT AND MEASUREMENT OF DEPRIVATION

INTRODUCTION

STUDIES that are being conducted currently on psychological impact of deprivation have their roots in three interrelated areas, viz., animal studies on learning and motivation, researches on children reared in 'restricted' environment, either in geographically remote and isolated areas or in non-stimulating environment of institutionalized children, and sensory deprivation researches. Taking cues from these studies, there has, of late, been an upsurge of interest in analyzing the psychological consequences of socio-cultural and economic disadvantages. It reflects a growing concern of our society in the problem of socio-cultural and economic inequalities and the strains produced by the same. An overview of contemporary psychological literature on deprivation reveals that the problem of deprivation is being approached from divergent theoretical angles with different strategies used for its measurement.

The papers in this section deal with the problems involved in conceptualisation and measurement of deprivation. They bring together diverse viewpoints that are reflected in different studies.

Ramashray Roy, a political scientist, deals with the intricacies involved in studying poverty and inadequacies of unidimensional definitions. Reviewing various accounts of poverty, he suggests a more pragmatic approach which involves combining both individual and socio-institutional properties that create conditions that perpetuate poverty.

R.C. Tripathi discusses how conceptual confusion in this area has emerged. Deprivation studies not only imply categorization of some marginal groups, but also conceptualization of deprivation environment.

Durganand Sinha is highly critical of the artificiality of a lot of studies in psychology which have taken the individual or the environment in isolation and emphasizes the need for studying the "entire individual-environment complex". For the purpose, he suggests an ecological model of deprivation and discusses its relevance for devising interventions.

Anandalakshmy sounds a warning against importing concepts of deprivation based on studies made in other cultures and generalizing from findings of studies conducted in industrial-technological societies of the West. She makes a plea for defining deprivation in ecological terms, points to a number of pitfalls in studying the deprived groups and suggests some methodological tips. She also presents a taxonomic model for conceptualizing deprivation variables.

L.B. Tripathi identifies certain significant methodological problems which have to be tackled in order to make deprivation studies scientifically sound and functionally meaningful. He examines various ways of categories and quantifying deprivation and discusses problems involved in macrocosmic and microcosmic approaches. While he accepts the utility of macro variables, he argues that measurement of the extent of deprivation at the individual level is essential.

A number of studies have taken somewhat uncritically certain indices of socio-economic status (SES), for characterizing deprivation, and have tried to establish their relationship with various measures of performance. Frequently a kind of monotonic and linear relationship with SES and psychological and other variables is taken for granted. Chatterjee questions this assumption and points to the possibility of non-monotonicity of relationships. Reviewing studies over a decade (1965-74), he examines the evidence for monotonicity or non-monotonicity between SES and performance measures.

The papers taken together highlight conceptual issues and intricate problems of measurement in psychological studies of deprivation in the controlled environment of the laboratory and in complex natural settings.

ONE

Ramashray Roy

THE MEANING AND MEASUREMENT OF POVERTY

OF LATE, academic interest in the study of poverty has increased sharply. This is no doubt due to the persistence of poverty despite planned developmental efforts of the last twenty five years, on the one hand, and the insufficiency of purely economic perspective in illuminating the phenomenon of poverty, on the other. The recognition that poverty is multifaceted has drawn scholars from several disciplines to examine and analyze the nature of poverty and suggest ameliorative measures.

While this is welcome, the determination of what constitutes poverty and what are its causes and consequences remains extremely uncertain. Three main factors account for this. First, a unidimensional measurement of poverty misses several factors that have an important bearing on the phenomenon of poverty. Second, once the definitional range of poverty is expanded, the confusion between causes of poverty and its consequences is likely to be accentuated. And, finally, the relativity of the concept of poverty itself makes the investigation of what constitutes poverty a difficult exercise.

As a result of these difficulties, it is not always possible to assess the relevance of intervention for reducing or eliminating poverty. If poverty is defined unidimensionally, the inadequacy of intervention becomes easily apparent. If the definition is expanded to include broad, open categories, it becomes difficult to separate cause from problem and problem from solution. It is true that the recognition of poverty as a complex, multi-dimensional phenomenon "serves to emphasize, for example, the self-perpetuating nature of the phenomenon and the enormity of the difficulties in the study of human problems. But, by the same token, one is not altered to those strategic pressure points which offer a means for development and a chance for effective intervention." (Schwarzweller, 1969, p. 18).

It is therefore necessary to avoid these pitfalls in the study of poverty. The purpose of this paper is to examine these difficulties and suggest an approach that can prove more helpful in conceptualizing the phenomenon of poverty in a useful way.

It is very common to define poverty as a unidimensional property. As Wilbur (1973) notes, "... for practical purposes it is easy and convenient to use an indicator, like income, as a criterion and to define poverty in terms of those who are below or above specific threshold..." (p. 6.). Having restricted poverty to those with low incomes, a multiple of correlates, such as, housing, education, employment, health, fertility, mortality, etc., are assembled. Here again it is not clear whether these factors are correlates or consequences of poverty. It is also not clear whether these factors should form a part of the definition of poverty or not. If they are a part of the definition, then the positing of the idea of correlates or consequences is redundant. Even the programme note on poverty and unemployment of the ICSSR has chosen to be silent on this point.

Apart from this, there are other difficulties. Poverty can be identified in one of the two ways. First, one could devise some objective criteria of ordering various groups of the population in a particular geographical area on the continuum of affluence-poverty and determine the pattern of the distribution of societal wealth. However, such a determination in itself will not help in ascertaining what is poverty. It can only suggest the extent to which inequality characterizes the distribution of wealth in a particular society. Even if some central tendency of such a distribution is taken as a cut-off point and we treat all those below it as poor, the problem remains intractable. It is not, on this basis alone, possible to answer the question, why should one treat all those below that cut-off point as poor.

One could also begin with a definition of what constitutes a "good life" and suggest what material resources are necessary for sustaining such a life. This, however, raises insoluble philosophical tangles pertaining to the role of material well-being in happiness, contentment, etc. Particularly, in the context of some societies or outlooks that put much store in abstinence and non-acquisition of material wealth, the determination of the nature of poverty will be virtually impossible.

Second, there is the subjective aspect of the definition of poverty. This refers to the subjective comparison by different individuals and groups with respect to their location in social space relative to others. Since it is subjective, such a comparison has neither a fixed boundary nor a determinate standard. It is, therefore, not possible to make this subjective comparison a basis for objective determination of the phenomenon of poverty even though this implies comparison and provides rationale and impetus for political action.

One could, however, try to skirt these problems by simply arguing that, above all philosophical tangles and subjective variability, there is the simple fact that there are minimum requirements in terms of food, housing, medical care, education, etc., that are necessary for subsistence, if not for a comfortable life. Proceeding on this basis one could possibly develop measures to arrive at a reasonable definition of poverty. While such a procedure will seemingly be objective, in fact, it offers no solution to the difficulty of defining poverty. An objective measure of poverty is possible only when the components constituting the domain of poverty are invariant over time and space. Even the so-called "objectively derived" norm of 2400 calories for maintaining good and active body encounters some difficulty. Experience shows that variations in food habits, which form as a result of adaptation to ecological constraints, are so diverse that they seldom conform to this seemingly objective criterion and yet provide enough sustenance to a large number of the working population.

The concept of the level of subsistence is no doubt helpful in identifying those who are destitute. However, implicit in this concept is the assumption that there are objective criteria on the basis of which one ascertains what is necessary. The consideration of what is necessary is not so much a matter of objective assessment as of social conventions. ". . . What is deemed 'necessary', once sheer physical survival is assured, is a matter of convention, not of principle; and conventions are socially formed" (Coates & Silburn, 1970, p. 24).

The determination of need and, therefore, of poverty is thus socially influenced. As Galbraith observes :

> . . . people are poverty-striken when their income, even if it is adequate for survival, falls markedly below that of the community. Then they cannot have what the larger community regards as the minimum necessary for decency; and they cannot wholly escape, therefore, the judgement of the larger community that they are indecent. They are degraded, for, in the literal sense, they live outside the grades or categories which the community regards as acceptable.

Thus the determination of poverty on the basis of some objectively ascertained level of subsistence misses an important point. As Coates and Silburn (1970) emphasize, "there is some easily discovered, absolute and apparently universal, line below which there is poverty and above which there is not, is fundamentally to misunderstand the problem" (p. 22). It is particularly morally indefensible in a society where inequality in the distribution of societal wealth is enormous, and which allows abject poverty in the midst of plenty. The only tenable absolute standard is an optimum one based upon the maximum social achievement. "Placed in this context, the stringently calculated subsistence level poverty line is seen to be an aberration on the part of those whose yearning for precision and parsimony exceeds not only their common humanity, but also their desire for sociological sophistication" (Coates and Silburn, 1970, p. 28).

That beyond the subsistence level, there is another poverty has been long recognized. As Marx (1946) observed long ago :

> A noticeable increase in wages presupposes a rapid growth of productive capital. The rapid growth of productive capital brings about an equally rapid growth of wealth, luxury, social needs, social enjoyments. Thus, in comparison with the needs of development of society in general although the enjoyments of the worker have risen, the social satisfaction that they give has fallen in comparison with the increased enjoyments of the capitalists which are

> inaccessible to the worker. Our needs and enjoyments spring from society and not by the objects of their satisfaction. Because they are of social nature, they are of a relative nature (pp. 268-269).

The implications of what Marx says are several. First, the conception of poverty in a stabilized (stagnant ?) economy will be different from the one in a developing economy. This is true of both time and space differences. If a country happens to be developing fast economically, it is reflected in the rising levels of income. This in turn, changes the dimensions of poverty. Or, alternatively, when a backward economy begins to develop economically increasing monetization enhances the range and the reach of market economy incorporating in the process even those communities which previously may have been economically self-contained. The dependence of these communities on the larger market forces and their need to earn an income to satisfy their changed consumption needs may radically change the meaning and structure of poverty. Similarly, the concept of poverty, say, in the United States and India will differ.

Second, there is also the fact that there are different degrees of poverty. Such related concepts as indigence, penury, and destitution connote variable degrees of poverty. Starvation, death from exposure, and loss of life due to some other total lack of resources are the only absolute forms of poverty. Beyond these, there are variable degrees of poverty. The various kinds of differences in the meaning and structure of poverty emanate, as Valentine (1970) points out, from

> the total amounts of consumable resources available in relation to the population, the distribution of control over resources within the social structure, the proportion of society's membership whose level of disposable resources stands below such standards and the degree of contrast in welfare between higher and lower social strata (p. 13).

Beyond the phenomenon of absolute poverty, there is the fact of relative poverty. The customary dichotomy of the poor and the non-poor is an oversimplification that distorts reality. It is a continuum, each point of which denotes poverty or affluence in relation to the other. Thus, poverty is a comparative concept that refers to a relative quality. To quote Valentine (1970) again :

> As a quality, however, the condition of being poor does have a central significance. The essence of poverty is inequality. In slightly different words, the basic meaning of poverty is relative deprivation. The poor are deprived in comparison with the comfortable, the affluent and the opulent.

Third, following Valentine, the primary meaning of poverty can be stated to be a "condition of being in want of something that is needed, or generally recognized as having value." (p. 12). This definition recognizes that the value system prevailing in a society has a great bearing on what is desired. Since value system itself is the product of the interplay between technology, production system and consciousness, it follows that the nature of value system will be different in different societies. This is so because societies differ in their resource endowment, the kind of technology used to exploit and transform their natural resources and the institutional mechanisms evolved to operate the production system and regulate distribution. Because of the differential configuration of all these factors the level of poverty will vary from society to society and therefore, its definition too. Recognizing the relativity of poverty and the impingement of societal values on the sense of relative deprivation, Straus defines poverty as "deprivation of those minimal levels of health, housing, food, education, and recreation compatible with the contemporary technology, beliefs, and values of a particular society in a specific locality" (Straus, 1969, p. 7).

Apart from these difficulties, there is also the question of the self-perpetuating properties of poverty. Broadly speaking, two explanations of the phenomenon of poverty can be identified. The first explanation, as propounded and popularized by Oscar Lewis, pertains to the concept of the culture of poverty. The culture of poverty, as Lewis argues, is not merely a matter of deprivation or disorganization, but is something positive with its own rewards. According to Lewis (1966),

> The culture of poverty is both an adaptation and a reaction of the poor to their marginal position in a class-stratified, highly individualized, capitalist society. It represents an effort to cope with feelings of hopelessness and despair which develop from the realization of the improbability of achieving success in terms of the values and goals of the larger society, (p. 34).

Through its impact on children, the culture of poverty tends to be self-perpetuating. In Lewis' account, those who live by the "culture of poverty" are pictured as removed and alienated, ignorant and uninterested, uninvolved and apathetic towards dimensions, such as, interest in politics, class consciousness, ethnic and national identification, of the wider world. In his words, "The lack of effective participation and integration in the major institutions of the larger society is one of the crucial characteristics of the culture of poverty." He notes further that "people with a culture of poverty are provincial and locally oriented . . . they know only their own troubles, their local conditions, their own neighbourhood . . . usually they do not have the knowledge, the vision or the ideology to see the similarities between their problems and those of their counterparts elsewhere—they are not class conscious" (pp. 37-38).

Another explanation of poverty is contained in the "cycle of poverty theory". It posits the notion of predestination of certain people to a life of (economic) poverty. The idea seems to be that one inherits poverty through his colour, caste, his socio-economic status, or the occupation of his parents. While there is little systematic explanation of this concept, there seems to be a general agreement that social status is associated with certain level of income, education, family structure, and community reputation. These become a part of the vicious circle in which each factor acts on the other to perpetuate the social structure and the individual family's position. The cycle argument holds that disadvantages are cumulative.

No doubt, both these explanations are partly true. However, both of them fail in providing adequate explanation of the phenomenon of poverty. The culture of poverty, as a sub-set of the larger culture, provides human beings with a design of living with a ready-made set of solutions for human problems. This view fails to recognize that the distinctive patterns of social life at the lowest income levels are determined by structural conditions of the larger society beyond the control of low-income people, not by socialization in primary groups committed to a separate cultural design. It is simply not true to say that the poverty sub-culture is self generating in the double sense that socialization perpetuates both the cultural patterns of the group and consequent individual psychological inadequacies blocking escape from poverty. The escape from poverty is much more dependent on the degree to which the poor people have access to societal resources. There is much truth in the suggestion that the dis-advantaged position of the poor is maintained primarily by the behaviour of the higher strata, acting in their own interest as they see it, to preserve their advantages by preventing a redistribution of resources.

A similar criticism can be made of the vicious circle theory. What is important is not so much the location of an individual in socio-economic space, although incapabilities associated with low socio-economic status do block access to various societal resources. Much more important in this regard are the various institutional mechanisms that help individuals in lower socio-economic groups to overcome these incapabilities and facilitate the opening up of the channels of their upward status mobility. It is at this point that the larger social structural factors come into play to deny the poor the capacity to overcome their incapabilities and block their mobility

The proponents of the culture of poverty seem to imply that some indicators or correlates of poverty, such as unemployment, underemployment, unskilled work, low status occupations, meagre wages, lack of education, crowded living quarters and deteriorated housing, etc., can be understood as parts of a "design for living", "handed on from generation to generation" through socialization. But the question is: Are these indicators or correlates better understood as problems or as solutions for problems? Lewis, together with the expositors of lower-class sub-culture, seem to believe that these are the lower class cultural solutions to the basic bio-economic problem of survival. It can, however, be argued that lack of work, lack of income and the rest pose conditions to which the poor must adapt through whatever socio-cultural resources they control. That is, these conditions are the phenomena of the environment in which the poor live, determined not so much by behaviour and values of the poor as by the structure of the total social system. It may also be suggested that this larger structure is perpetuated primarily by the economic and political actions of the non-poor.

It is thus clear that the self-perpetuating property of poverty is the function exclusively of neither the culture of poverty nor of the cycle of poverty. It is true that the accident of birth in lower socio-economic groups incapacitates the poor from taking advantage of various opportunities of status mobility. It may also be true that their location in lower socio-economic space instils in them an outlook of despair and resignation, breeds in them feelings of incompetence and marginality, makes them incapable of participating in the activities of the larger society, and inclines them to violence. As such, there can be no doubt that living in poverty has its own destructive effects on human capacities and that these impairments become part of the whole process perpetuating deprivation. However, the origin of poverty is rooted much more in the unequal distribution of societal resources and the continuance of this inequality is associated with social structural factors.

We have so far sketched some of the difficulties associated with the definition of poverty. As has been pointed out, a unidimensional or a single factor definition of poverty is inadequate. Similarly, to define poverty in terms of subsistence level is also problematic since it fails tc take into account the relative aspects of poverty. When the definitional range is enlarged to accommodate values, cultures and structures, the likelihood of confusion between cause and problem, on the one hand, and problem and consequences, on the other, enhances.

The definitions advanced by Valentine (1970) and Straus (1969) incorporate value aspects that refer to a socially determined frame of reference within which the phenomenon of poverty acquires meaning. However, such definitions, as Schwarzweller (1969) argues, deal only with culturally defined goals and avoid any mention of culturally defined or normatively sanctioned means.

> Poverty . (can be) shown to be more a problem steaming from inadequate, insufficient means (for example, social, cultural, and psycnological advantages) than from unsatisfied ends. Indeed, one might argue very convincingly that poverty is the inability of an individual or family to manipulate the external environment; the consequences of such a "poverty" are a high probability of incidents of culturally defined misfortunes and, likewise, a high probability of failure to achieve access to culturally defined goals.

In view of these difficulties, it is desirable to reformulate the definition in such a way that permits meaningful investigation. Poverty has both the absolute and the relative aspects. As an absolute category, it is rooted in a particular society's resources and their distribution. While it is possible to define the minima required to live a tolerable life, this does not help us in capturing the relative aspects of poverty. The relative aspect is associated with the prevailing pattern of the distribution of societal resources which differs from one society to the next. As such the definition of poverty in its relative aspect must be grounded in the conditions obtaining in a particular society. This calls not for a very rigid definition of poverty but for fixing the parameters which would permit a meaningful investigation into the phenomenon of poverty. Thus, the function of definition as related to the phenomenon of poverty is not to identify in absolute terms the precise components of poverty but to yield a formulation that makes investigation possible. In view of these considerations, poverty can be defined as a relative lack of or inaccessibility to resources and/or inability to utilize resources to achieve what is needed or desired.

Defined in this way the phenomenon of poverty is linked together with the causes that produce poverty, the phenomenon of poverty itself, the value and structural framework of society and the consequences of poverty. As such, poverty becomes something more than a concept. Following Wilbur (1973), it is desirable to conceive of poverty not as a concept but as a system, an abstract, a construct possessing multiple properties. As a construct, it is invulnerable to measurement; however, it can be identified through its properties which are capable of measurement. This requires the specification of the properties through which the domain of poverty is to be measured.

As is apparent from the discussion above, a fruitful approach to the study of poverty must combine investigations of both individual-relevant and social-institutional-specific properties that together create conditions which perpetuate poverty. The problem of poverty is more than the problem of access of individuals and families to certain resources as well as their ability. Access and ability themselves are influenced and determined by larger societal forces that enter into the exploitation of resources and the distribution of wealth. As such, social-institutional characteristics are as much, if not more, important as individual-relevant characteristics. It is, therefore, necessary to delineate, both at the individual and societal level, the resources available, pattern of their mobilization and poverty, properties that emanate from inability to mobilize these resources. Only then poverty can be measured and analyzed.

REFERENCES

Coates, K., & Silburn, R. *Poverty : The forgotten Englishman.* Harmondsworth : Penguin Books, 1970

Galbraith, J.K. *The affluent society.* Harmondsworth : Penguin Books, 1962.

Lewis, O. *La Vida : Puerto Rican family in the culture of poverty.* New York : Random House, 1966.

Marx, K. *Selected works.* London : Lawrence and Wishart, 1942, (vol. 1), 268-269.

Schwarzweller, H.K. 'Comment' In T. Weaver, & A. Magid, (Eds.) *Poverty : New interdiscriplinary perspectives.* San Fransisco : Chandler Publishing Co., 1969.

Straus, R. The problem of conceptualizing poverty. In T. Weaver, & A. Magid, (Eds.) *Poverty : New interdisciplinary perspectives.* San Fransisco : Chandler Publishing Co., 1969.

Valentine, C.A. *Culture and poverty : Critique and counter-proposal.* Chicago : The University of Chicago Press, 1970.

Wilbur, G.L. (Ed.) *Poverty : A new perspective.* Lexington : The University Press of Kentucky, 1973.

TWO

R.C. Tripathi

THE CONCEPT OF DEPRIVATION
Some Issues

EVERY so often in the social sciences a particular area of research starts receiving a little more focused attention. This generally happens on two counts. The area in question is socially significant, or "relevant", to use a more popular term, or because it holds theoretical promise for opening up some new lines of research. In the first case, the objective before the social scientist is to develop a social concern, while in the second case a theoretical model. Whatever the stance of the social scientist, the nature of research inevitably gets influenced by the goal of the scientist. For example, a psychologist who will like to take upon himself the role of an advocate against inequality, discrimination, disadvantage with a view to developing a policy for intervention and change has little use for the operationalization or conceptualization of variables. Because the variables he works with are categorical level variables, often marginal groups like Harijans, Muslims or tribals, taking recourse to sophisticated measurement procedures changes the very nature of these variables which does not help him in his role of an advocate of social change. However, for a scientist interested in developing a model and understanding basic relationships, these categorical variables are not independent enough (Anandalakshmy, 1974), and therefore, of little use.

Although, the boundary between research based on social advocacy or a scientist's urge to unfold fundamental relationships is admittedly thin, and sometimes arbitrary and unnecessary, it would appear that it has been responsible for the *muddle* found in the area of deprivation research. If it has led to a search for the deprived groups, it has also led to the investigation of all kinds of deprivations. The "Psychological Abstracts" index lists over two dozen types of deprivation, such as stimulus, cultural, egoistical, economic, social, political, linguistic, educational, material and environmental. To this one can add various types of need deprivation such as, food, water, sexual activity and the like.

Another source of confusion in the concept of deprivation is with respect to preferences for certain criteria for classifying the deprivation states. Deprivation is classified in terms of the following criteria :

Organismic v. environmental

Deprivation is said to be the property of the organism or the environment. If the deprivation is organismic, one refers to the conditions which are responsible for lack of fulfilment of needs. Deprivation in this case is that of the organic inputs and it leads to tissue deficits. Under this category would fall food/ nutrition, water, sex, and sleep deprivation. Tissue deficit is assumed to be a noxious state and drives the organism to take appropriate steps to reduce it. Secondly, the locus of deprivation may be environmental. Here the dimension of categorization employed is generally the richness versus poorness of environment e.g., the case of rural-urban or slums and non-slum areas. One generally operationalizes environmental deficit in terms of level of living (housing, employment, education, etc.) or in terms of the absence of objects and persons (e.g., parents) which should be present in the normal course. More often than not, the two types of deprivations are treated as belonging to mutually exclusive sets and no effort is made to relate appropriate variables in these realms or even to see how they influence psychological processes in interaction with each other.

Objective v. subjective

Deprivation is also sought to be distinguished in terms of objective and subjective criteria. The distinction is actually based on how far the measurement of deprivation is independent of the individual's subjective states. The emphasis on objective deprivation is intimately linked with the concept of minimum basic requirement for psychological functioning. One looks for a line which could serve as a "cut off" line to demarcate deprived from the non-deprived. The assumption is that one knows what is required and in what amount. In case of subjective deprivation it is presumed that only an individual knows what he wants and in what amount. If the "desired" falls below his subjective standard, he feels deprived. He may have arrived at the reference after comparison with relevant others or even independently. The concept sometimes implies that comparison with others is a necessary condition for subjective deprivation. However, one can also conceive of standards which are arrived at by individuals themselves. This may happen when one takes into consideration the subjective states resulting from the acceptance of organic inputs. Consider, for example, prescribing the amount of food a beggar must eat to feel satisfied. The distinction between objective and subjective is tenuous for example, it is generally assumed that objective deprivation leads to a drive state of an organism. However, there are many studies to support that deprivation per se does not lead to a drive state but perception of it does. Nevertheless, even perception requires objective referents from the real world.

Absolute v. relative

This distinction comes closer to the objective versus subjective distinction with the only possible exception that absolute deprivation seems more possible in case of primary needs and less in case of secondary needs, in which case "relative" deprivation appears to be more appropriate.

While there is nothing wrong with a classification and assigning of labels, what seems to have happened in case of the above classifications is that they have been reified as descriptors of deprivation as it is obtained in the real world.

THE DEPRIVATION-ENVIRONMENT

The problems with the concept of deprivation are not confined to using of marginal groups as deprived or making distinctions based on familiar categories. The problem also lies with the definition and conceptualization of the deprivation-environment. A deprivation-environment is often conceptualized and measured by building a catalogue of things and possessions in a home or neighbourhood. This is the standard procedure which is used by many authors in developing SES scales (Pareek & Rao, 1974). Whiteman and Deutsch's (1968) deprivation-index, which has been widely used, is based on the amount of variety available in the environment. The assumption here is that the lesser the value of the parameters, the greater the deprivation. Generally, the parameters of deprivation-environment are given unit weight so that all parameters are assumed to exercise the same effect on the dependent variable. What is missed is that it is not the values of parameters but the degree of inter-relatedness of parameters in the deprivation environment which may be crucial in understanding psychological development. Emery and Trist (1965) have proposed a typology of environments based on the degree of interconnectedness of various environmental elements. The environment which has the minimum amount of connectedness is termed by them "placid-random" because the resource distribution in such environment is random and, therefore, not predictable. The other environments, in order to their complexity are called "placid-clustered" with cluster resources, "disturbed-reactive" with multiple contingencies among their components and finally "turbulent fields" which are most complex and have the highest degree of connectedness. Thus, it is the degree of inter-relatedness of parts which makes for the complexity of an environment. To the extent an environment is less complex, it may be said to be deprived in relation to more complex environments. In none of the measures of deprivation-environment inter-relatedness of various elements has been taken into consideration. Inadequate conceptualization of environment has also been responsible for misleading conclusions and inappropriate generalizations. Where comparisons are made within an environment the danger of misleading conclusions are small because of the uniform nature of environment, although even within an environment-type one has to allow for variations. However, when between environment comparisons are made the danger of inappropriate conclusions is very great. Consider an individual who has been reared in a "placid-clustered" environment. Since the existing complexity of the environment is of low order, the associated behavioural complexity of individuals reared in such environments will also be low. An individual in such environments will require simpler cognitive and adaptive strategies. If one compares individuals from this environment with individuals coming from relatively more complex environments a clear difference in the behavioural complexity will be observed. It would be wrong to castigate the individuals in less complex environments as inferior to the ones in more complex environment because both are equally effective within their own settings. There is also evidence that as organisms move from one environment to other environments which are more complex behaviourally, they have difficulty in discovering the laws that govern the behaviour of that system, and, therefore have difficulty in adapting, whether they move from simple to complex or from complex to simple environments. The skills which individuals develop are appropriate to *an* environment and not to *all* environments.

Another problem with the concept of deprivation-environment is that researchers often conceptualize environment as given or static. An individual is said to adapt by reacting to what *exists* in a proactive fashion. In this connection, the concept of "enacted environment" put forward by Weick (1969) seems to be very relevant. According to Weick, enacted environment is created by the human actors through their actions and interactions to which they adapt in a retroactive fashion. Adoptive behaviour results in terms of the state of evolution of environment at a particular point in time. In any organized social setting, people occupy different positions in social space. Since rewards and control of resources is a function of position in social space, some people are more fortunately placed than others. The interaction of the "dominant partners" in social exchange with their more "recessive" partners results in a certain type of "lived experience". These discrete "meaningful lived experiences" form the basis of enacted environment. The deprived, for that matter others also, do not act on the basis of what is, but what has been. Nevertheless, most of the deprivation measures focus on the present state rather than on the state and experiences of the organism.

If deprivation is to be understood, one needs to distinguish between a deprived and a non-deprived state. While studying deprivation in natural settings, one takes for granted that the deprived groups will be different from the non-deprived groups with respect to drive level. The acid test, however, is rarely applied. Two principles from the behaviour theory are used in this connection. First, with deprivation, behaviour should vary in strength or amplitude in a monotonic fashion. However, this is not always true, as Chatterjee (1977) reveals. There are various psycho-social stimuli which are believed to contribute to the well being of the individual but whose excess influences quality of life in a negative way such as, parental care, communication, ambiguity, freedom of action, security, population density. There is, therefore, a great need to isolate variables with which deprivation may correlate in a non-monotonic fashion, besides the variables with which it has a monotonic relationship. Assuming that deprivation will relate with psychological variables only in monotonic or non-monotonic fashion is too simplistic a view.

Finally, various intervention programmes are suggested to alleviate the ill effects of deprivati on or social disadvantage. The behaviour theory holds that the presence of incentives should be reinforcing under deprivation. However, the social system hardly, if ever, works this way. It is the "haves" who control all the resources. Therefore, it is they who decide what behaviours to reinforce and when. Such reinforcements are likely to be few and far between and, therefore, will play only a small role in the psychological development of the deprived. Thus, both in terms of our understanding of the concept of deprivation and amelioration of the negative effects of deprivation, we seem to be a long way away.

REFERENCES

Anandalakshmy, S. How independent is the independent variable? In W.J. Dawson & W. Lonner (Eds.) *Readings in cross-cultural psychology.* Hongkong : University of Hongkong Press, 1974.

Chatterjee, B.B. *Methodological implications of using socio-economic status scale as a control variable in disadvantage-deprivation studies.*

Paper presented at the Symposium on "Psychological Studies on Deprivation." Department of Psychology, Allahabad University, Allahabad, November, 1977.

Emery, F.E., & Trist, E.L. The causal texture of organizational environments. *Human Relations*, 1965, 18, 21-32.

Pareek, U., & Rao, T.V. (Eds.) *Handbook of psychological and social instruments*. Ahmedabad : Samasthi, 1974.

Whiteman, M. & Deutsch, M. Social disadvantage as related to intellective and language development. In M. Deutsch, I. Katz, & A.R. Jensen (Eds.) *Social class, race and psychological development*. New York : Holt Rinchart & Winston, 1968.

Weick, K. *The social psychology of organizing*. Reading, Mass.: Addison-Wesley, 1969.

THREE

Durganand Sinha

TOWARDS AN ECOLOGICAL FRAMEWORK OF DEPRIVATION

ETYMOLOGICALLY, the word "deprivation" is derived from the verb "to deprive" which means to dispossess or strip (a person or an object), and it implies a "felt loss". The reference obviously is to certain deficiencies in the environment, which are not only there but are also experienced as such by the individual. It relates to certain features or aspects of the environment that are absent or inadequate in certain degree which causes an impact on the functioning of the individual. Thus, when one talks of deprivation, the emphasis is on the relevant aspects of the environment which are deficient or wanted in some respects. Therefore, any conceptualization of deprivation should have due emphasis on the environment or the setting in which the individual operates. Unfortunately, despite behaviour being conceived in psychology as a result of interaction between the organism and the environment, one of the main weaknesses of this discipline for long has been the undue concern for individual variables and giving a short shrift to environment. If at all, only lip service is paid to environmental variables. Lewin's topological approach did try to set things on proper footing. But the individual and personalistic bias still persists. It is particularly the case with researches of psychologists in this country, as reflected in frequent papers and dissertations produced, that simply deal with the person and personality (and frequently using a vague omnibus expression like "psychological") variables, whether it be related to job satisfaction, need for achievement, academic performance, adjustment and the like. Most of these ill-conceived researches implicitly at least imply that the individual functions as if in a vacuum. An individual's psychological processes can have meaning only if they are conceived in their proper setting or are viewed in terms of their interactions with the environment. Lewin's concept of "life space" does not seem to have made much impact on our thinking.

Further, in a lot of our studies, we find focus on a single variable at a time and attempt to "control out" all the others. This fear of "contamination" especially of the multifarious environmental variables underlies the fact that most of the psychological studies are of a nature which is removed from actual life situations. Concern for single variable has been largely responsible for generating artificiality in our studies so that the phenomenon studied remains removed from real life. 'More-than-one variable' experiments are certainly there. But even they have frequently not taken due cognizance of the environmental matrix. While the subject has gained in scientific rigour and taken it nearer to its goal of scientific precision and exactitude, it has been at a considerable cost. It has certainly made for scientific rigour, but often has in the process lost in relevance, so that it is frequently difficult to generalize to settings other than the one in which the experiment has been performed, and those concerned with practical applications of the results often find it useless when it comes to evolving an intervention programme. The emphasis on rigour has led to experiments that are elegantly designed but often limited in scope. Either the findings are too trite and commonplace, or of such a character that they are not generalizable to actual life situations. It is from this perspective probably that Bronfenbrenner in his invited address to the 1974 Convention of the American Psychological Association characterised much of contemporary developmental psychology as "the science of the strange behaviour of children in strange situations with strange adults for the briefest possible periods of time" (Bronfenbrenner 1974a). If one substitutes the word "individual" or "organism" for "children", the statement is equally applicable to the bulk of contemporary psychology.

The main purpose of this discussion is to bring home some of the shortcomings of modern psychological researches, and to emphasize that behaviour is to be viewed not simply in terms of individual factors, nor the environmental factors as having isolated impact on the individual, but in the entire individual-environmental complex as a constant two-way interplay. Ecology, conceived as the study of biological forms in relations to their physical environment, or to put it in Lewinian terminology, as the study of these aspects of individual's environment which are important parts of his life space, provides a useful framework for conceptualizing most of the psychological processes. In its wider connotation, ecology is not confined to merely physical environment, but comprises the socio-cultural setting in which the individual operates. Two things are prominent in ecology: (a) a conceptualization of psychological adaptation in terms of person-environment congruence, and (b) a concern with effective coping (Holahan, 1977). Ecological perspective views psychological processes in true transactional terms. For example, in contrast to defining adjustment exclusively on the basis of internal personality dynamics, adjustment is construed in terms of transactional relationship between the individual and environmental setting in which he functions. Specifically, psychological adjustment may be defined as the state in which an individual's needs and proclivities for action are congruent with the demands and opportunities of the particular settings in which he operates. In addition, the ecological view emphasizes effective coping rather than adjustment or pathology.

Ecology provides a useful framework for understanding the psychological processes related to deprivation, and it has certain additional advantages in that it not only makes our research efforts more realistic, but also helps in suggesting some intervention strategies. In analysing the impact of deprivation on certain perceptual skills, the author (Sinha, 1978) has followed closely a model suggested by Bronfenbrenner (1974a). The nature of environment provides the necessary sensory inputs, stimulation and experiential base for the development of perceptual skills of various kinds. The enduring environment of the child or his ecology may be conceived in terms of two concentric layers. The "upper" and the more visible layer contains his home, school, peer groups and so on, each providing three dimensions, namely, physical space and material, social roles and relationships of the child vis-a-vis other people, and his activities. The "supporting" or the "surrounding" layer embedding the former is provided by the geographic and physical environment and the institutional setting of the child in terms of his social class, caste and the general services and amenities available to him.

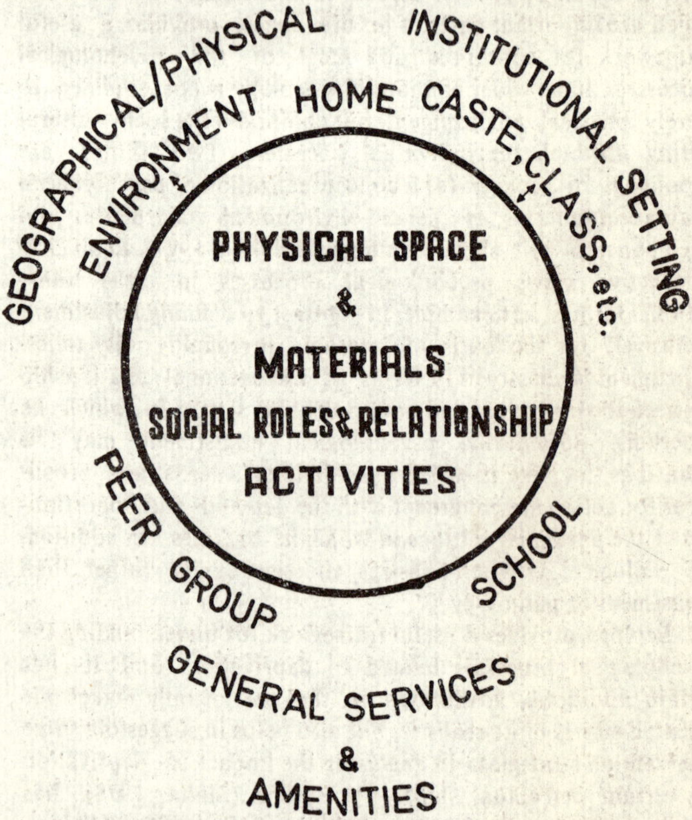

Fig. 3.1

Home and its conditions in terms of over-crowding, space available to each member of the family, toys, pictorial and cultural materials in the home, technological devices used for general living and the like would constitute the most important visible "upper layer" influence on the individuals matched probably only by the nature and quality of schooling, and the facilities to which the individual child is exposed. In home as well as in the school, the nature of interpersonal relationships and activities that are encouraged or inhibited would constitute another kind of influence emanating from the family and the school. The third factor constituting the other visible layer is the nature of interactions and activities prevalent in his peer groups right from his childhood onwards. These three factors, namely the home, school, and peer groups with physical facilities, nature of social interactions, and activities common in each, constitute the most important ecological influences on the psychological development of the child, and these influences are relatively easier to discern and examine. It may be borne in mind that there are other visible upper layer factors but are relatively minor in their import than the three outlined above.

These factors do not operate independently, but constantly interact not only with one another, but also are embedded in a larger and more pervasive setting constituting what have been designated as the "surrounding layers" of the child's ecology. They constantly influence the "upper layer" factors, but being pervasive and a little more diffused, their influences are not always clearly visible. The general geographical environment, nature of terrain which determine the mode of economic pursuits, space for play and other activities available to him outside the home including general congestion of the locality and density of population, space and facilities for play constitute the first element of the surrounding layer of ecology. To this may be added the topographical characteristics of the geographical environment (whether it is a flat, featureless, steppelike grassland or undulating mountains) whose influence on our susceptibility to certain geometrical-optical illusions has been demonstrated, and which form the basis of the famous "carpentered world" hypothesis of Segall, Campbell and Herkovits (1963). Second element in the surrounding layer is the institutional setting provided by caste, class and other factors each providing certain role expectancies and strains, and imposing certain limitations on the individual, and prescribing certain kinds of preferred activities. The third factor is constituted by the general amenities available to the individuals residing in those places like drinking water, power, municipal and civic amenities, means of entertainment, and so on. These surrounding layers comprise the general environment, and being pervasive and common, their influences are taken for granted and not easily noticed. To all these may be added the factor of the level of poverty and general economic conditions which underlie all these, and which have repercussions on all the upper and surrounding layer factors in various degrees.

It may be observed that the visible and the surrounding layer factors often combine and interact with one another, and shape not only the economic pursuits, way of life, but also the socialization processes and interpersonal relationships and the general cognitive and perceptual functioning of the individual. Differentials in these, singly or in combination with others, are likely to have definite impact on the cognitive and perceptual competence of the individual as well as affect his motivations, style of coping with problems, and the general personality development.

Viewed in this perspective, the ecology of various socio-economic groups in India can be said to have a two-tiered concentric layer. For example, general poverty and the attendant congestions of the locality to which people belong, the limitations and roles enjoined by caste, and the facilities provided by the civic authorities to the areas where people reside can be viewed as the surrounding layer of ecology. Again, the conditions and facilities prevalent in home, the role relationships prevalent therein, and the activities encouraged or discouraged would constitute the outer and visible layer of ecology. Similarly, the conditions of the school and the nature and quality of schooling, as well as the nature of peer groups to which the child belongs would be regarded as other factors of outer layer ecology. The contrast in ecologies in both the layers is easily visible in comparing children from caste-Hindu families with those from the scheduled castes or the so-called "untouchables". For centuries, the scheduled castes have been living under conditions of intense social disadvantages, and prevented from sharing in the mainstream of socio-cultural and economic life of the Hindu society. The poor socio-cultural atmosphere in which they have lived for ages has resulted in their constituting the bulk of what is today called "the weaker sections of society" in India. Despite recent legislative and administrative measures to ensure their equality and eradicate discriminations against them, provide them with new roles and the provision of certain "privileges" to bring them rapidly up to the level of other social groups, they still suffer from many socio-cultural disadvantages which can collectively be regarded as "cultural deprivation". As Whiteman and Deutsch (1968) have observed, "social deprivation implies that the association between social grouping and specific environmental factors is not directly causal, but is mediated by more basic societal conditions such as unemployment, poverty, and inequality of opportunity in various areas". Apart from social disadvantages, poverty is another important factor constituting the environment of the scheduled caste children. But as Das and Singh (1975) have pointed out, the socio-cultural atmosphere in which a caste-Hindu lives would still be superior even between poor caste-Hindu and scheduled castes.

Thus, the socio-cultural disadvantages due to over-crowded neighbourhood, meagre civic amenities, and caste/class differentiation, may be regarded as the "surrounding or supporting layer" of the ecology of the child belonging to the scheduled castes. The upper or visible layer is provided by poor and deficient housing, the inferiority and discriminations which they still experience in various social relationships, and the inadequate schooling facilities available to them mainly because of poverty and indifference of their family towards getting them educated.

The above framework has been utilized by the author in a series of studies on the development of certain perceptual skills on urban, rural, and tribal children of various caste/religious statuses and exposed to differing qualities of schooling. One of these studies has been reported separately. In a recent paper (Bronfenbrenner, 1977) has suggested a more refined model. He argues that "the understanding of human development demands going beyond the direct observation of behaviours on the part of one or two persons in the same place; it requires examination of multiperson systems of interaction not limited to a single setting and must take into account aspects of the environment beyond the immediate situation containing the subject". He proposes scientific perspective of *ecology of human development* which can provide a useful framework for conceptualizing the psychological consequences of deprivation on human level. The author has followed closely his formulations regarding the same key concepts. Ecology of human development has been defined as "the scientific study of progressive mutual accommodation, throughout the life span, between growing human organism and the changing immediate environments in which it lives, as this process is affected by relations obtaining within and between these immediate settings, as well as the larger social contexts, formal and informal, in which the settings are embedded" (Bronfenbrenner, 1977).

The conception of environment that is implicit here is considerably broader and more differentiated than that usually found in psychology. As Bronfenbrenner (1977) has stated "the ecological environment is conceived topologically as a nested arrangement of structures, each contained within the next." Following the terminology of Brim (1975), four successive levels have been proposed : *microsystem*, *mesosystem*, *exosystem* and *macrosystem*. According to Bronfenbrenner (1977) a microsystem is "the complex relations between the developing person and environment in an immediate setting containing that person (e.g., home, school, workplace, etc.)". The factors of place, time, physical features, activity, participant and role, constitute the elements of the setting. In a psychological experiment, usually these elements are neglected, and roles other than those of the experimenter and the subject that may be operative upon the participants are disregarded, and "behaviour is examined primarily in terms of process, (e.g., modes of interaction, reinforcement schedules, response rates) rather than content (e.g., the nature and purpose of the task)" (Bronfenbrenner 1977, p. 514).

A mesosystem is conceived as comprising "the interrelations among major settings containing the developing person at a particular point in his or her life" (Bronfenbrenner, 1977, p. 514). It may encompass interactions among families, school, peer group, religious group and so on. It is a system of microsystems.

An exosystem as defined by Bronfenbrenner (1977) is "an extension of the mesosystem embracing other specific social structures, both formal and informal, that do not themselves contain the developing person but impinge upon or encompass the immediate settings in which that person is found, and thereby influence, delimit, or even determine, what goes on there. Major institutions of the society constitute the structure, and they encompass among others the world of work, neighbourhood, the mass media, agencies of the government, the distribution of goods and services, communication facilities, and informal social networks" (p. 515).

A macrosystem differs from these foregoing systems in that "it refers not to specific contexts affecting the life of a particular individual but to general prototypes, existing in the culture or subculture, that set the pattern for the structures and activities occurring at the concrete level". A macrosystem refers to "the overarching institutional patterns of the culture or subculture such as the economic, social, educational, legal, and political systems, of which micro-meso, and exosystems are the concrete manifestations. A macrosystem is conceived not only as structures but also as carriers of information and ideology, explicit or implicit, that endow meaning and motivation to various social agencies" (Bronfenbrenner, 1977, p. 515).

It is not necessary to dilate upon the properties of each of these four systems. It would suffice to point to the characteristic of reciprocity and constant interaction within factors of each system and between the systems. In the present context, it is contended that deprivation can be conceived as certain deficiencies characterizing one or more of these systems with which the individual has to cope constantly. More the number of factors involved, greater would usually be the level of deprivation. Further, it is to be noted that deficiencies in the four systems or in factors within each one of them can best be conceived not in simple additive terms but as having an interactive relationship with each other. It is felt that with this four-level ecological perspective underlying any study of the effects of deprivation, the phenomenon is likely to be viewed in all its complexity and reality. Without sacrificing scientific rigour, relevance of the study would be assured.

The second framework of deprivation in your levels of ecosystems is not essentially different from the earlier formulation in terms of two concentric layers. It has, however, the advantage of being more differentiated, capable of conceptualizing various factors of deprivation in more specific, concrete, and realistic terms. Studies and experiments designed within this framework are not likely to suffer from the usual defect of artificiality and irrelevance.

Before concluding, it may be pointed out that the model that is conceptualized is not a rigid one. It represents essentially a perspective and a viewpoint which is relevant to a number of different content areas and problems. Ecological perspective, as Holahan (1977) has pointed out, is also applicable across different levels of problem analysis, including role relationships in an organised setting, the effects of physical environment upon behaviour, and the pervasive influences of culture and history on community processes.

The perspective has the utility in helping to evolve intervention programme which focuses on the individual's level of functioning. It draws our attention to the necessity of improving such skills that the individual needs to cope with particular institutional or environmental blocks for achieving the desired objectives rather than towards personality factors per se. If it is observed that a particular environmental setting has precipitated severe psychological handicaps in a large number of individuals, the intervention strategy would focus towards changing those characteristics of the environment that present serious obstacles to individual functioning. Moreover, effort will also be directed to identify and bolster those aspects of the physical and socio-cultural systems that can help the individual meet the demands of the situation more effectively. In this context, as Spielberger and Iscoe (1970) have observed, a psychologist can assume newer and innovative roles. Kelly's (1968) intervention project in Michigan on two high schools situated in areas which were environmentally highly discrepant supporting divergent types of effective coping behaviour provides a good example of the utility of this framework. This, the potential social policy relevance of the ecological perspective in contrast to the intra-psychic position augurs well in the context of increased emphasis on social relevance. As Holahan (1977) concludes, "facility in integrating a sound conceptual basis with social action enhances its viability".

REFERENCES

Bronfenbrenner, U. *Experimental human ecology : a reorientation to theory and research on socialization*, Invited Address, American Psychological Association, New Orleans, August, 1974 (a).

Bronfenbrenner, U. Developmental research public policy and the ecology of childhood. *Child Development*, 1974, **45**, 1-5 (b).

Bronfenbrenner, U. Towards an experimental ecology of human development. *American Psychologist*, 1977, **32**, 513-531.

Brim, O.G. Micro-structural influences on child development and the need for childhood social indicators. *American Journal of Orthopsychiatry*, 1975, **45**, 516-524.

Das, J.P., & Singh, P.S. Caste, class, and cognitive competence. *Indian Educational Review*, 1975, **10**, 1-18.

Holahan, C.J. The role of ecology in community psychology : a tale of three cities. *Professional Psychology*, 1977, **8**, 25-32.

Kelly, J.G. Towards an ecological conception of preventive interventions, In J.W. Carter (Ed.) *Research contributions from psychology to community mental health*. New York : Behavioural Publication, 1968.

Segall, M.H.. Campbell, D.T., & Herskovits, M.J. Cultural differences in perception of geometric illusions. *Science*, 1963, **139**, 769-771.

Sinha, D. Some social disadvantages and development of certain perceptual skills. *Indian Journal of Psychology*, 1977, **52**, 115-132.

Spielberger, C.D., & Iscoe, I. The current status of training in community psychology. In I. Iscoe, C.D. Spielberger (Eds.) *Community Psychology : Perspectives in training and research*. New York : Appleton-Century-Crofts, 1970.

Whiteman, M., & Deutsch, M. Social disadvantages as related to intellective and language development. In M. Deutsch., I Katz., & A.R. Jensen (Eds.) *Social class, race, and psychological development*. New York : Holt, Rinehart and Winston, 1968.

FOUR

S. Anandalakshmy

THERE'S A METHOD TO THE MEASUREMENT

POLONIUS, observing Hamlet's peripatetic ramblings and hearing that the Prince of Denmark had gone mad, was not totally convinced. Methinks, he said, there's a method to his madness. In echoing Polonius' statement in the title, the intention is to draw attention to the non-randomness in the selection of methods used in the study of deprived populations. It is possible to be systematic and selective with methods because there is pattern and predictability to life in deprived conditions. Life in deprived economic conditions is in the Indian context fairly consistent and routine, and not chaotic, arhythmic and anarchic as sometimes described in the academic literature of the West.

Defining deprivation

Deprivation is primarily an economic concept. There are other factors that tend to form a cluster with the economic one, but the nature and composition of these clusters vary from one country to another. Each country, each region must have its own definition of poverty calculated in terms of the incomes and costs pertaining there. As an example, in the United States, the poverty standard is defined as three times the cost of the minimum diet. In other words, if a family has to spend more than one-third of its income on an adequate diet for its members, it is considered to be below the poverty line. In Canada, it is estimated that families spending more than 70 per cent of their income on the three basic heads of food, clothing and shelter would fall below the poverty line.

These criteria of poverty would be obviously unsuitable to our country. In a study on poverty, Dandekar and Rath (1971) calculated a minimum consumer expenditure that would secure an adequate diet. This amount is lower in the rural areas. According to their estimates, 40 per cent of the rural population and 50 per cent of the urban population are living below the minimum. In absolute terms, this adds up to 200 million people or more. In the U.S., approximately one-sixth of the population is poor, while in India about one half of all the people can be so described, and this difference persists in spite of the criteria of poverty varying so greatly in the two countries. These contrasts are focused at the start as a cautionary measure against the generalizations of the findings of research in the industrial-technological West to the situation in India.

The above definition of deprivation can be given a little more depth by the concepts of time and energy into the equation. When a family does not get adequate nutrition even when all the members spend their resources of time, energy and money on breadwinning activities, it knows poverty as a total experience. Energy levels as well as time for leisure activities are of necessity limited. Almost every member contributes to the family income. In a large majority of such cases, even the children are involved in procuring cash or kind for their wherewithal for survival. There are economic pressures that force them to join the labour force early, and the children of the poor have no childhood.

This definition is relevant to India. It is apparent that in countries that have strict legal sanctions against child labour, such a definition would have no validity. In the same way, we must exercise caution in importing the concepts of deprivation from other cultures. In the last decade, a concept used with great frequency among social scientists with a concern for didactic social action is the term, the culture of poverty. It gained currency with the publication of Oscar Lewis' studies—Children of Sanchez and La Vida (Lewis, 1965). His empathy enabled him to get people to talk to him of their most personal concerns, and his insight then translated their statements into a framework. What followed has been something of a disadvantage to the analysis and understanding of people in low economic conditions. It was assumed that there is virtually an autonomous sub-culture among the poor, one that is both self-perpetuating and self-defeating. The traits associated with it are a sense of resignation, fatalism, an inability to put off immediate gratification, a low motivation for education, and inadequate preparation for an occupation and no plan for the future. If these traits were merely descriptive of a specific culture, with the facts extrapolated from family histories, there would be no debate. But in the use of the term culture to describe poverty is implicit the concept of homogeneity of characteristics of the poor. Also suggested by this model is a closed circle relationship between the individual and society. Invidious aphorisms such as "the culture of poverty is the poverty of culture" were found even in the academic writings, and these in turn became handles for those with prejudice to the poor. The culture of poverty is not a culture in the sense in which the anthropologists use it. It is not unique, not specific to a time, place or tradition and is not socio-geographically isolable. The concept serves no heuristic purpose save that of providing an academic garb to what may be called "classism", a parallel of racism and casteism. There are, of course, the specific and tangible aspects of poverty, the physical aspects. Urban poverty, for instance, generally seems to include sub-standard housing, overcrowded living space, a high noise level, and inadequate civic services. Poverty should thus be defined in economic and ecological terms. The effects of living in conditions of poverty certainly need investigation, but the assumption that universal traits of personality and behaviour will result from such an experience is unwarranted.

A review of the research in poverty reveals that among the traits attributed to the poor are some of the following : low self-esteem, a sense of inefficacy and passivity, preference for the familiar and simplification of experience, relationship structured in terms of power, restriction of language and linguistic modes of communication and reliance upon non-work friendships and kinship contacts for social support and resources (Hess, 1970). This cluster of traits is doubtless empirically substantiated. But the problem with stereotypes of this kind is that they are treated almost as personality traits of the poor, rather than as traits that follow the structural constraints of the social system. The values of the poor are considered as factors which tend to perpetuate poverty from generation to generation. This view has been criticised. According to Valentine (1971), what is distinctive of life at the lowest socio-economic levels is determined primarily by the structure of society as a whole and by forces beyond the control of the poor; not by the poor teaching a separate cultural design of each generation. Peattie (1971) also holds that the poor develop value systems which have to do with their life situations and that they adjust their values and aspirations to the limits of the possible.

It is difficult to agree with Hess' viewpoint that the relationship of the poor are structured in terms of power; it would be more correct to say that the relationships of the poor with the rest of society are structured in terms of power. It is the essential powerlessness of the poor which forces them into fatalistic attitude towards their own lives. When a man has no control over the events that govern his own life, he resorts to fatalism, magic, or irrationality (Anandalakshmy, 1973). Values may be the consequences of certain experiences, not the antecedents.

Some of the problems arising in theorizing about the effects of deprivation originate in the sociology of research. Those who plan and conduct research are never from deprived groups themselves, and subtly their own norms and codes become the standard against which others are assessed. Sometimes, a contrast effect is so dramatic on first encounter that it gets magnified in description. There is also a tendency to compare the ideal in one's own culture with the actual in the others. Examples of this are available in descriptions of the school behaviour of lower class children in centre-city schools in urban America, contrasted with the middle class children. As the urban educators developed the idea of the culture of poverty, and cultural deprivation, to explain the less satisfactory performance of lower class and black children in American schools, the concept of "the vacuum ideology" of the educators in the Indian reservations arose (Wax & Wax, 1971). This propounded that American Indian children had no culture of their own and were blank when they came to school.

The parallels to the Indian situation would be clear. The same type of negative stereotyping persists, especially with reference to caste and class. Many teachers and administrators believe that the children of the poor are genetically inferior, and that they have neither the ability now the motivation to benefit from the educational system. It is not difficult to imagine that these become self-fulfilling prophesies. Psychologists researching in this area of interest have a special responsibility to be clear-headed and objective, since their findings may have some influence on policy. That there is a prejudice to the deprived sections of our society, as seen in the negative stereotypes, is evident; this prejudice is largely shared by those in power and we must caution ourselves not to add grist to their mill, at least not without a sound empirical base.

Answering the question "How" ?

From our own field experience, we have arrived at some working principles that appear to be theoretically sound as well as empirically feasible. One could refer to this as folk wisdom if one so wishes.

If the communities one chooses to select for study are very different from one's own, one makes the effort to learn these differences, so that one can communicate and move around in that culture. This is anthropological commonsense. When the average researcher goes to a deprived group to study it, he is an outsider to it . He is perceived as an outsider and must be willing to accept it. The identification of his purpose for being there and the information he seeks to gather will have in a sense, to be approved by his respondents. It is not something that is automatic, or derivative in the situation, but something he will have to work on. He may be moving from a complex, impersonal, urban culture to a peasant culture, that is, face-to-face. An outsider to such a culture is by definition a stranger. Strangers are treated with suspicion, and the only way to deal with him is to find out a great deal about him so that he is no longer a stranger. He will be asked his caste, occupation and income, his marital status and family size. Once his credentials are established, he can go about with his data collection. Until the time of his acceptance by his first respondent, any information he has got may not be an actuality. So, the temporal dimension in research is of the essence in working with simpler communities. Some time must be allocated for establishing rapport, but this cannot be fixed earlier, as it is totally dependent on the inter-personal situation. Once accepted by some in the group, being accepted by the others takes less time. Word gets around, and the communication network within the community is one of the most effective systems.

In the minds of the ordinary resident of the village, the researcher is associated with the government, the power structure and the establishment. A certain degree of suspicion is, therefore, to be expected. In addition if the investigator asks him questions, in order to test his information than to find out something he genuinely wishes to have information on, the adult villager finds the situation unfamiliar and uncomfortable. A formal school is the only place where we are trained to answer questions when the questioner already knows the answers. Those not willing to play "word games" may just clam up.

If establishing rapport and informally interviewing people can be so complicated, the question of using standard psychological tests is fraught with problems. If the tester or his materials are unfamiliar and frightening to the child, his coping with the situation may also affect built-in expectations in all tests that a person's performance is at his level of competence. We assume that the individual has given his best response, and this assumption may not be valid, especially when the tester and the tested represent two ends of the scale of social hierarchy.

Another problem that one has to confront straightaway, is the logistic one of finding a place to administer the test. Most tests would require the subject to be alone and undisturbed for a while. This is next to impossible in most Indian homes. The child will be surrounded by his siblings, friends and neighbours, who will help him to answer the items he cannot, on his own. In our study, making people to understand that we did not want the right answer, but wanted to study the child's way of answering was one of the hardest things to convey. One of the ways by which we dealt with the problem, was to have two persons in the field, one of them to distract the children with a game, while the other one did the testing. This was not always possible or always necessary, but is only an instance of the kind of resourcefulness that is essential if the research is to be good. Team work is effective, in any case, and where the investigators are female and young, working in a team is eseential. They are better accepted for being with one or more others like themselves. Since writing down the responses is not always possible, it makes for reliability and greater veracity of the data. It also gives their visit the structure of a social visit. There is one other issue in this connection. The closer the investigator's appearance and clothes to those she is interviewing, the greater their expectation that she would conform to their own social codes. The codes do not apply to an absolute outsider, and those who wish to become insiders might also find themselves expected to behave with the same properties required of an insider.

These are only minor tips. The major requirements of field work are, of course, high motivation, respect for individuals and the culture under study, and a willingness to be human and flexible at all times.

Refining the variables

In many recent methodological discussions, especially with reference to cross-cultural psychology, the difference between *emic* and *etic* approaches have been mentioned (Jahoda, 1977). These terms, derived from the linguistic terms, phonemic and phonetic, have been used by anthropologists for more than a decade. The emic approach is to consider culture-specific items of behaviour, while the etic approach would take into account cultural universals. One should be able to see what is going on in a certain society and then convert them into the more generalized and academically universal variables. Generally, one finds the psychological studies unaware of such differences. Tests standardized abroad, sometimes decades earlier, are used or sometimes tests standardized in India on the educated urban upper classes. The relevance of test items to the children being tested is rarely questioned. The studies on tribal and scheduled children have several instances of low performance levels. If the tribals devised a test based on knowledge of wild life, hunting skills and finding one's way back to the homestead from the middle of the jungle, I wonder how many of us would pass the test. It is true that the standard measures of intelligence are good predictors of school performance, because they are somewhat similar in the kinds of information sought. We often test the children to see if they will fit into the school system, or to identify those with differential abilities. The tests are useful and can be used for diagnostic purposes, but in many cases they have been used indiscriminately. While groups are described as low in intelligence, be they members of a regional residence group, a caste group or an occupational group. At its root, the problem may be a semantic one, one of confusing the scores on a particular test with the potential for intelligent functioning, but the danger arising from the labelling phenomenon must be apparent now. There are scores of studies which conclude that lower class and lower caste children are lower in intelligence. In a society, where there is total vertical mobility and talent finds its level, income and intelligence will be related to status. Even the open industrial countries of the West have not attained this ideal of mobility: race, religion and sex are factors in mobility.

In India, the situation is compounded by the variable of caste. In a subtle way, and sometimes not so subtly, caste puts the ceiling on educational and occupational achievement, especially in the rural areas. So, when the child is assessed on tasks in which the constraints of his caste and class act as disadvantages, his performance will not reflect his innate potential. In as much as caste is an ascribed status, his test scores may be "ascribed" especially if he is from the lowest rung of the hierarchy and has not had the opportunity to develop individuality and self-esteem. The socially disadvantaged score low on positive variables, high on negative ones, whether cognitive or personality variables. So they say, I feel that it is as much an artifact of the test items themselves, couched in school language, and most likely administered at the school. What began as a concern for the under-privileged has been quietly converted into a prejudice against them. We may need to start with an emic approach : to take into account items of subjective relevance and to suppress our own ethnocentricism in the interpretation of the findings.

Differentiating proximal and distal variables

One of the problems in the study of poverty and deprivation has been the combination of macro-units and micro-units in the same design (Anandalakshmy, 1974). In many cases, the antecedent variables are too global and the dependent variables too minute to make any theoretical insights possible. Another model for the analysis of our theoretical constructs is that of proximal and distal variables. The model is presented in Table 4.1 briefly and is intended only as a pre-theoretical frame work for the discussion of the major issues.

Sociologists generally study the relationships among the variables in Column A or those between A and E, i.e., between distal environment attributes and distal behaviour attributes. Clinical Psychology is usually concerned with the study of attributes within C and their relationships or between C and D. Developmental Psychology has a focus on the relationships of B with C, or B with D or E. It is possible to visualize a study that begins with the consideration of A, then goes on to B,C and D and finally draws some tentative conclusions about their relationship to E as well.

If on the other hand the psychologist moves from A to C, without identifying the factors in B that may be necessary conditions, he is bound to arrive at some unwarranted generalizations. Since we have the techniques by which to assess individuals, we should amend and extend them to the study of the proximal environment as well.

Most of the deprivation studies have tended to take the distal variable of poverty conditions or socio-economic status as the independent variable, without a consideration of the proximal factors in the situation. If we are to move ahead we must look at the cases who prosper, despite economic constraints, and by prosper, in this context, is to score high on positive trait measurements. For instance, in a recent study on the effects of nutritional status on cognitive functioning of infants, we found that even when socio-economic status, nutritional intake, and the related anthropometric measurements were all clearly below par, a child who performed well on the

TABLE 4.1 : **Illustrative taxonomic model**

Environment A Distal	Attributes B Proximal	Person Attributes C	Behaviour D Proximal	Attributes E Distal
Race	Social evaluation	Skills	Aggressiveness	Social failure
Social class	Reactions	Beliefs	Withdrawal	Delinquency
Urban ecology	Parental teaching modes	Motives	Discrimination	Inter-group hostility
Ethnic status	Teacher expectations Affectional climate	Interests Attitudes Identities	Reading deficiency	Psychopathology

(Adapted from the US Department, HEW publication, 1968)

cognitive tasks, tended to have a strong emotional bond with the mother and stimulating interactions with her. So, even when a social class or economic level is taken as the variable on which the sampling is done, the actual insight into the nature of the problem under investigation came only with the breaking up of the environment into smaller units. For the better understanding of micro-variables, one must be willing to look for the finer details. Apart from the field methods mentioned earlier in the paper, it is the change in the perspective of the study and in the scaling down of the size of the variable that we can come to terms with the issues of measurement. There *is* a method to the measurement.

REFERENCES

Anandalakshmy, S. How independent is the independent variable? In W.J. Dawson, & W. Lonner, W. (Eds.) *Readings in cross-cultural psychology*. Hong Kong : University of Hong Kong Press, 1974.

Anandalakshmy, S. *The process of modernization : Perspectives from India.* Paper read at the Workshop on the Interface between Culture and Learning, East-West Center, Honolulu, Hawaii, 1973.

Dandekar, V.M. & Rath, N. *Poverty in India.* Bombay : Indian School of Political Economy, 1971.

Hess, R.D. Social class and ethnic influence upon socialization. In P.H. Mussen (Ed.) *Carmichael's manual of child psychology*. New York : John Wiley & Sons, 1970.

Jahoda, G. In pursuit of the emic-etic distinction. In Y.H. Poortinga (Ed.) *Basic problems in cross-cultural psychology*. Amsterdam & L. Isse : Swets Zeitlinger, 1977.

Lewis, O. *La Vida : A Puerto Rican family in the culture of poverty.* New York : Random House, 1965.

Peattie, L.R. The structural parameters of emerging life-styles in Venezuela. In E.W Leacock (Ed.) *The culture of poverty : A critique.* New York : Simon and Schuster, 1971.

U.S. Department of Health, Education and Welfare. *Perspectives on human deprivation : Biological, psychological and sociological.* Washington, D.C. : Govt., 1968.

Valentine, C.A. The 'culture of poverty', its scientific significance and its implications for action. In E.W. Leacock (Ed.) *The culture of poverty : A critique*. New York : Simon and Schuster, 1971.

Wax, M.L., and Wax, R.H. Cultural deprivation as an educational ideology. In E.W. Leacock (Ed.) *The culture of poverty : A critique.* New York : Simon and Schuster, 1971.

[illegible] which the [illegible] process [illegible] the [illegible] [illegible] [illegible] [illegible] Clearly, the [illegible] [illegible] [illegible] [illegible] [illegible] [illegible] [illegible] [illegible] [illegible] [illegible] the [illegible] [illegible] [illegible] the size of [illegible] [illegible] [illegible] [illegible] [illegible] [illegible] [illegible] [illegible] [illegible]

REFERENCES

[illegible] (1974) [illegible]

Amerasinghe, [illegible] [illegible] [illegible] [illegible] Press, Cambridge, 1974.

[illegible]

[illegible] (ed.), [illegible] New York [illegible]

[illegible]

[illegible] [illegible] [illegible] 1974.

[illegible]

FIVE

L. B. Tripathi

SOME METHODOLOGICAL PROBLEMS OF DEPRIVATION STUDIES

INTRODUCTION

OVER the past twenty five years there has been phenomenal increase in the quantum of psychological research on the behavioural and cognitive impacts of deprivation. This upsurge has yielded data leading to contradictory results and mushroom growth of theories. Inconsistencies in results and confused theoretical speculations may be primarily due to a variety of methodological problems and short-comings with which the contemporary deprivational studies are fraught. Scientific endeavours to look into the relationship between deprivation and the emergence, growth and level of psychological functions are of recent origin. Therefore, neither has the concept of deprivation become sharpened and crystallize enough to include in its orbit all its phenomenal or empirical referents in order to be accepted as a respectable scientific concept, nor has the methodology employed in measuring deprivation, as well as in designing deprivation studies, become sophisticated enough to yield unequivocally valid and reliable data. In the present paper an attempt has been made at identifying those methodological problems and shortcomings which have to be tackled in order to make deprivation studies scientifically sound and functionally meaningful.

Research efforts in the area of the psychological effects of deprivation have proceeded in two distinct directions. On the one hand, deprivation has acquired the status of an operational concept and has been treated as an experimental variable in controlled laboratory conditions. On the other hand, it has also acquired the status of a natural phenomenon or a variable. It is manipulated through some selection procedure and is usually treated as a nominal, or at best, as an ordinal variable (Whiteman & Deutsch, 1968). The laboratory treatment of deprivation has given rise to the term of sensory deprivation in which so widely divergent operations are used that the popularly known term of sensory deprivation has become a misleading term. The concept of deprivation in natural settings has also been so freely interpreted that for a student of psychology it has now become almost impossible to understand its exact meaning. In both types of researches the numerosity of methodological problems and issues has been on the increase as the research output has increased. Although these two lines of distinctly separable research developments may be viewed as having a common ancestry, and proceeding towards a common future, they have come to be beset by different sets of methodological problems.

Broadly speaking, laboratory studies of deprivational effects are truly experimental while its studies in natural settings are largely correlational. From this obvious fact it can easily be surmised that the methodological problems, issues and considerations confronting the investigators in these two types of researches must be of different complexions and complexities. It is, therefore, reasonable to treat them under separate headings. It is true that sources of the emergence of many problems in these two types of investigations are more or less similar but they assume different characteristics in their functional forms. Since the quantum of experimental investigations into the effects of deprivations on psychological functions have a longer history and have attained greater precision than the deprivation-research in natural settings, their methodological problems have become more crystallized. In a number of papers these problems and issues have been discussed at length. A paper by Rossi (1969) presents an excellent account of the major methodological problems in experimental research in the area of sensory deprivation. However, the focal theme of our discussion will be on behavioural impacts of deprivation as it occurs in an individual's natural life setting.

During recent years emphasis on studies of deprivation has shifted from laboratory to deprivation in real life conditions of individuals, and numerous research papers on the effects of deprivation on a host of psychological functions have been published. However, a critical survey of these studies reveals two sets of methodological problems. The first set of problems originates from diversities in the meanings of the term deprivation and the criteria used in its identification as well as its measurement. The second set of problems originates in actual conduct of such deprivation studies. The former is primarily an issue of devising ways and means for attaining precision in the measurement of the nature and extent of deprivation, while the latter set of problems is concerned with the adequacy in control of the confounding variables and eliciting reliable and valid responses to various objectively scored test items.

CONCEPTUAL DIVERSITY AND MEASUREMENT PROBLEMS

In the studies of deprivational effects in natural settings psychologists and other behavioural scientists have conceptualized the term 'deprivation', not as scientists, but as litterateurs imposing subjectively determined connotations to the term and selecting arbitrary criteria for separating the deprived from the non-deprived. More often than not, knowingly or unknowingly, psychologists have become much more motivated by expediency and convenience rather than by methodological soundness and exactitude in determining the empirical referents of deprivation. As a consequence of this, a multitude of terms have emerged each purporting to signify deprivation in this or that sense leading to diversity in measurement criteria and devices. It would not be out of place to present a flavour of the terminological diversity by sampling some of the terms that have been used as synonyms of deprivation as it occurs in the life span of individuals. This terminological sample will help us in understanding the difficulties that are likely to arise in devising ways and means for quantifying and assessing the nature and extent of deprivation to which an individual has been subjected in his life. Some of the terms used are : effective deprivation (Gewirtz, 1961); cognitive deprivation (Green, Hofmann & Morgan, 1967); cultural deprivation (Riessman, 1962; Kogan, & Kogan, 1970; Wight, Gloniger & Kneene, 1970; Das, 1973); economic deprivation (Symmonds, 1968); educational deprivation (Getzels, 1969); emotional deprivation (Stott, 1974); environmental deprivation (Deutsch, 1965); inequality (Miller, 1968); parental or maternal deprivation (Yarrow, 1961); malnutrition (Das & Pivato, 1977; Dobbing, 1967; Bladslee, 1967); medical deprivation (Suchman, 1966); poverty (Bee, 1974); prolonged deprivation (Misra & Tripathi, 1977a; Tripathi & Misra, 1975, 1976); psychological deprivation (Langmeier, 1972; Goldfarb, 1945; Langmeier & Matezeck, 1975); relative deprivation (Crosby, 1976); social pathology (Coleman, 1971); social and cultural disadvantage (Havighurst, 1964; Gordon, 1968; Uzgiris, 1968; Sinha, 1977a; Singh, 1976); social deprivation (Rankin, 1970; Tulkin, 1972).

All these terms have inevitably led to different criteria for isolating the empirical referents in developing deprivation measurement devices. These empirical referents and units of measurement, differ from one author to the other, and at times the confusion is so pervasive that what is conceived to be deprivation in one approach is not necessarily considered to be so in the other.

Most of the investigators have used the concept of deprivation, irrespective of the difference in deprivational magnitude, as a nominal or categorical variable. It has been tacitly assumed that deprivation is a characteristic which is either present and effective in an individual's life, or it is non-existent. They classify their universe of study in two groups, i.e., deprived and non-deprived. For such a classification of people they adopt a single criterion of this or that kind, and on the basis of that criterion they separate the deprived from the non-deprived. Let us examine some of these criteria and evaluate their adequacy in measuring deprivation.

Residential area

A number of investigators (e.g., Wight, *et al.*, 1970; Gordon, 1968; Adams, 1971; De Board, 1968) have employed residential area as the sole criterion for distinguishing deprived individuals from the non-deprived ones. It cannot be denied that living in certain areas may have some degree of correlation with deprivation but it cannot be considered as the valid basis for identifying the 'deprived'. More often than not, location of one's residence is a matter of heritage and in a relatively non-mobile society, such as one in India, some residences, even in the worst areas of a township or a village, have all the facilities necessary to keep materialistic deprivation away from life, and at times presenting a contrast to the adjoining residences creates a sense of enrichment in its inhabitants leading to perhaps significant psychological impacts.

Institutionalization

Recently a number of studies have been reported in which institutionalization of children has been characterised as deprivational. Observed differences between the institutionalized children and those living in their own families have been ascribed to deprivation. Orphanages (Sinha & Shukla, 1974), foster homes (Talmadge, 1969), child care centres (Langmeier & Matezeck, 1968) are some of the institutions identified as deprivational. Undoubtedly such institutions present deprivational setting to a great extent but it cannot be said that they are always deprivational. However, it is intuitively obvious that deprivation can occur and does occur in ordinary family life also. The best that can be said about this criterion is that such institutions and normal families create different types of life conditions and provide not only different types of experiential deprivation but patterns also. There are a host of other variables also along which the two settings differ, and therefore it does not seem sound and scientifically justifiable to consider them distinguishable in terms of deprivation alone.

Membership of some cultural/social/economic group

One of the most frequently employed criteria of deprivation is membership of some specified group. Individuals have been considered as deprived on the grounds of low socio-economic status (Gordon, 1968), being Negro (Wilcox, 1971 ; Green & William, 1965), belonging to a minority community (Goff, 1954) or to an aboriginal tribe (Nurcombe, 1970) or to a particular caste (Das, Jachuk & Panda, 1970 ; Rath & Dash, 1972 ; Sinha,

1977). It cannot be denied that certain segments of the social structure in any country are correlated with deprivational life-experiences but it does not require much effort to discern that in modern socio-political atmosphere membership of specific groups or communities does not present insurmountable barriers for enriching oneself and becoming non-deprived. Every community today has a fairly sizeable number of families which provide enriching conditions of life-experiences. Moreover, deprivation cannot be considered as of a fixed category but as a dimension or a set of several dimensions along which quantitative differences may exist. Such categorical criteria fail to provide quantitative discrimination among the people of the so-called deprived categories.

Having realized the inadequacy of treating deprivation as a nominal variable a number of investigators have started using a variety of other criteria for separating the deprived from the non-deprived with varying magnitudes and use indices of deprivation. This may be considered as the first set of serious attempts at quantification of deprivation. Davis (1968) used a set of seven point rating scales for assessment of deprivational background, even though these rating scales covered only a very narrow range of background factors. A more refined attempt was made by Munsey (1971) in which he developed a Cultural Deprivation Index independent of ethnic group membership and included education, income, and area of residence. Whiteman and Deutsch (1968) developed another cultural deprivation index in which a number of basic societal conditions were included. They argued that 'the association between social grouping and specific environmental factors is not directly causal but is mediated by some more basic societal conditions, such as unemployment, poverty and inequality of opportunity in various areas. With the removal of such conditions the association between social grouping and disadvantaging factors may vanish' (Whiteman & Deutsch, 1968 ; p. 91). Thus, they consider social deprivation as a relative term. They included six variables so combined in a measuring device as to yield a composite score known as "deprivation index". The index has been used by them in the roles of specifier, mediator, independent contributor and also as an interactive variable. The six criterion variables used in the index were : housing condition, educational aspirational level for the child, number of children under 18 years of age in the family, number of cultural experiences, dinner time conversation and attendance of the child in kindergarten. These criterion variables qualified to be included because they related to, (i) an important psychological function, such as reading, and (ii) social groups with varying socio-economic status. The development of the scale was made on a meagre sample of 294 children and no attempt at its cross-validation was made.

On similar lines, Rath and Samant (1975) have developed a cultural deprivation index suitable for Indian setting. Having derived some concepts and techniques from pertinent literature they selected 14 factors of socio-cultural disadvantage or deprivation. Following the method of equal appearing intervals, 42 categories, referring to the selected 14 factors were prepared, and 90 judges (postgraduate students) gave their ratings. Scale values derived from these ratings were determined for each category. The deprivation score of an individual was equal to the mean scale values obtained for all the 14 factors. A later study indicated that family income, father's education, place of residence, and caste of subjects were significantly related to performance on Raven's Progressive Matrices and verbal development. Undoubtedly this scale is an improvement over the other scales, and has included experiential areas in which deprivation may be considered critical for psychological functions. However, it is also open to criticism on more than one ground. For instance, this index was derived on the basis of the responses of judges. While this is an accepted procedure in attitude scaling it cannot be recommended for measurement of deprivation, for the reason that deprivation as conceptualized and understood by judges cannot be considered identical with that which occurs in real-life settings. Judges, being well-to-do and highly educated persons, cannot be considered as having first hand experience of deprivational existence. Their ideas of deprivation are mostly based on secondary sources of information and anecdotes mixed with various kinds of imageries. Therefore, it is essential that in measurement of deprivation the reference point must be the deprived group and not the judges. Items should be selected on the basis of close scrutiny of the living conditions prevailing in the environment of deprived individuals. Moreover, there are a number of important experiential areas that have not been included in this scale.

Although indexing of deprivation is decidedly an improvement over earlier categorical treatment of deprivation, there are still many shortcomings in this approach. In brief, five methodological shortcomings can be mentioned. Primarily, in indexing of deprivation the coverage of criterion variables is partial and narrow, and, therefore, limits the conceptual status of the term deprivation. Secondly, the scoring procedures have not been fully objectified. Elaborate administration and scoring procedures have not been standardized as a result of which investigator's subjectivity still affects the indexing process. Thirdly, the approach can be best characterized as treating deprivation as a nominal variable on the basis of a number of criteria instead of one. As a consequence, varying magnitudes of deprivation cannot be discriminated on the basis of such indices. Fourthly, the current indices of deprivation have left out the experienced or felt or phenomenological aspects of deprivation which have to be considered as important factors in shaping and directing human behaviour. Finally, the indexing of deprivation has laid emphasis on the prevalent status of the individual on the criterion factors and has not paid attention to the temporal aspects of deprivation. It can easily be imagined that any individual, no matter of what chronological age, must have had deprivational experiences not at the time of deprivational indexing but lasting over varying periods of time. Thus, deprivation can be conceptualized as having a temporal dimension which has been neglected in the current efforts at measuring it. It is interesting that in experimental studies of sensory deprivation while its temporal aspect has loomed very large, studies of deprivation in natural settings have ignored it. This shortcoming of the available tools has created a big barrier in attaining precision and comprehensiveness in deprivation measures.

Recently, having realized the methodological limitations inherent in the above mentioned approaches to the measurement of deprivation, Misra and Tripathi (1977a, b, 1978) have tried to standardize a Prolonged Deprivation Scale (PDS) in which deprivation has been taken as a more refined, comprehensive and experience-oriented concept. They have also laid the due emphasis on the temporal dimension of deprivation.

They have made an attempt at identifying the various aspects of environment in relation to which individuals become enriched or impoverished (deprived). In this scale they have included fifteen aspects of natural settings with special reference to life experiences in this country. These aspects comprise (1) housing condition, (2) home-environment, (3) economic-sufficiency, (4) food, (5) clothing, (6) educational experiences, (7) childhood experiences, (8) rearing experiences, (9) parental characteristics, (10) interaction with parents, (11) motivational experiences, (12) emotional experiences, (13) religious experiences, (14) travel and recreation, and (15) miscellaneous socio-cultural experiences. These areas have been split into 96 items along which the investigator is required to rate, on five-point scales, the information culled from the respondent on the basis of interview and observation. The scale is so designed that it can be used with maximum profit, if used at the residence of the respondent. The scale has been standardized on 471 respondents belonging to the age group of 15 to 25 years. This sample was drawn from all kinds of villages, large and small, developed and under-developed, multi-caste dominated and single caste dominated, near townships or away from them. After standardization, data from 600 more respondents were collected. The entire data were subjected to factor analysis. Two factors have emerged which have been designed as physical and psychological. The scale has been validated in variety of ways.

It can be unhesitatingly asserted that PDS presents a marked improvement over other scales and can be profitably used in all kinds of societies provided that its items are translated into the language of the locality in which research has to be conducted, and the investigators are well versed with the local dialect, customs, mores, and have the capacity to establish rapport with the respondent. However, there is still room for improvements in it. Even though the authors have tried to be as exhaustive as possible, it cannot be claimed that all possible deprivational areas of life have been included in it. The scale is based on the assumption that deprivation is a global phenomenon and has been so treated. Naturally, on the basis of this scale subjects with different types of deprivations cannot be discriminated.

On an apriori basis, it can be asserted that each area of deprivation might have differential effects on psychological functioning. But on the basis of this scale such hypotheses cannot be tested. Another limitation that can be pointed out is concerned with the conceptual framework of deprivation within which this scale has been developed. The scale treats lack of physical facilities as well as impoverished experiences as something absolute and does not give due consideration to deprivation as a relative phenomenon.

Macroscopie v. microscopic levels of measurement

In literature on the effects of deprivation on cognitive growth one comes across a rather convenient and expedient method of separating the deprived from the non-deprived persons. Some nominal variable, such as race or caste or religion or residential locality or institutionalized-noninstitutionalized upbringing during childhood, is taken as the sole criterion on the basis of which persons are placed in either deprived or non-deprived category. This is justified as measurement of deprivation at its macroscopic level. This technique of measurement was conceived and conventionalized in the United States of America where two easily distinguishable races, i.e., white and black, exist. The blacks or Negroes have been labelled as deprived while the whites as the non-deprived people. Faithfully following this technique, a number of psychologists in India have considered the members of scheduled castes or scheduled tribes as constituting the universe of deprivation, and other castes as that of non-deprivation or enrichment. However, the subtle but significant differences between the two societal structures, i.e., Indian and American, have escaped their notice. The distinction between the whites and the blacks in the United States of America is racial, has historical roots separating them economically, culturally, politically and more often than not segregating the blacks physically as well as educationally. On the whole, the American society is dichotomous having two distinct social ethos, one with the traditions of "had-been masters", attitudes of superiority and with the rights, privileges and conveniences of "had-been owners", while, the other one with the deeply etched scars of "had-been-slaves", experiences of inferiority and with the liabilities, hardships and inconveniences of the "had-been-owned". Thus, in that country if the two ethos are considered separately, one consisting of the deprived and the other of the non-deprived, there does not appear to be any methodological snag, though on other methodological grounds of precision and soundness, the practice can be subjected to valid criticism. However, this kind of generalization or description can not be validly transferred in case of the social structure in India. The Indian society can be more aptly described as hierarchical. It is true that usually, the lower the hierarchial status of a caste, the greater is the probability of its being impoverished economically, culturally and educationally. But this relationship is not absolute. Therefore, the dichotomization of Indian subjects on the basis of caste or religion does not have the merits of the white-black dichotomization.

Apart from this short-coming on the grounds of differences in the two societies, there is another danger which is inherent in the macroscopic methodological approach. It is self evident that when one talks of macroscopic method of measuring deprivation, one has to necessarily accept some criterion on the basis of which social groups are distinguished in two or more categories. Naturally enough, the level at which categorization is made, is at the group level and not at the level of individual. The criterion (or, the classificatory variable), as such, entails the inevitable corollary that the behavioural variable also gets treated at the group level, and no valid inference can be drawn concerning the individual. Prime facie this seems to be all right, but it creates a situation which is likely to disturb the foundation of psychology itself.

The basic difference between psychology and sociology lies in the level at which behavioural data are analyzed. Sociologists analyze their data at the group level while psychologists are primarily concerned with the behaviour of individuals. If psychologists start using their antecedent and consequent variables at the level of groups alone without treating these variables at the individual plane, the distinction between psychology and sociology is certain to disappear and psychology will subsequently lose its identity in the context of social psychological research. Thus, use of macroscopic approach denies the scope for predicting the behaviour of the individual, or explaining and controlling it. It is within this framework that measurement of the nature and extent of deprivation at the individual level becomes essential.

One must not be misled to the conclusion that the studies that have employed macroscopic level of measurement in investigations of deprivational effects have no psychological value. As a matter of fact, these studies are pioneers in the growth of psychological research in India. In any new area of research the initial sets of investigators are bound to be methodologically coarse. Methodological sophistication emerges as a function of research insight that develops through sustained research activity in a particular area. It is only at this stage that psychologists are in a position to talk of microscopic treatment of deprivation in developing tools and techniques for measuring it. It is in this sense that one has to proceed from coarse-grain-analysis to fine-grain-analysis as, Sinha (1977b) advocates.

The question of optimum experience

The most common strategies adopted in studying the role of life-situation-created deprivation-variables in the origin and growth of psychological functions are two: (i) to separate the deprived group from the non-deprived group; administer tests to them or record their performance under controlled conditions and statistically compare their average performance, or (ii) to determine the degree of deprivation for each subject as well as their individual performance and calculate correlation values between deprivation scores and scores on the chosen psychological measures. On the basis of obtained statistical differences or correlations it is usually concluded that deprivation leads to impaired performance or exerts significant influence on behaviour. It is in consonance with the most commonly assumed theoretical position that certain types of experiences or facilities are essential for proper growth of psychological functions. This assumption leads to a number of theoretical problems but it is not the purpose of the present paper to raise them. In addition to these problems, it has a number of methodological implications also for the measurement of deprivation.

Let us assume that we have chosen some dimension or

specific area, such as parental or cultural or nutritional deprivation along which an individual's deprivation level has to be determined. Let us further assume that we have arbitrarily decided to contain the entire dimension between zero and maximum degree of deprivation and divided it into seven equal appearing intervals envisaging increasing degree of deprivation. Now the most natural methodological question is what type of experiences of living facilities should be considered as involving zero degree of deprivation? This is in a way the problem of fixing the nature and kind of optimal experience. From purely methodological point of view its determination presents a knotty problem. Can it be determined in an absolute manner or has it to be a point relative to the conditions prevailing in those particular natural settings in which deprivation has to be measured? In either case, even though it may appear like hair-splitting, the determination of the zero point of deprivation or the level of optimal experience, seems to be a Gordian knot at the present stage of methodological know-how. This methodological problem is important enough to merit further elaboration.

It can be easily imagined that deprivation in any area of life is a bipolar dimension. At its one end lie those experiences which have to be assumed as maximally deprivational, while, at the other end, lie those experiences which are to be considered as maximally enriching. If it is so, it becomes a deprivation-enrichment dimension. Naturally, there must be a transition point where deprivation as well as enrichment are at a zero level. It is below that point that deprivation becomes more in amount and above which enrichment begins and gradually increases. It is intuitively clear that determination of this point is problematic as has been the case in measurement of attitudes. Since the problem has been tentatively resolved in the measurement of attitudes, it can also be done in measurement of experiences along the deprivation-enrichment continuum, provided that we adopt an approach which assumes that deprivation is an absolute phenomenon. However, the whole idea of deprivation-enrichment dimension becomes disrupted if one accepts deprivation as relative (Crosby, 1976). Within this theoretical framework experiential enrichment becomes a meaningless concept, because relative deprivation being more or less a comparison phenomenon becomes some kind of motivational variable and absence of such motivating factors in any human being will amount to having zero motivational arousal level which can occur in sleep, coma and death only.

Measurement of various types of deprivation

In the preceding discussion, we have hinted at terminological confusion prevailing in the realm of deprivation reflected in such terms as, of cultural deprivation, social and economic disadvantage, emotional, motivational, nutritional or parental deprivation. It can be safely assumed that these various types of deprivation imply differences in areas of deprivation involving lack of specified or specifiable kinds of stimulation patterns. Once we accept this position and by extending the generalization on the basis of results obtained from experimental investigations of sensory deprivation, to the areas of deprivation in natural setting, we hypothesize that the different types of stimulation patterns cumulatively received in specific areas, mentioned above, affect different types of psychological functions. As such, it becomes imperative that the experiential regions covered by these various types of deprivations be carefully mapped out and the boundaries of these regions be clearly demarcated. It is only then that measurement of various types of deprivation and their functional relation with specific psychological characteristics can acquire scientific respectability, and help in more minute and deeper analyses of such functional relationships.

METHODOLOGICAL PROBLEMS IN CONDUCTING DEPRIVATION STUDIES

A review of psychological studies concerned with the effects of deprivation on cognitive, motivational and personality functions reveals that the current research strategies are fraught with a variety of methodological crudity and limitations which, more often than not, create contaminating and confounding effects. Therefore, the obtained results become more of artifacts than manifestations of genuine relationship. In this connection, two sets of problems can be isolated which, so far, have not received due attention. The first set of problems arise from the type of equipment, test materials and experimental tasks that are used in measuring the various functions and behaviours. The second set of problems arise from the kinds of investigators who conduct such studies and also from the kinds of respondents that are identified as deprived ones, especially under rural settings.

Equipments and test materials

Equipment and materials that we generally use for tapping perceptual, learning, problem-solving, representational or intellective functions are usually those that have been designed and developed by teachers and research scholars of psychology. The tests and equipments contain components which are mainly available to educated and richer segments of society that mostly live in fairly affluent conditions have acquired respectable degree of formal education. Since a majority of the deprived respondents come from rural background and are not well educated, it is self-evident that for them these test components and equipments are novel and distracting. Let us assume that we have to measure intelligence or capacity for depth perception or concept formation or any kind of cognitive skill in deprived persons. In any of these cases, we may use some standardized intelligence test, paper-pencil material containing pictures or outlines, memory drum, tachistoscope or some performance test, such as, pass-along test. In this assumed situation, we may follow one of the two strategies, i.e., either we bring the respondent to some psychological laboratory or we take the laboratory to the natural setting where our respondent lives. In the former case, not only the test equipment and materials are completely novel to the subject but the laboratory surroundings also are unfamiliar. It is a well known fact (Hebb, 1958; Bindra and Spinner, 1958; Berlyne, 1951, Dember, 1960) that novelty of material and situation can lead to performance decrement. Any difference in performance between two groups may not necessarily be due to deprivational factors but due to unfamiliarity of the respondents with the test equipments and materials. These methodological problems were realized long back. In 1964, Deutsch and his associates pointed out that standardized tests currently in use present three practical difficulties when they are used with disadvantaged minority groups: (i) they may not provide differentiation and the range of minority group scores, (ii) their predictive validity for minority groups may be quite different from that for the validation and standardization groups, and (iii) the validity of interpretations strongly depends upon an adequate understanding of social and cultural background of the group in question. Having realized these and other limitations, Sinha (1977b) has made quite a few innovations and adaptations in preparation of test materials for use on deprived groups in Indian setting and has also stressed the need for culturally appropriate tools for data collection (Sinha, 1960, 1977a).

Investigator elicited problems

While doing research in one of the most backward areas of the country, namely; the rural areas of eastern Uttar Pradesh, Misra and myself (Misra & Tripathi, 1980 ; Tripathi & Misra, 1975, 1976) were confronted with a variety of problems which threatened to thwart our research efforts in the very beginning. These problems were not specific to our research only. They are of generic importance and relate to the total set of interaction between investigators and respondents. Research investigators are usually Master's or Ph.D. degree holders in psychology or other social sciences, who are completely different in dress, diction and deportment from the respondents. They create the impression of being government officials or other types of organizational functionaries. This difference gives rise to very strong barriers in easy and smooth communication between the investigators and respondents. Because of this difference, the illiterate and experientially deprived members of the chosen community become suspicious, inhibited and evasive not only in answers to various questions put to them as part of interview schedule or test items, but also in making themselves available for various tests and experimental sessions. Even if the investigator is able to quell these initial hurdles by skilfully handling the problem of rapport, the initial difference in the three *Ds* mentioned above creates a feeling of a respect for the investigator which vitiates or confounds the responses to test materials. This kind of confounding effect has been referred to as *courtesy-effect* by Doob (1968). This effect implies that such respondents are likely to give the interviewer the kind of response they believe he seeks rather than what they really believe in. Apart from these difficulties the well known response styles, such as acquiescence and social desirability, have been shown to vitiate such research situations to a large extent.

In the context of interaction between the investigator and respondent there is another factor which has not received as much methodological caution and care as it deserves. It is a well known fact that individuals coming from the deprived segments of society are deficient in vocabulary and verbal expression (Whiteman & Deutsch, 1968) and also in verbal learning with respect to hierarchy of verbal association, associative clustering, and syntactical mediation (Jensen, 1968). Hess and Shipman (1965) observe that 'the meaning of deprivation is the deprivation of meaning in a cognitive environment'. A number of authors such as Baratz and Baratz (1970), Goodman (1969), Labov (1970), Shuy (1969) and Stewart (1968), on the basis of their researches on poor children, conclude that such children come to school with a dialect which differs from standard English. This finding, which appears logically sound as well as appealing to common sense, can be generalized more fruitfully to rural stratum of Indian society. If investigators are not well versed in the dialect of the respondents, quite naturally there would be communication gaps and misinterpretations. Under such circumstances, investigators are liable to get many more expected responses and thus become prophets of self-fulfilling prophecies, as is the case in a number of situations pointed out by Rosenthal and Jacobson (1968). Perhaps, on the basis of such confounding factors, one can explain the fact that most of the researchers working with human subjects drawn from deprived groups always obtain data that are expected on the basis of their hypotheses. Special care is required to have investigators who are efficient in the dialect of the respondents.

The problem of control in deprivation studies

As has been pointed out earlier, deprivation studies in natural settings are totally or partly correlational. The deprivation variable, no matter in what sense it is taken, is manipulated through some selection procedure and dichotomous or trichotomous groups of subjects are formed. These groups are subjected to experimental treatments or administered different psychological tests. When we select deprived subjects on the basis of this or that criterion, usually other factors also vary, and, consequently, interpretation of results on the basis of criterial variable becomes misleading. The problems of control have been ignored in those studies in which deprivation or social disadvantage has been treated as a categorical variable on the basis of caste (Rath & Dash, 1972) or caste and parental income (Das, *et al.*, 1970) or type of school and socio-economic status (Verma & Sinha, 1977) or age, caste and type of schooling (Sinha, 1977) or institutionalization (Sinha & Shukla, 1974) or residential area (Soares & Soares, 1969). In such studies, deprivation or disadvantage is assumed to be a direct function of some social or economic stratification. It does not require much effort to infer that even though deprivation may have positive correlation with the above mentioned criteria and many more, it does not necessarily follow that everyone belonging to a particular group or stratum is deprived. For example, let us take the case of parental income as the basis of separating or distinguishing the deprived from non-deprived. Imagine the case of a family which consists of three members consisting of father, mother and child with income of Rs. 200 per month and another family consisting of grandparents, parents and four children with an income of Rs. 500 per month. Obviously the former child would be considered economically deprived while the latter one becomes advantaged or non-deprived. In this case, naturally the family size is the crucial variable which has been left out uncontrolled. Experiences gained in a larger family have to be different from experiences gained in a smaller family, both in quality, as well as, quantity. Such examples are innumerable. The point worth bearing in mind is that such strategies in selecting samples of deprived and non-deprived subjects leave out many relevant variables that ought to be controlled or made a part of the strategy of deprivation assessment.

Even in those studies where deprivation is measured in the form of indices on the basis of a variety of criteria combined together (Rath & Samant, 1975; Misra & Tripathi, 1977a; Whiteman & Deutsch, 1968), the problem of controlling the relevant variables becomes very complex and involved, not only because deprivation studies in natural settings are essentially correlational, but because there is every possibility that different areas of life, where deprivation takes place, interact among themselves. In the first instance, since these researches are conducted using the *R-R paradigm* and deprivation is the independent variable, i.e., the first *R* in the paradigm, and other innumerable *R* variables become relevant to the variations in the second *R*. The first *R* variable is manipulated through selection, other *R* variables may be effectively controlled, but this is not always the case. In many studies where cognitive processes are studied as functions of deprivation level, personality variables which have been undoubtedly shown to affect cognitive functions are seldom controlled, though, personality too has been shown to be a function of deprivation. On the other hand, it can also be asserted that deprivation-areas interact with one another even though it has not yet become clear as to what is the exact nature of this interaction. If it is true, it becomes self-evident that picking up the deprived and non-deprived groups on the basis of one life area alone, such as, economic or maternal deprivation, does not provide scores for matching the two groups of subjects in terms of the experiential content in relation to other areas of deprivation. And, therefore, the probability remains very high for sources of error to become systematic without the investigator's knowledge. For precision, accuracy and validity, it is necessary that we direct our efforts, towards more microscopic treatments and analyses in deprivation studies.

REFERENCES

Adams, A.A. "The effects of planned background experiences on economically disadvantaged kindergarten children". Unpublished Doctoral Dissertation, Missisippi State University, Missisippi, 1971.

Baratz, S.B., & Baratz, J.C. Early childhood intervention : The social science base of institutional racism. *Harvard Educational Review*, 1970, 40, 29-50.

Bee, H. *Social issue in developmental psychology*. New York : Harper and Row, 1974.

Berlyne, D.E. Novelty and curiosity as determinants of exploratory behaviour. *British Journal of Psychology*, 1951, **41**, 68-80.

Bindra, D., & Spinner, N. Response to different degrees of novelty : The incidence of various activities. *Journal of Experimental Analysis of Behaviour*, 1958, **1**, 341-350.

Bladslee, A.L. Nutritional time bomb. *Today's Health*, 1967, **45**, 7.

Coleman, J.C. *Psychology and effective behaviour*. Bombay : D.B. Taraporevala, 1971.

Crosby, F.A. Model of egoistical relative deprivation. *Psychological Review*, 1976, **83**, 85-113.

Das, J.P. Cultural deprivation and cognitive competence. In N.R. Ellis (Ed.) *International review of research in mental retardation*. (Vol. **6**) New York : Academic Press, 1973.

Das, J.P., Jachuk, K., & Panda, T.P. Caste, cultural deprivation and cognitive growth. In H.C. Haywood (Ed.) *Social cultural aspects of mental retardation*. New York : Appleton-Century-Crofts, 1970.

Das, J.P., & Pivato, E. Malnutrition and cognitive functioning. In N.R. Ellis (Ed.) *International review of research of mental retardation*. (Vol. **8**) New York : Academic Press, 1977.

Davis, R.E. Social deprivation and cognitive functioning in lower class children. *Dissertation Abstracts*, 1968, **29**, 1105-1406.

Deutsch, M., Fishman, T.A. Kogan, L.S. North, R.D., & Whiteman, M., Guidelines for testing minority group children. *Journal of Social Issues*, 1964, **20**, 129-145.

Deutsch, C.P. *Effects of environmental deprivation on basic psychological processes : Some hypotheses*. Paper presented at the annual meeting of American Educational Research Association, Chicago, Illinois, 1965.

DeBoard, L.W. "The achievement syndrome among Negro and White culturally disadvantaged boys." Unpublished Doctoral Dissertation, Vanderbilt University, 1968.

Dember, W.N. *The psychology of perception*. New York : Holt, Rinehart & Winston, 1960.

Dobbing, J. Growth of the brain. *Science Journal*, 1967, **5**, 81-86.

Doob, L.W. Just a few of the presumptions and perplexities confronting social psychological research in developing countries. *Journal of Social Issues*, 1968, **24**, 71-81.

Getzels, J.W. The social psychology of education. In G. Lindzey, & E. Aronson, (Ed.) *The handbook of social psychology*. (Vol. **5**) New York : Addision Wesley, 1969.

Gewirtz, J.L. Learning analysis of the effects of effective privation in childhood. *Acta Psychologia*, 1961, **19**, 404-405.

Goodman, K.S. Dialect barriers to reading comprehension. In J.C. Baratz & R.W. Shuy (Eds.) *Teaching black children to read*. Washington D.C. : Centre for Applied Linguistics, 1969.

Goff, R.M. Educational implication of the influence of rejection on aspiration levels of minority group children. *Journal of Experimental Education*, 1954, **23**, 179-183.

Goldfarb, W. Psychological privation in infancy and subsequent adjustment. *American Journal of Ortho-psychiatry*. 1945, **15**, 247-255.

Gordon, J.E. The disadvantaged pupil. *Irish Journal of Education*. 1968, **2**, 68-105.

Green, L., & William, W.E. Negro academic motivation and scholastic achievement. *Journal of Educational Psychology*, 1965, **56**, 241-243.

Green, R.L. Hofmann, L.J., & Morgan, R. Some effects of deprivation on intelligence, achievement and cognitive growth. *Journal of Negro Education*, 1967, **36**, 5-14.

Havighurst, R.J. Who are the socially disadvantaged ? *Journal of Negro Education*, 1964, **33**, 210-217.

Hebb, D.O. *A text book of psychology*. Philadelphia : W.B. Saunders, 1958.

Hess, R., & Shipman, V. Early experiences and the socialization of cognitive modes in children. *Child Development*, 1965, **36**, 869-885.

Jensen, A.R. Social class and verbal learning. In M. Deutsch, I. Katz, & A.R. Jensen (Eds.) *Social class, race and psychological development*, New York : Holt, Rinehart & Winston, 1968.

Kogan, J., & Kogan, N. Individual variation in cognitive processes. In P.H. Mussen (Ed.) *Carmichael's manual of child psychology*. (Vol. **1**) New York : John Wiley & Sons, 1970.

Labov, W. *The study of nonstandard English*. Illinois National Council of Teachers of English, 1970.

Langmeier, J., & Matezeck, Z. *Psychological deprivation in childhood*. Praha : SZN, 1968.

Langmeier, J. Personalities of deprived children. In F.J. Monks *et al.* (Eds.) *Determinants of behavioural development*. New York : Academic Press, 1972.

Langmeier, J., & Matezeck, Z. *Psychological deprivation in children*. New York : Holsted, 1975.

Miller, J.O. *Cultural deprivation and its modification : Effects of intervention*. Paper presented at the International conference on 'Socio-cultural aspects of mental retardation'. Nashville, March, 1968.

Misra, G., & Tripathi, L.B. The concept of prolonged deprivation and its measurement. *Indian Journal of Behaviour*, 1977, **1**, 48-60 (a).

Misra, G., & Tripathi, L.B. *Manual of prolonged deprivation scale*. Agra : National Psychological Corporation, 1977 (b).

Misra, G., & Tripathi, L.B. *Psychological consequences of prolonged deprivation*. Agra : National Psychological Corporation, 1980.

Misra, G., & Tripathi, L.B. Prolonged deprivation scale. *Indian Journal of Psychology*, 1978, **53**, 65-76.

Munsey, W.L. Development of an index of cultural deprivation independent of ethnic group membership. *Dissertation Abstracts*, 1971, **32**, 3051.

Nurcombe, B. Deprivation : An essay in definition with special consideration of the Australian aboriginals. *Medical Journal of Australia*, 1970, **2**, 88-92.

Rankin, N.O. The effects of selective social deprivation in a natural setting. *Dissertation Abstracts*, 1970, **30**, 4820-4821.

Rath, R., & Dash, A.S. *Cognitive growth and class room learning of naturally deprived children in the primary schools*. Paper presented at the East West Center for Cross-Cultural Studies, Honolulu, 1972.

Rath, R., & Samant, C. "Cultural deprivation index". Unpublished manuscript. Department of Psychology, Utkal University, Bhubaneshwar, 1975.

Riessman, F. *The culturally deprived child*. New York : Harper & Row, 1962.

Rosenthal, R., & Jacobson, L. Self-fulfilling prophecies in the classroom : Teacher's expectations as unintended determinants of pupil's intellectual competence. In M. Deutsch, I. Katz, & A.R. Jensen (Eds.) *Social class, race and psychological development*. New York : Holt, Rinehart & Winston, 1968.

Rossi, A.M. General methodological considerations. In. J.P. Zubek, (Ed.) *Sensory deprivation : Fifteen years of research*. New York : Appleton-Century-Crofts, 1969.

Shuy, R.W. Linguistic background for developing reading materials for black children. In J.C. Baratz, & R.W. Shuy (Eds.) *Teaching black children to read*. Washington D.C. Centre for Applied Linguistics, 1969.

Singh, A.K. *Social disadvantage, intelligence and academic achievement*. Paper presented at the 14th annual conference of the Indian Academy of Applied Psychology, Indian Institute of Technology, Kharagpur, 1976.

Sinha, D. *Indian villages in transition : A motivational analysis*. New Delhi : Associated Publishing House, 1969.

Sinha, D., & Shukla, P. Deprivation and development of skills of pictorial depth perception. *Journal of Cross-Cultural Psychology*, 1974, 5, 434-450.

Sinha, D. Social disadvantages and development of certain perceptual skills. *Indian Journal of Psychology*, 1977, 52, 115-132 (a).

Sinha, D. Orientation and attitude of the social psychologist in a developing country : The Indian case. *International Review of Applied Psychology*, 1977, 26, 1-10(b).

Soares, A.T., & Soares, L.M. Self perceptions of culturally disadvantaged children. *American Educational Research Journal*, 1969, 6, 31-45.

Stewart, W.A. Continuity and change in American Negro dialects. *The Florida Reporter*, 1968, Spring.

Stott, L.H. *The psychology of human development*. New York : Holt, Rinehart, & Winston, 1974.

Suchman, E.A. Medical deprivation. *American Journal of Orthopsychiatry*, 1966, 36, 665-672.

Symmonds, M. Disadvantaged children growing in a climate of hopelessness and despair. *American Journal of Psychoanalysis*, 1968, 28, 15-24.

Tripathi, L.B., & Misra, G. Cognitive activities as a function of prolonged deprivation. *Psychological Studies*, 1975, 21, 54-61.

Tripathi, L.B., & Misra, G. Some cognitive processes as functions of prolonged deprivation. *Indian Journal of Psychology*, 1976, **51**, 129-143.

Talmadge, M., Hayden, B.S., & Schiff, D. Longitudinal analysis of intellectual and educational achievement change in culturally deprived and emotionally disturbed boys. *Perceptual and Motor Skills*, 1969, **29**, 435-440.

Tulkin, S.R. An analysis of the concept of cultural deprivation. *Development Psychology*, 1972, **6**, 326-339.

Uzgiris, I.C. *Socio-cultural factors in cognitive development*. Paper presented at the International conference on 'Socio-cultural aspects of mental retardation'. Nashville, Ten A. 1968.

Verma, L., & Sinha, M.M. Effects of SES on perceptual differentiation contingent upon induced frustration in children. *Indian Psychological Review*, 1977, **15**, 27-35.

Whiteman, M., & Deutsch, M. Social disadvantage as related to intellective and language development. In M. Deutsch, I. Katz, A.R. Jensen (Eds.) *Social class, race and psychological development*. New York : Holt, Rinehart & Winston, 1968.

Wight, D.W. Cloniger, M.F., & Kneene, P.J. Cultural deprivation : Operational definition in terms of language development. *American Journal of Orthopsychiatry*, 1970, **40**, 77-86.

Wilcox, R. *Psychological consequences of being a black American*. New York : John Wiley & Sons, 1971.

Yarrow, L.J. Maternal deprivation : Toward an empirical and conceptual re-evaluation. *Psychological Bulletin*, 1961, **58**, 459-490.

SIX

B.B. Chatterjee

METHODOLOGICAL IMPLICATIONS OF USING THE SOCIO-ECONOMIC STATUS SCALE AS A CONTROL VARIABLE IN DISADVANTAGE-DEPRIVATION STUDIES

INTRODUCTION

IN RECENT times socio-economic status (SES) has been finding increasingly frequent use in a variety of psychological, sociological and socio-educational investigations. Generally, SES tends to be used as a control variable for ordering or fractionating the study sample. If the design uses several strata of the sample, the implicit aim appears to be a search for a significant main effect of varying SES reflected in significant difference in the dependent variables under study. A large proportion of these studies appears to follow this implicit attempt for establishing a main effect attributed to varying SES.

A smaller proportion of studies utilizing SES as a control variable may or may not assume the existence of a main effect, but may assume the existence of a significant interaction effect, between SES and the dependent variables under study. In most investigations, an interaction effect is only a by-product of the statistical analytic procedures used, there being no explicit theory for logical expectation of such an interaction, or of its characteristic, such as its direction, strength, etc.

There is still a much smaller class of investigations, where the implicit assumptions about the nature of relationship between SES and the variables under study are more complex and sophisticated, even if they are not fully spelled out in the language of statistics. A curvilinear relationship may be assumed to exist between SES and concomitant variations in the dependent variables under investigation. Thus, both high SES and low SES groups may be postulated to have high scores on the dependent variable, but the middle range of SES may be postulated to have low scores on the same variable. Or it may be the reverse. In one case, the fit is described best by a U-shaped curve, in another by a V-shaped curve. In the realm of studies using the SES as an ordering variable, such curvilinearity of relationship has been recognized, if not explicitly at the design and statistical analysis stage, but at the verbal explanation stage. Reasonably satisfactory level of achievement in school subjects in middle class homes, contrasted with relatively indifferent performance in poorer and affluent homes, involves such a curvilinear hypothesis, though few studies use this language explicitly. This also applies to many other psychological variables such as adjustment, personality traits, social interactions, level of aspiration, etc.

Need for methodological clarification

A considerable number of investigations on the effect of deprivation, disadvantage and handicaps, at the social-economic-cultural levels, have accepted the monotonic assumption, that of a linear relationship characterizing SES and psychological-sociological-educational functions and achievement, rather unquestioningly. The lower the SES level, the poorer the home; the greater the deprivation, disadvantage and handicap : this should be faithfully reflected in a significant main effect due to SES, or a significant interaction between SES and the dependent variables.

But the possibility of the relationship between SES and degree of deprivation or disadvantage being non-monotonic or curvilinear cannot be ruled out, on logical grounds. Indeed, at the verbal explanatory level, such recognition is already there. Psychologists have started stating clearly that a tribal culture, may be disadvantaged in economic terms, or in terms of material possessions, but need not necessarily be deprived or disadvantaged at the 'cultural' level, that is, in terms of the cultural stimulation and enrichment that it can provide to its members. The culture of the urban slum, or of the backward rural area, may have built-in disadvantages, in terms of money and materials, but perhaps not so in terms of availability of stimulation which may instigate behaviour and learning, and adjustment of perhaps different types.

Failure to recognise this possibility of non-linearity, and non-monotonicity or relationship between SES and other dependent variables may lead to erroneous conclusions.

In certain cases, combining of results over the entire range of the SES scale may result in the actual relationship present being masked, and at times may lead to wrong conclusions being drawn about the very character of the relationship. This simplistic assumption of a linear, monotonic relationship between two classes of variables is more serious. Studies start with the naive assumption about the existence of a one-to-one correspondence between values on the SES scale and degree of deprivation-disadvantage-handicap. This is not always the case: there are many exceptions.

In the present paper, the results of a search for such evidence, about linearity-monotonicity versus non-linearity-non-monotonicity of relationship between SES-subsumed under the deprivation-disadvantage-handicap on the one hand, and achievement-performance-functioning on the other, are being presented briefly. The search is confined to literature of the period 1965 to 1974 only. It is only a preliminary, indicative study.

SES, DEPRIVATION, DISADVANTAGE, HANDICAP AND ACHIEVEMENT

During the last decade and a half considerable research effort has been spent on studying the impact of variables like SES, deprivation, disadvantage, and handicap, which are related to social, economic, ethnic, or residential factors, on achievement and performance in a variety of psychological and educational tasks. The types of study conducted, and the nature of the findings with regard to group or class dependent differences in performance or achievement, in predicted directions as evidence of monotonicity or otherwise, of the relationship between independent and dependent variables, have been presented in Table 6.1.

Data shown in Table 6.1 is not a complete listing. Some of the studies are actually "within (a single) group" study, and no

TABLE 6.1 : **Findings of studies on achievement and performance as a function of socio-economic status, disadvantage, deprivation, deficit and handicap**

Source	Independent/Control variable & sample	Dependent variable(s)	Evidence for monotonicity or non-monotonicity
1	2	3	4
I. Socio-economic status studies			
(A) *Need for achievement and level of aspiration*			
1. Gruen *et al.* (1970)	SES; children	Level of aspiration; learning tasks	SES unrelated to learning with same MA group
2. Srivastava & Tiwari (1967)	SES; students	N-achievement	Non-monotonicity; middle class higher than upper class higher than lower class
(B) *Academic performance*			
3. Baird (1967)	Family income; College students	Academic, non-academic achievement	Complex-relation, non-monotonic with regard to

(*Contd.*)

1	2	3	4
			test scores, but non-tonic with regard to grades
4. Chopra (1966)	SES; HS students	H.S. Exam. marks	Monotonocity
5. Coffin, Dietz & Thompson (1971)	SES; Negro X graders	Academic achievement	Monotonic; no relation with intellectual ability
6. Gough (1971)	SES; HS students	HS graduation	No clear evidence
7. Herr & Tobias (1970)	SES; VI graders	General achievement test through programmed-instruction	Little evidence for monotonicity
8. Harrison (1968)	SES (lower, middle) 10th graders	Educational and occupational aspiration; school performance	Monotonic : middle SES group higher than lower in all variables
9. Hood (1966)	SES : college students	College achievement	Weak evidence for monotonicity
10. Jeffares-Fost & Cosens (1970)	SES; I graders	Auditory discrimination Reading achievement	Monotonicity present
11. Kulkarni & Naidu (1970)	SES; HS students	Mathematics achievement	No monotonicity

(Contd.)

1	2	3	4
12. Oakland (1969)	SES: I & VI graders	Auditory discrimination; reading ability	Monotonicity clear
13. Stevenson, William & Coleman (1971)	SES; disadvantage	Learning and performance tasks	No monotonicity
14. Vervoort (1966)	SES	School achievement	Clearcut monotonicity
(C) *Cognitive abilities and development*			
15. Adler (1970)	SES; 5 year olds	Auditory retention	Group difference for digit span; no group difference for sentence test
16. Bresnahani & Blum (1971)	SES; I graders	Concept acquisition	(1) Monotonicity (2) High group performance worsens, with more reinforcement
17. De Armengal & Goldstein (1974)	SES; Spanish kindergarten children	Test of imitation, comprehension and production	Clearcut monotonicity
18. Figurelli and Keller (1972)	SES; 6-8 yr. olds	Conservation concept	Strong monotonicity
19. Gaudia (1972)	Social class race; low SES; Indians and Whites; I-II graders	Piaget's conservation tasks	Monotonicity, Negroes retarded by one year

(*Contd.*)

1	2	3	4
20. Johnson (1974)	SES; kindergarten children	Categorizing ability	Clearly monotonic performance similar in all SES groups
21. MacDonald, Hines & Kenoyer (1974)	SES; 3 years old children	Concept learning	Monotonic but not for visual reception
22. Mallet & Drew (1974)	SES; III & VI graders	Classificatory Behaviour	Compensation in lower SES groups
23. Nelson & Lechelt (1970)	SES; III graders	Number discrimination value of coin estimation	Monotonicity; value of coins underestimated by low SES groups
24. Spence (1970)	SES; III graders	Discrimination task	No relationship
25. Wexley (1974)	SES; 3-5 yr. olds	8 tests of cognitive skills	Monotonic compensation possible
(D) *Intellectual performance/IQ*			
26. Barger & Berg (1971)	SES; kindergarten children	IQ Verbal	No monotonicity
27. Lichtenwalner & Maxwell (1969)	SES; pre-school children	Creativity; object identification originality test	Strong monotonicity

(*Contd.*)

1	2	3	4
28. Chopra (1968)	SES; students	Intelligence, high School exam. marks	Monotonic, urban groups better than rural groups
29. DeLacey (1971)	High contact aborigines & low SES White Australians	Classificatory ability, verbal intelligence	Monotonicity for IQ, no such relation for classificatory test
30 Ireton, Thuring *et al.* (1970)	SES; 8 months-4 years olds	Mental development	Monotonicity with regard to IQ
31. Kaltsounis (1974)	SES; VIII grade; Black & White	Torrence's Test of Creativity	Non-monotonic; Black *S*s better in fluency and originality
32. Kenneth & Cropley (1970)	SES; 11-15 yr. old	IQ	Clear monotonicity
33. Keogh & McMillan (1971)	SES; Race children	IQ	No monotonicity
34. Kinnie & Sternlof (1971)	SES; 4-5 yr olds; Negro, White	IQ	Compensation in lower SES groups through test familiarization
35. Mumbauer & Miller (1970)	SES; 4 yr olds	General intellectual functions	Clear monotonicity
36. Palmer (1970)	SES; Negro elementary children	Intellectual performance	Linear relation in earlier stages, no relation in later stages

(Contd.)

1	2	3	4
37. Stennett (1969)	SES; IX graders	IQ change	Clear cut monotonicity
38. Telegdy (1974)	SES; kindergarten children	Academic readiness; human figure drawing; picture completion; copying	Strongly monotonic
(E) *Language ability*			
39. Guthrie (1971)	SES; Negro V & VI graders	Language concept	No evidence of monotonicity in concept formulation test, high SES group learned faster
40. Howard & McKinnon (1970)	SES; kindergarteners	Language ability	Strong monotonicity
41. Larsen & Herman (1974)	SES; adult Danes	Language comprehension	No relationship
42. Rodgers, Slade & Conry (1975)	SES; I graders	Oral language comprehension	Monotonic
43. Teasedale & Katz (1968)	SES; ethnic groups I graders	Psycholinguistic test	Monotonicity for auditory components. No group difference for visual and motor components
44. Worley & Storey (1967)	SES; I graders	Language facility	Clear monotonicity

(*Contd.*)

1	2	3	4
II Disadvantaged			
(A) *Academic performance*			
45. Aleamoni & Bowers (1974)	Disadvantage; Black college students	Academic performance	Evidence unclear
46. Buck & Austin (1971)	Economic disadvantage; Negro students	School achievement	Within group study no evidence for between group difference
47. Carver (1968)	Disadvantage; Junior HS Boys	Reading proficiency	Monotonicity
48. Cohen (1959)	Disadvantage I graders	Visual perception Reading ability	Within group study; remediation possible
49. Dispenziert *et al.* (1971)	Disadvantage; college students	College performance	Not much evidence for monotonicity
50. Justman (1966)	Disadvantage	Academic aptitude Reading ability	Weak evidence for monotonicity
51. Kultner (1970)	Ethnic groups; Negro and Amer. Indian	Scholastic test	American Indians better than Negroes
52. Kune, Bruch & Thelen (1974)	Disadvantaged; adults	Academic achievement	Evidence unclear

(*Contd.*)

1	2	3	4
53. Neale & Mussell (1968)	Disadvantaged; children	Reading achievement; attitude towards school	Compensation with special programme possible
54. Williams (1972)	Poverty, IV & VI Graders	Educational achievement	Within same neighbourhood poverty level, no difference between Negroes and Whites, Compensation possible
(B) *Cognitive abilities and development*			
55. Blank & McCandless (1970)	Deprivation	Abstract thinking cognitively dissected perception; coding; problem solving	Evidence for compensation in deprived group through special remedial programme
56. Brodsky (1969)	SES; cultural disadvantage	GSR, task performance	Monotonicity present
57. Hicks & Docklader (1968)	Cultural deprivation; pre-schoolers	Preference for complex and novel stimuli	Monotonicity found
58. Jacobson *et al.* (1971)	Poverty; 3-4 yr olds	Concept learning social interaction; I.Q.	Remediation by special programme; not much evidence for SES related group differences

(*Contd.*)

1	2	3	4
59. Kunz & Moyer (196?)	Economic disadvantage kindergarteners	Intelligence; language; creativity; curiosity	Monotonicity in 3 sub-tests partially monotonic in 3 other sub-tests, no relation in 8 sub-tests
60. Martin (1970)	Disadvantage; I graders	Questioning skills	Clear monotonicity
61. Milgram, Shore & Malasky (1971)	Disadvantaged; kindergarten I grade children	Story recall	Monotonic for 4 measures; difference greater for language compared to thematic categories
62. Minuchin (1971)	Disadvantage; 4 yr. old Negroes	Curiosity; exploratory behaviour	Non-monotonicity
63. Rogers (1968)	Disadvantage; IV graders	Drawing aesthetic judgement; visual orginality and fluency	Monotonic in drawing ability only, in visual fluency, non-monotonic relation compensation possible
64. Secure & Wales (1971)	Cultural disadvantage; V graders	Concept attainment	No monotonicity
65. Thomas (1971)	Disadvantage; kindergartener	Conceptual development	Strong monotonicity

(*Contd.*)

1	2	3	4
66. Torrance & Torrance (1972)	Disadvantage; 6-13 yr. olds	Creative problem solving	Within group study
(C) *I.Q.*			
67. Bruininks & Feldman (1970)	Disadvantage; children	Creativity, intelligence and achievement	Within group study
68. Bruininks & Lucker (1970)	Disadvantage	IQ	Within group study, rise in correlation with rise in age
69. Chopra (1969)	Cultural deprivation; 15-17 yr olds	IQ	Difference between high and middle; no difference between low and middle SES groups
70. Milgram (1971)	Disadvantage; Negro 3-8 yrs	IQ	No clear evidence for monotonicity
71. Thorndike (1969)	Disadvantage; pre-schoolers	IQ	No monotonicity
(D) *Perceptual skills*			
72. Bruininks (1969)	Disadvantage; boys	Perceptual skill, reading ability	Monotonicity, which decreases if verbal intelligence partialled out

(*Contd.*)

1	2	3	4
73. Elkind & Deblinger (1969)	Disadvantage; Negro II graders	Reading, perceptual ability	Disadvantage can be remedied by special programme
74. Thomas, Chissom & Booker (1974)	Disadvantage; adults	Perceptual motor tasks; Academic readiness	Unclear evidence; high correlation between two dependent variables in disadvantage groups only
(E) *Verbal ability*			
75. Gupta & Stern (1969)	Disadvantage; young children	Spoken language	Within group study
76. Sapon (1959)	Disadvantage; $2\frac{1}{2}$-$3\frac{1}{2}$ yr. olds	Verbal behaviour	Unclear evidence for monotonicity
77. Shriner & Miner (1968)	Disadvantage; pre-schoolers	Morphology of language use	Monotonicity

comparison with more advantaged or less advantaged or a control sample is made. Many of these "within group" studies are investigations in remediation programmes meant for compensating the deficiencies hypothesized to characterize certain groups. A quick perusal through Table 6.1 will indicate that the hypothesized inter-dependence between SES, disadvantage, deprivation, handicap and performance, being clearly monotonic in nature is not a universal phenomena. In Table 6.2, the percentages of cases that fall into different categories in terms of the nature of the evidence have been shown.

TABLE 6.2 : **Proportion of studies falling in different categories with regard to evidence about monotonicity or non-monotonicity of relationship between independent and dependent variables : Performance and Achievement**

Type of Finding	Number	Percentage of Total (77)
1. Clear monotonic relation	31	40.25
2. Monotonicity in some variables, lack of monotonicity with other variables in same study	8	10.38
3. Evidence about monotonicity unclear	10	12.98
4. Absence of monotonicity	12	15.58
5. Non-monotonicity of relationship	5	6.49
6. Within group study : remediation successful	9	11.68
7. Remediation unsuccessful	2	2.59

It will be seen from Table 6.2 that about 40 per cent of the studies show clear-cut evidence of the hypothesized monotonic relationship between the two classes of variables. Evidence for absence of any such relationship is also not meagre. At least in 23 per cent of the studies, there is not much evidence of monotonicity. The studies on remediation tell an interesting story : compensation being positively attainable in

TABLE 6.3 : **Findings of studies on various psychological functions related to SES, deprivation, disadvantage, handicap and deficit**

Source	Independent/control variable and sample	Dependent variable	Evidence for Monotonicity on-Non Monotonicity
1	2	3	4
I. Socio-economic status studies			
(A) *Social acceptance and psychological control*			
1. Nuttal *et al.* (1970)	SES, Puerto Rican Adolescents	Social acceptance and psychological control	Monotonicity found
2. Purnell (1970)	SES; VII-IX graders	Preference for self-peers and adults	Evidence for monotonicity unclear
3. Trowbridge (1970)	SES; elementary graders	Self concept	Compensation possible
(B) *Imbibing values*			
4. Alarcon (1969)	SES; adolescents	Life goals	No monotonicity
5. Barger and Hall (1966)	SES; college students	Value orientation	Monotonicity
6. Ermalinski and Ruscelli (1971)	SES; pre-schoolers	Imbibing values	Monotonicity found

(*Contd.*)

1	2	3	4
(C) *Semantic differential*			
7. Williams (1971)	SES; V graders	Semantic differential	Strong monotonicity
(D) *Focus of control*			
8. Bartel (1971)	SES; I, II, IV, VI graders	Locus of control; Iowa test of basic skills	No monotonicity
9. Forbes & Mitchell (1971)	Poverty SES; Negro Adults	Blame attribution feelings of anger; aggression	Unclear evidence for monotonicity
(E) *Delinquent behaviour*			
10. Voss (1966)	SES; VII graders	Delinquent behaviour	Non-monotonic relation for girls, monotonic for boys
II. Disadvantages			
(A) *Self perception*			
11. Boney (1967)	Disadvantage; Negro children	Rejection, inferiority curiosity	Monotonicity present
12. Soares & Soares (1969)	Disadvantage; elementary, secondary children	Self concept	Non-monotonicity

(Contd.)

1	2	3	4
13. Soares & Soares (1970)	Disadvantage; HS students	Self-concept teacher's view of same	Weak non-monotonicity in teacher's view
14. Soares & Soares (1971)	Disadvantage; elementary and secondary school children	Self perception	No monotonicity
15. Soares & Soares (1971a)	Disadvantage; children	Self and inter personal perception	Compensation equally effective in all groups
16. Soares & Soares (1970b)	Disadvantage; elementary graders	Self concept	Non-monotonicity found
(B) *Personality traits*			
17. Epps (1970)	Disadvantage students	Interpersonal relationship	Remediation highly successful
18. Goldstein & Chorost (1966)	Cultural disadvantage; I-III graders	Social adjustment	Compensation with low SES groups
19. Gruber & Kirkendall (1973)	Disadvantage IX-XI graders	Personality	No monotonicity

(*Contd.*)

1	2	3	4
(C) *Semantic differential*			
20. Greenberg *et al.* (1965)	Deprivation IV-V grade Negroes	Attitude, semantic differential	No monotonicity
21. Nelson & Storey (1969)	Disadvantage : Rural-Urban group	Problems (Mooney's check list)	Monotonicity
(D) *Locus of control/expectation*			
22. Milgram *et al.* (1970)	Disadvantage 6 year olds	Level of aspiration, locus of control	No monotonicity
23. Soares & Soares (1971b)	Disadvantage; youth	Expectation	Clear non-monotonicity

most programmes, there being two studies where no such compensation was observed.

The situation is, by and large, similar with studies in which various psychological functions rather than achievement or performance are made the dependent variables. This is made clear in the summary of findings presented in Table 6.3.

A perusal of Table 6.3 will be facilitated by the summary of the nature of evidence about monotonicity or otherwise presented in Table 6.4.

TABLE 6.4 : **Proportion of studies falling in different categories with regard to evidence about monotonicity or non-monotonicity of relationship between independent and dependent variables : Psychological functions**

Type of Finding	Number	Percentage of Total (23)
1. Clear monotonic relation	3	13..04
2. Monotonicity in some variables, lack of monotonicity in some other variables with same study	3	13.04
3. Evidence about monotonicity unclear	1	4.34
4. Absence of monotonicity	8	34.78
5. Non-monotonicity of relationship	4	17.40
6. Within group studies : remediation possible	4	17.40

Table 6.4 shows that in psychological functions other than achievement and performance, the impact of SES-deprivation-disadvantage-handicap, is still more unclear. At least in one-fifth of the studies sampled, there is some evidence for a reversal effect, that is, non-monotonicity of the relationship between the two classes of variables. It is also clear that remediation programmes are able to compensate for deficits generated by poverty and impoverishment.

Direction of future research

Scholars who take interest in this area of research will have noted the stress on the variety of remediation programmes geared to the needs of special groups. Studies of Grotberg (1965), Willerson (1965), Taylor *et al.* (1965), Deutsch (1965), Houston, (1970), Guinagh (1971) and Wade (1969), belong to this genre, and point to the enormous scope of carefully carried out remediation action programmes in removing educational and psychological disparities of varying degree. One methodological problem that needs to be tackled at this stage is the need of devising proper culture-fair tools, which will be free from bias with regard to any particular group.

Secondly, the need for a detailed, indepth debate in the concept of disadvantage, deprivation, handicap and deficit has become pressing. The structure and ingredients of these overlapping concepts have to be analysed. In this connection, the points raised by Stella Chess (1969) in her article "Disadvantage of the 'disadvantaged' Child" deserve attention. She has suggested that blanket use of such terms "produces a stereotype which leads to the classification of children from diverse backgrounds into a limited category". She has cautioned that "to assess any individual child it is essential to know both the group characteristics and the variations within the group".

Such an analysis may lead to the proper designs of studies, in which naive and unverified assumptions will be replaced by operational categorizations with the right type of instruments. In this way methodology of the studies in this area will become sophisticated.

REFERENCES

Adler, S. Auditory retention ability in five-year-old lower and middle class children : A pilot study. *Journal of Communication Disorders*, 1970, 3, 133-139.

Alarcon, R. Life goals of adolescents of different socio-economic levels. *Revista Latino Americans de Psicologis*, 1969, **1**, 55-61.

Aleamoni, L.M., & Bowers, J. E., The evaluation of special educational opportunities programme for disadvantaged college students. *Research in Higher Education*, 1974, **2**, 151-164.

Baird, L. L. Family income and the characteristics of college-bound students. *Acta Research Reports*, 1967, **17**, 26.

Barger, B., and Hall, E. The inter-relationships of family size and socio-economic status for parents of college students. *Journal of the Marriage and the Family*, 1966, **28**, 186-187.

Bruininks, R. H. Auditory and visual perceptual skills related to the reading performance of disadvantaged boys. *Perceptual and Motor Skills*, 1969, **29**, 179-186.

Bruininks, R. H., & Feldman, D. H. Creativity, intelligence, and achievement among disadvantaged children. *Psychology in the Schools*, 1970, 7, 260-264.

Bruininks, R. H., & Lucker, W.G. Changed stability in correlations between intelligence and reading test scores among disadvantaged children. *Journal of Reading Behaviour*, 1970, 2, 295-305.

Berg, N. L. & Berg, S. D. Comparison of verbal intelligence of young children from low and middle socio-economic status. *Psychological Reports*, 1971, **28**, 559-562.

Blank, M., & McCandless, B.R. A methodology for fostering abstract thinking in deprived children. *Ontario Institute for Studies in Education Monograph*, 1970, **9**, 1-15.

Boney, J. D. Some dynamics of disadvantaged students in learning situations. *Journal of Negro Education*, 1967, **36**, 315-319.

Bresnahani, J. L. & Blum, W. L. Chaotic reinforcement : A socio-economic leveller. *Developmental Psychology*, 1971, **4**, 89-92.

Brodsky, M. Cultural deprivation and arousal level. *Proceedings of the 77th Annual Convention of the APA*, 1969, **4**, 315-316.

Bartel, N. R. Locus of control and achievement in middle-and-lower-class children. *Child Development*, 1971, **42**, 1099-1107.

Berman, G., & Eisenberg, M. Psycho-social aspects of academic achievement. *American Journal of Orthopsychiatry*, 1971, **41**, 406-415.

Buck, M. R., & Austin, H. R. Factors related to school achievement in an economically disadvantaged group. *Child Development*, 1971, **42**, 1813-1826.

Carver, R. P. Evaluation of a listening comprehension test for disadvantaged Junior High School boys. *American Institute of Research*, **68**, 1968.

Chess, S. Disadvantages of "the disadvantaged child". *American Journal of Orthopsychiatry*, 1969, **39**, 4-6.

Chopra, S. L. Socio-economic background and failure in the high school examination. *Educational and Psychological Measurement*, 1966, **26**, 495-497.

Chopra, S. L. Measured intelligence and academic achievement as related to rural-urban residence. *Rural Sociology*, 1968, **36**, 214-217.

Chopra, S. L. Cultural deprivation and academic achievement. *Journal of Educational Research*, 1969, **62**, 435-438.

Cohen, S. A. Studies in visual perception and reading in disadvantaged children. *Journal of Learning Disabilities*, 1969, **2**, 498-507.

Coffin, B. S., Dietz, S. C., & Thompson, C. L. Academic achievement in a poverty area school : Implications for counselling. *Journal of Negro Education*, 1971, **40**, 365-368.

de Armengai, M., Goldstein, F. & Lombana, I. Comparison of imitation, comprehension and the production of grammatical contrast by children from high and low socio-economic status. *Revista Latinoamericans de Psicolgia*, 1974, 6, 239-254.

De Lacey, P. R. Classificatory ability and verbal intelligence among high contact aboriginal and low socio-economic white Australian children. *Journal of Cross-Cultural Psychology*, 1971, 2, 393-396.

Dispenziert, A., Giniger, S., Reichman, W., & Levy, M. College performance of disadvantaged students as a function of ability and personality. *Journal of Counselling Psychology*, 1971, 18, 298-305.

Deutsch, C.B. Education for disadvantaged groups. *Review of Educacational Research*, 1965, 35, 140-146.

Elkind, D., & Deblinger, J. A. Perceptual training and reading achievement in disadvantaged children. *Child Development*, 1969, 40, 11-19.

Epps, E. G. Interpersonal relations and motivation : Implications for teachers of disadvantaged children. *Journal of Negro Education*, 1970, 39, 14-25.

Ermalinski, R. & Ruscelli, V. Incorporation of values by lower and middle socio-economic class preschool boys. *Child Development*, 1971, 42, 629-632.

Figurelli, J.C., & Keller, H.R. The effects of training and socio-economic class upon the acquisition of conservation concept. *Child Development*, 1972, 43, 293-298.

Forbes, G. B., & Mitchell, S. Attribution of blame, feelings of anger, and direction of aggression in response to inter-racial frustration among poverty level Negro adults. *Journal of Social Psychology*, 1971, 83, 73-78.

Gaudia, G. Race. Social class and age of achievement of conservation on Piaget's tasks. *Developmental Psychology*, 1972, 6, 158-165.

Goldstein, K. M. & Chorost, S. B. Preschool and background factors in the school adjustment of culturally disadvantaged children. *Proceedings of the 7th Annual Convention of the APA*, 1966, 275-276.

Gouch, H.G. Socio-economic status as related to high school graduation and college attendance. *Psychology in the Schools*, 1971, 8, 226-231.

Graff, V. A., & Feldman, S. C. Effective reading for the socially deprived child. *Journal of Rehabilitation*, 1965, 31, 13-14.

Greenberg, J.W., Gener, J. M., Chall, J., & Davidson, H. H. Attitudes of children from a deprived environment toward achievement related concepts. *Journal of Educational Research*, 1965, 59, 57-62.

Grotberg, E.M. Learning disabilities and remediation in disadvantaged children. *Review of Educational Research*, 1965, 35, 413-425.

Gruber, J.J., & Kendall, D.R. Relationship within and between the mental and personality domains in disadvantaged high school students. *American Corrective Therapy Journal*, 1973, 27, 136-140.

Gruen, G., Ottinger, D., & Zigler, E. Level of aspiration and the probability learning of middle and lower-class children. *Development Psychology*, 1970, 3, 133-142.

Guinagh, B.J. An experimental study of basic learning ability and intelligence in low socio-economic status children. *Child Development*, 1971, **42**, 27-36.

Gupta, W., & Stern, C. Comparative effectiveness of speaking vs. listening in improving spoken language of disadvantaged young children. *Journal of Experimental Education*, 1969, **38**, 54-57.

Guthrie, J. T. Relationship of teaching method, socio-economic status, and intelligence in concept formation. *Journal of Educational Psychology*, 1971, **62**, 345-351.

Harrison, F. Aspirations as related to school performance and socio-economic status. *Sociometry*, 1968, **32**, 70-79.

Hicks, R.A., & Docklader, S. Cultural deprivation and preschool children's preferences, for complex and novel stimuli. *Perceptual and Motor Skills*, 1968, **27**, 1321-1322.

Herr, A., & Tobias, S. Achievement via programmed instruction and socio-economic status. *Psychology in the Schools*, 1970, **7**, 53-56.

Hood, A.B. Comparison of the academic achievement of certain types of students in different types of colleges. *Proceedings of the 7th Annual Convention of the APA*, 1966, 289-290.

Houston, S.H. A re-examination of some assumptions about the language of the disadvantaged child. *Child Development*, 1970, **41**, 947-967.

Howard, M.J., Hoops, H.R., & McKinnon, A.J. Language abilities of children with differing socio-economic backgrounds. *Journal of Learning Disabilities*, 1970, **3**, 328-335.

Ireton, H., Thwing, E., & Gravem, H. Infant mental development and neurological status, family socio-economic status, and intelligence at age four. *Child Development*, 1970, **41**, 937-945.

Jacobson, L.I., Berger, S.E., Bergman. R.L., Milham, J., & Greeson, L.E. Effect of age, sex, systematic conceptual learning, acquisition of learning sets, and programmed social interaction on the intellectual and conceptual development of pre-school children from poverty backgrounds. *Child Development*, 1971, **42**, 1399-1415.

Jeffares-Fost, D.J. & Cosens, G.V. Effects of socio-economic status and auditory discrimination training on first-grade reading achievement and auditory discrimination. *Alberta Journal of Educational Research*, 1970, **16**, 165-178.

Johnson, R. Categorizing ability of kindergarteners of high and low socio-economic status. *Psychological Reports*, 1974, **35**, 311-316.

Justman, J. Academic aptitude and reading test scores of disadvantaged children showing varying degrees of mobility. *Journal of Educational Measurement*, 1965, **2**, 151-155.

Kaltsounis, B. Race, socio-economic status and creativity. *Psychological Reports*, 1974, **35**, 164-166.

Kenneth, K.F., and Cropley, A.J. Intelligence, family size, and socio-economic status. *Journal of Biosocial Sciences*, 1970, **2**, 227-236.

Keogh, B.K. & MacMillan, Donald L. Effect of motivational and presentation conditions on digital recall of children of differing socio-economic, racial, and intelligence groups. *American Educational Research Journal*, 1971, **8**, 27-38.

Kinnie, E.J., & Sternlof, R.E. The influence of non-intellective factors on the IQ scores of middle and lower-class children. *Child Development*, 1971, **42**, 1889-1995.

Kulkarni, S.S., & Naidu, C.A. Mathematics achievement related to students socio-economic and attitude variabies : A pilot study. *Indian Journal of Psychology*, 1970, **45**, 53-66.

Kultner, R.E. Comparative performance of disadvantaged ethnic and racial groups. *Psychological Reports*, 1970, **27**, 372.

Kune, J.T., Bruch, M.A., & Thelen, M.H. Vicarious induction of academic achievement behaviour in disadvantaged adults. *Journal of Counselling Psychology*, 1974, **21**, 507-510.

Kunz, J., & Moyer, J.E. A comparison of economically disadvantaged and economically advantaged kindergarten children. *Journal of Educational Research*, 1969, **62**, 392-395.

Larson, S.F., & Hermann, J. Social status and language comprehension. *Scandinavian Journal of Psychology*, 1974, **15**, 161-168.

Lichtenwalner, J.S., & Maxwell, J.W. The relationship of birth order and socio-economic status to the creativity of preschool children. *Child Development*, 1969, **40**, 1241-1247.

MacDonald, R., Hines, B., & Kenoyer, C. Socio-economic status as related to two levels of conceptual attainment. *Journal of Genetic Psychology*, 1974, **125**, 195-199.

Mallett, J., & Drew, C.J. Classification behaviours in third and sixth grade lower and middle socio-economic status school children. *Journal of Child Orthopsychiatry*, 1974, **15**, 123-131.

Martin, F. Questioning skills among advantaged and disadvantaged children in first grade students. *Psychological Reports*, 1970, **27**, 617-618.

Milgram, N.A., Shore, M.F., Riedel, W., & Malasky, C. Level of aspiration and locus of control in disadvantaged children. *Psychological Reports*, 1970, **27**, 243-350.

Milgram, N.A., Shore, M.F., & Malasky, C. Linguistic and thematic variables in recall of a story by disadvantaged children. *Child Development*, 1971, **42**, 637-640.

Milgram, N.A. IQ constancy in disadvantaged Negro children. *Psychological Reports*, 1971, **29**, 319-326.

Minuchin, P. Correlates of curiosity and exploratory behaviour in preschool disadvantaged children. *Child Development*, 1971, **42**, 939-950.

Mumbauer, C.C., & Miller, J.O. Socio-economic background and cognitive functioning in preschool children. *Child Development*, 1970, **41**, 471-480.

Neale, D.C., & Mussell, E. Effects of big-brother relationships on the school related attitude of disadvantaged children. *Journal of Special Education*, 1968, **2**, 397-404.

Nelson, H.M., & Storey, S.E. Personality adjustment of rural and urban youth : The formation of a rural disadvantaged sub-culture. *Rural Sociology*, 1969, **34**, 43-55.

Nelson, T.N., & Lechelt, E.C. Socio-economic status, value, and response to number. *Perception and Psychophysics*, 1970, **8**, 76-80.

Nuttall, R.L., Smith, D.H. & Nuttall, E.V. Family background, parent child relationship, and academic achievement among Puerto Rican junior and senior high school students. *Proceedings of the Annual Convention of the APA*, 1970, **5**, 307-308.

Oakland, T.D. Auditory discrimination and socio-economic status as correlates of reading disability. *Journal of Learning Disabilities*, 1969, **2**, 325-329.

Palmer, F.H. Socio-economic status and intellectual performance among Negro preschool boys. *Developmental Psychology*, 1970, **3**, 1-9.

Parnell, R.F. Socio-economic status and sex differences in adolescent reference-group orientation. *Journal of Genetic Psychology*, 1970, **116**, 233-239.

Rogers, D.W. Visual expression : A creative advantage of the disadvantaged. *Gifted Child Quarterly*, 1968, **12**, 110-114.

Rodgers, D., Slade, K., & Conry, R. Oral language, reading ability, and socio-economic background in Grade I class. *Alberta Journal of Educational Research*, 1974, **20**, 316-326.

Sapom, S.M. Contingency management in the modification of verbal behaviour in disadvantaged children. *International Review of Applied Linguistics*, 1969, **7**, 37-44.

Securre, S., & Walls, R.T. Concept attainment of culturally advantaged and disadvantaged children, utilizing artificial and life like stimulus tasks. *Journal of Educational Psychology*, 1971, **62**, 531-538.

Shriner, T.H., & Miner, L. Morphological structures in the language of the disadvantaged and advantaged children. *Journal of Speech and Hearing Research*, 1968, **11**, 605-610.

Soares, A.T., & Soares, L.M. Comparative study of the self-perceptions of disadvantaged children in elementary and secondary schools. *Proceedings of the 77th Annual Convention of the APA*, 1969, **4**, 659-660.

Soares, A.T., & Soares, L.M. Interpersonal self-perceptions of disadvantaged and advantaged high school students. *Proceedings of the Annual Convention of the APA*, 1970, **5**, 457-458.

Soares, A.T., & Soares, L.M. Self-concepts of disadvantaged and advantaged students. *Proceedings of the Annual Convention of the APA*, 1970, **5**, 653-654.

Soares, L.M., & Soares, A.T. Self-concepts of disadvantaged and advantaged students. *Child Study Journal*, 1970-71, **1**, 69-73.

Soares, A.T., & Soares, L.M. Comparative differences in the self-perceptions of disadvantaged and advantaged students. *Journal of School Psychology*, 1971, **9**, 424-429.

Soares, A.T., & Soares, L.M. Expectancy, achievement, and self-concept correlates in disadvantaged and advantaged youths. *Proceedings of the Annual Convention of the APA*, 1971, **6**, 561-562.

Spence, J.T. The distracting effects of material reinforcers in the discrimination learning of lower and middle-class children. *Child Development*, 1970, **41**, 103-111.

Srivastava, P.K., & Tiwari, M.L. Socio-economic stratification of need achievement. *Psychological Studies*, 1967, **12**, 9-16.

Stevenson, H.W., Williams, A.M. & Coleman, E. Inter-correlations among learning and performance tasks in disadvantaged children. *Journal of Educational Psychology*, 1971, **62**, 179-184.

Stennett, R.G. The relationship of sex and socio-economic status to IQ change. *Psychology in the Schools*, 1969, **6**, 385-390.

Taylor, J.B., Levy, P., & Wykert, J. Psychological problems in low-income families : A research report. *Bulletin of the Menninger Clinic*, 1965, **29**, 312-339.

Teasedale, G.R., & Katz, F.M. Psycholinguistic activities of children from different ethnic and socio-economic background. *Australian Journal of Psychology*, 1968, **20**, 155-159.

Telegdy, G.A. The relationship between socio-economic status and school readiness. *Psychology in the Schools*, 1974, **11**, 351-356.

Thomas, J.R., Chissom, B.S., & Booker; L. Perceptual-motor and academic relationships for disadvantaged children classified as learning disabled and normal. *American Correction Therapy Journal*, 1974, **28**, 95-99.

Thorndike, R.L. The effect of Headstart training on the cognitive growth of disadvantaged children. *Journal of Educational Research*, 1969, **62**, 387-389.

Thomas, E.C. Conceptual development in advantaged and disadvantaged kindergarten children. *Perceptual and Motor Skills*, 1971, **32**, 711-717.

Torrance, E.P., & Torrance, P. Combining creative problem-solving with creative expressive activities in the education of disadvantaged young people. *Journal of Creative Behaviour*, 1972, **6**, 1-10.

Trowbridge, N. Effects of socio-economic class on self-concept of children. *Psychology in the Schools*, 1970, **7**, 304-306.

Vervoort, C.E. Social determinants of learning in primary education. *Gwein*, 1966, **14**, 314-326.

Wade, S.E. Media and the disadvantaged : A review of literature. Stanford : *ERIC* 1969.

Wexley, K., Guidubaldi, J., & Kehle, T. An evaluation of Montessori and Day care programs for disadvantaged children. *Journal of Educational Research*, 1974, **68**, 95-99.

Williams, M.M. Race, poverty, and educational achievement in an urban environment. *Proceedings of the Annual Convention of the APA*, 1972. **7**, 467-468.

Williams, W.S. A semantic differential study of the meaning of personality test items to children from different socio-economic groups. *Journal of Psychology*, 1971, **79**, 179-188.

Worley, S.E., & Story, W.E. Socio-economic status and language facility of beginning first-graders. *Reading Teacher*, 1967, 20, 400-440.

Willerson, D.A. Programs and practices in compensatory education for disadvantaged children. *Review of Educational Research*, 1965, 35, 426-440.

SECTION TWO

PSYCHOLOGICAL CONSEQUENCES
Cognitive and Motivational

INTRODUCTION

ESTABLISHING a functional relationship between deprivation and various measures of psychological functioning has been a favourite area of research by psychologists in India. The strategy of these studies has been to take some index or indices of deprivation as an independent variable and try to establish its association with differentials in performance on measures of perceptual, linguistic or cognitive competence and personality characteristics.

Undernourishment of various degrees is a common concommitant of deprivation, and for a long time, adverse effect of malnutrition on performance has been taken almost as axiomatic. However, research in this area has yielded somewhat ambiguous findings. J.P. Das and Priyani Soysa's study on *kwashiorkor* children in and around Colombo reveals that an episode of malnutrition does not make a unique contribution to cognitive performance. It emphasizes the importance of the total environment of the undernourished child during the period of his growth.

Differences in the linguistic behaviour associated with socio-cultural disadvantage have been actively researched in recent years in linguistics, psychology and sociology. Annamalai makes a critical appraisal of the concept of linguistic deprivation and contends that the findings of Bernstein on code difference among various social classes imply nothing more than 'style' differences and have no bearing on intelligence. However, he concedes that such differences may contribute to specific linguistic problems in learning situations in school in case of the lower class children. In this context, compensatory education and its pitfalls are discussed.

On a somewhat related issue, Shantilata Sahu uses Osgood's composite test of primary and semantic generalization and three-stage-mediational ability to report that the effects of social disadvantage vary with age as well as the task.

Two of the studies presented in this section deal with cognitive and perceptual competence. Girishwar Misra reviews the evidence related to the effect of deprivation on cognitive competence and proposes the concept of prolonged deprivation. His findings suggest that prolonged experiential deprivation adversely affects cognitive performance. Similarly, taking caste-status and quality of schooling as indices of socio-cultural disadvantage, Durganand Sinha finds age, caste and schooling as significant main effects on performance on some perceptual tasks. His study also presents some evidence for what he calls the 'broomstick effect', i.e., high and low caste differences getting accentuated in favour of the former with advance in age and schooling.

Though, general cognitive functioning of the individual in relation to deprivation seems to be the most researched area by the psychologists, deprivation has also been related to motivational variables. Durganand Sinha and Girishwar Misra review the main studies conducted in India and abroad which throw light on the motivational and personality characteristics of the deprived.

Socio-psychological problems related to the education of the disadvantaged have received a good deal of attention in the West but have remained somewhat neglected by Indian researchers. Namita Pande and R.C. Tripathi's paper focuses on the school climate and its impact on classroom behaviour especially with reference to the scheduled caste children. They report that the scheduled caste children generally perceived the school climate as unsupportive which had a dampening effect on their motivational levels. In this context, a model for the scheduled caste under-achievement is also suggested by them.

The picture of the effects of deprivation that emerges from these papers is a complex one, and due caution is to be exercised in interpreting the findings. It may, however, be said that general deprivation and various kinds of socio-cultural disadvantages do adversely influence the cognitive and personality functioning of the individual. The results taken together suggest that the deprived do not suffer much from learning disabilities but more from deficit in performance which can be removed through appropriate intervention programme.

SEVEN

J.P. Das and *Priyani Soysa*

LATE EFFECTS OF MALNUTRITION
A Biomedical and Psychological Study* **

A REVIEW of the important studies on the effect of malnutrition on cognitive competence will lead one to the conclusion that a direct relation between the two has not been established (Das & Pivato, 1977). It is difficult to separate the effects of complicating social factors which are invariably associated with malnutrition in the lower socio-economic classes. Further, the presumed damage to the brain structures cannot be directly shown in cases of human malnutrition. The indirect evidence is based on the demonstration that malnutrition which occurs during the most vulnerable period of brain development is most harmful for the development of intellectual functions; this has not received much support (Birch & Gussow, 1970). In fact, the bulk of the evidence relating the age at which the child was hospitalized for malnutrition and later performance at school is at best inconclusive (Hertzig, Birch, Richardson & Tizard, 1972). Finally, where the data indicate that the

* The project was supported by Grants S-73-0059 from the Canada Council. Assistance of Dr. R.F. Jarman, University of British Columbia in statistical analysis of the data is gratefully acknowledged. Informed consent of parent (s) and school authorities was obtained for testing the children.

** A revised version of this paper entitled Late Effects of Malnutrition on Cognitive Competence has been published in *International Journal of Psychology*, 1978, 13, 295-303. Permission of publishers to reprint the material is gratefully acknowledged.

malnourished child is inferior in intellectual tasks, a causal relation has been questioned. Instead of malnutrition, the probable causes could be the loss of learning time while the child was hospitalized, a lack of attention and motivation (Birch & Gussow, 1970).

We wish to illustrate the complications commonly found in designing studies in area before presenting our study. Let us consider the project in Jamaica (Richardson, 1972) which is perhaps the best controlled study in existence up to now. In this project, the index children, that is, those who had been hospitalized for an episode of malnutrition, were compared with their siblings as well as with healthy children. A large number of the siblings were illegitimate children. The index and the sibling had a common mother, but for several siblings the father was not common. One of the findings was that, the siblings were higher in IQ than the index cases. The difference could be explained as much in terms of heredity as by the relatively superior nutritional status of the siblings.

In an article published in *Pediatrics*, Richardson and colleagues came to the conclusion that the obtained differences in IQ between index and control children cannot be directly attributed to differences in nutritional status during the first two years of life. The index children may differ from their controls in attributes other than nutrition (Hertzig, *et al.* 1972).

One of these attributes could be the intellectual stimulation at home. Richardson (1976) mentions that those index children who had an intellectually stimulating home environment were equal in intellectual performance to a group of control children who had a home condition characterized by low intellectual stimulation.

The data in this regard are suggestive rather than conclusive of an environmental determinate of intellectual performance. One has to ask further as to what factors determine the level of intellectual stimulation at home. Does the intelligence level of parents covary with the quality of home environment? Can we establish that the parental IQ of the index children from 'stimulating homes' was the same as the parental IQ of healthy children who came from an 'unstimulating home'?

It seems to us that most of the well-known studies in this area have not controlled for the differences in sociological factors, such as home environment. In the well-known study by Stoch and Smythe (1963), the index children lived in poorer homes, came from broken families, and had unemployed parents. The control children, on the other hand, lived in better homes, and none of the children were illegitimate, compared with 13 out of 21 of the index children who were illegitimate. It is no wonder the IQ's of the index children were lower than the IQ's of the control children.

It seems to us that wherever a difference between malnourished children and their controls is found, the researcher should examine closely the contribution of genetic and environmental factors separately. This has not been done in many studies. For instance, in the famous study by Chase and Martin (1970), it is reported that the mean IQ of mothers of malnourished children was lower than the mean IQ of mothers of non-malnourished children, a fact which casts some doubt on the validity of attributing low intelligence in the child to malnourishment. Similarly, on Moncheberg's (1972) project in Chile, IQ of mothers of malnourished children was found to be related to the nutritional status of the child as evidenced by the child's height. This means that mothers with low IQ had shorter children. Height of the child in that case was partly related to the child's intelligence, which in turn is related to mother's IQ. Therefore, short height reflected the genetic relation between mother and child and by itself was not entirely due to malnutrition. In any case, the study in Chile compared a control group of middle class children with slum children. It is anyone's guess as to the proportion of contribution of nutrition and heredity to the difference that was found between the control and the malnourished children in intelligence.

A prospective study is often recommended as the best possible strategy to disentangle the effects of heredity and environment. Such a study is being carried out by Cravioto and DeLicardie (1972), preliminary results of which have already been announced showing that the malnourished children were poorer in at least language skills than their cohort controls. But in Cravioto's study one notes that the micro-environment of the malnourished children was inferior to that of the cohorts.

The question then, is : Does malnutrition further depress the cognitive function of disadvantaged children? The present paper tries to answer this question. Suppose severe clinical malnutrition marasmus or kwashiorkor do not have an additional effect over and beyond the effects of social-familial factors. Then the biomedical evidence linking an episode malnutrition with damage to the structure of the brain needs to be re-examined. A crucial study which will answer the above question should have two samples of children for comparison: one which is economically and socially disadvantaged and has survived an episode of severe clinical malnutrition, and another which is equally disadvantaged, but without a clinical history of episodic malnutrition. However, the second group, in order to be meaningfully compared as control with the first, must come from the same depressed neighbourhood. The two groups should have comparable family environments. The control is perhaps chronically undernourished, whereas the index group has a history of severe malnutrition resulting in hospitalization. We have examined four groups of children in Sri Lanka with the above consideration in mind.

METHOD

Sample

Forty-two index cases were chosen who were hospitalized for marasmus or kwashiorkor about five or six years before. They were living in and around Colombo at the time of testing. Their mean age was about 116 months (with a standard deviation of 13 months). A control group of 42 children for the index cases was taken from similar social and familial backgrounds, and in most cases, from the same neighbourhood. The children in the control group were matched only on age and sex with the index case. Further one-to-one matching was not carried out because such matching might infringe on some of the basic assumptions of sampling. Apart from the index cases and their controls two other samples were also examined. These were the siblings of the index cases who were between 7 and 12 years of age and their controls. Most of our cognitive tests were for ages 7 to 12, hence, older or younger siblings were not included in the study. In some cases the index child did not have a sibling, and in some cases, the index and the sibling were in different families. The average age of the 35 siblings so chosen was 120 months (with a standard deviation of 21 months). An equal number of control children for the siblings, matched on age and sex and in the majority of cases, living in the same neighbourhood, was also selected for comparison purposes. However, most of the cognitive data were available for only 33 siblings and their controls were compared. All children included in this study came from some of the most underdeveloped areas in and around Colombo.

The index children were traced from the admission records as in-patients of the malnutrition ward at Colombo Children's Hospital. The following entries for the index cases were found in the admission records: sex, chronological age, urban or rural residence, income, number of children in family, place of the child in the family, father's education, mother's education, child's education, marital status of parents, presence or absence of infections, type of malnutrition (that is, kwashiorkor or marasmus), immunization records, intake .of protein, four clinical signs (including conjectiva, lymphadenopathy, skin and liver), results of investigations (including stool, hemoglobin, hand serumalbumin), duration of stay in hospital, and age and weight at admission. A question may be raised as to the reliability of data from admission records. One of the authors, (Soysa) had closely supervised the first admission of the index children and had continued to be in charge of the malnutrition ward. Although it is impossible to be absolutely certain of the reliability of the entries, we would believe that the continuation of the same pediatrician in the supervisory role of the ward may substantially contribute to their reliability.

When the child was brought in for cognitive tests, an assistant sometimes recorded head and chest circumferences, and the child's weight and height. However, these records were not completed for all cases. An assessment of the current status of the child at the time of the cognitive tests would also be desirable. But unfortunately, medical indices for the index or the control children were not obtained.

Medical characteristics of index children

Although different degrees of protein-calorie malnutrition were seen in the years 1966 and 1967, which were the years of admission of our index children into the malnutrition ward, those who were hospitalized as in-patients were only the severe cases. In terms of Gomez's (1956) classification, the children were labelled "protein-calorie malnutrition grade 3" and in terms of weight they fell into Jelliffe's (1966) grades 3 and 4. More specifically, kwashiorkor was diagnosed on the basis of the presence of at least two of the following characteristics: growth retardation, oedema, muscular wasting, and psycho-motor change. The other associated characteristic features which are sometimes present were: hair and skin changes, hepatomegaly, anemia, hypoproteinemia, and vitamin deficiencies. Marasmus was diagnosed on growth retardation and wasting of muscles and subcutaneous fat, while hair changes were also occasionally associated with marasmus. Of our 42 index children who completed the psychological tests, 17 were florid cases of kwashiorkor, 10 were cases of kwashiorkor that had been reversed to marasmus and 15 were clear cases of marasmus.

Congitive tests

The practice of comparing index and control children on a standard intelligence test has been criticized (Hurwitz, 1976). Any global measure of IQ is apt to overlook specific cognitive processes which may indicate the difference between malnourished and control children in some but not all cognitive functions.

A battery of cognitive tests was given to the children. The battery provides an operational description of two major coding processes, namely simultaneous and successive (Das *et al.* 1975). Simultaneous processing is defined by Raven's Progressive Matrices, Figure Copying and Memory for Designs. The target tests of successive processing are Visual Short-term Memory, Digit Span and Serial Recall of short lists of words. An additional test, Cross-modal Coding was also given to the children. This is the test of intersensory integration previously used by Birch and Gussow (1970). The test measures both processes. Speed of processing is indicated by a Color Naming task in which the child is required to name 40 randomly arranged colour strips, 10 each from the four primary colours of red, green, yellow and blue.

The battery of tests has been factor analyzed several times, and the three factors of simultaneous, successive and speed have emerged. A model of cognitive functions (Das, *et al.* 1975) has been suggested. We expected that if one can notice some form of cognitive deficit in the severely malnourished children, it should be evident in one or more of the cognitive processes.

In addition to the cognitive tests, a measure of home environment was taken by administering a short questionnaire to the mother or father of the index child. The questionnaire was taken from Richardson (1972) and consisted of questions such as : "Does the child have toys of his own at home?" "Does anyone tell him stories?" "Is he taken out on trips?" The maximum score was 5, obtained by answering 'yes' to 5 questions; the minimum was zero, which was 'no' to all questions.

RESULTS

A major concern was whether the index children were inferior to the control children in cognitive tests; a second question was whether or not the siblings were inferior to the controls. The sibling-control comparison was made to discover if inherited factors or conditions in the micro-environment of the home of the malnourished child might adversely affect the cognitive performance of all children including that of the index child in the family.

Ideally, one should determine if the difference between the index child's performance and his control is greater than the difference between the performance of the sibling and his control. A series of *t*-test (adjusted for unequal variances) was made comparing the index child with his or her control. The results of comparisons are reported in Table 7.1. First of all, we wanted to find out if the index and the control were comparable in their special-familial variables such as income, number of children in the family, etc. It was observed that the index and the control children did not differ in terms of the biographical variables except father's education (index superior to control) and the number of years the child has attended school (control superior to the index). No consistent trend then, was evident in terms of biographical characteristics. The two groups of children did not differ in their home stimulation scores which is important. As far as the short home environment questionnaire goes, the micro-environments at home for the two groups were similar.

Of the nine cognitive tests, the control children were not superior even in a single test.

TABLE 7.1 : **Index and control children : Comparison of means**

Variables	Mean			
	Index	N	Control	N
Income (in rupees)	176.67	42	158.26	34
No. of children in family	5.83	42	6.40	25[1]
Ordinal position of child	4.31	42	3.70	37[1]
Father's education (yrs.)	4.75	41	3.17*	36
Mother's education (yrs.)	4.73	41	3.95	18
Progressive matrices	12.24	41	12.41	41
Figure copying	25.98	42	26.55	42
Memory for designs (errors)	18.55	38	15.70	37
Visual short-term memory	55.30	36	66.03	32
Digit span	3.80	41	4.18	39
Free recall	76.97	36	78.80	36
Cross-modal coding	2.90	41	3.61	41
Color naming (Secs.)	55.23	35	50.76	34
Home stimulation	1.07	42	1.12	41

1 Discrepancy is due to two reasons : (1) The informant who brought the child did not know how many other children were born after the index-control child. (2) In some cases, simple negligence in the case of the filed assistant to elicit the information.

Note : Significance levels reported are of t-values, Welch's t-prime adjustment for unequal variances.

* $p < .02$.

The next set of *t*-tests involved the sibling and his or her control. Means and sample sizes are given in Table 7.2. In terms of social-familial factors, there was again no difference between the sibling and the control children. This was also true for the home stimulation scores. On the cognitive tests, the control children were not significantly better than the siblings; none of the adjusted *t*-tests reached the 5 per cent level of significance.

TABLE 7.2 : **Siblings and their controls : Comparison of means**

Variables	Means			
	Sibling	N	Control	N
Income (in Rupees)	181.28	35	175.62	32
No. of children in family	6.00	35	6.04	24
Ordinal position of child	4.09	35	3.64	31
Father's education (yrs)	4.85	34	3.59	31
Mother's education (yrs)	4.53	34	4.59	34
Child's education (yrs)	2.77	30	3.64	25
Progressive matrices	12.57	35	13.76	33
Figure copying	27.09	35	27.03	33
Memory for designs (error)	15.71	35	13.32	31
Visual short-term memory	61.82	34	65.50	31
Digit span	4.17	35	4.38	34
Free recall	77.75	32	78.81	32
Color naming (secs)	56.59	34	50.89	28
Cross-modal Coding	3.41	34	4.65	31
Home stimulation	1.41	34	1.21	3

Note : None of the *t* values were significant

On the whole, the results clearly show that neither the index children nor the siblings were inferior to their controls.

Turning to intercorrelations within the index group, product moment correlations were computed between all biographical measures and cognitive tests. Those variables which had two or more significant *r*'s with other variables are presented in Table 7.3.

TABLE 7.3 : **Correlation (Pearson *r*) social-familial variables and cognitive tests**

Variable/Test			
Income x	Child's education	.310	40
	Figure Copying	.400	42
No. of children x	Ordinal position	.890	42
	Father's education	.380	41
	Color Naming	.346	35
Ordinal position x	Memory for Designs	.340	38
	Color Naming	.395	35
Father's education x	Mother's education	.350	41
	Cross-modal Coding	.320	43
Child's education x	Progressive Matrices	.403	39
	Figure Copying	.540	40
	Memory for Designs	.580	36
	Visual Short-term Memory	.670	34
	Digit Span	.480	39
	Free Recall	.510	34
	Cross-modal Coding	.600	39
Mother's education	Figure Copying	.320	41
	Cross-modal Coding	.365	40

It is interesting to note that the child's education has the largest number of correlations with other variables; in fact, except for one cognitive test, all other haves statistically significant correlation with the number of years for which the child has attended school.

Correlation as an index of association between two variables may be useful, but an ideal procedure for determining the relative influence of criterial variables on predicted variables is the computation of multiple regression. We wish to report multiple Rs now, which are of great interest. However, because the children missed some of the tests, and different children missed different tests, we had to modify the program for handling missing data. In situations like these, the reliability of the multiple R is not as good as when no missing data exist. Generally, within these constraints, the results of multiple regression are presented for consideration.

We will first consider the group of index cases. Do any of the medical variables predict the performance of the index children in cognitive test? Free Recall of words was predictable from the medical characteristics of the index children. The child's age at the time of testing, the duration of his stay at the hospital when he was admitted for malnutrition, and the age at admission jointly account for 59.66 per cent of the variance in Recall scores of the children. Most of the variance is contributed by chronological age at testing—the older child would recall better, generally. Age at admission makes a minor contribution, but nevertheless, an expected one—children who were older than the average at the time of hospitalization were also older at the time of testing. The role of duration of hospitalization should be investigated fully in another study. It may be possible that those who were hospitalized longer recovered better from kwashiorkor or marasmus.

The next multiple regression computations involved the predictability of cognitive test performance by social-familial or biographical characteristics of the index children. It is obvious that the number of years of formal education received by the index child overwhelmingly determines his performance in the cognitive tests.

The details of the step-wise regression analysis are presented in Table 7.4. Of all the cognitive tests, only one is not predicted by years of formal education the child has received at the time of testing; this is Color Naming. In all others, the child's education figures as a prominent criterion variable. The next set of important variables appear to be the ordinal position of the child in family, mother's education, and the presence of protein in the child's diet.

TABLE 7.4 : **Results of multiple R for index case : Prediction of cognitive test performance using social-familial variables (income, etc.)**

Predicted variable	Criterion variable	% of Variance predicted
Progressive Matrices	Child's education	16.22
Figure Copying	Child's education	29.10
Memory for Designs	Ordinal position in family; child's education; protein intake	50.71
Visual Short-term Memory	Child's education	44.89
Digit Span	Child's education	22.98
Free Recall	Child's education	26.20
Color Naming	Ordinal position in family	15.59
Cross-modal Coding	Mother's education; child's education	43.88

Medical data were not available for the siblings, the control children for index cases, or for the controls for siblings. Therefore, the multiple regression analyses for these three groups were done with the social-familial variables which were available. As before, these variables constituted the criterion variables for the purpose of predicting performance on the cognitive tests. The results for siblings are reported in Table 7.5. Quite clearly, these are similar to the results found for the index cases, in that the child's education again emerges as the predominant predictor for almost all the cognitive tests. The only addition to this variable is the father's education.

Predictions of the cognitive test performance of index cases were significant for Visual Short-term Memory and Home Stimulation. These were the only variables with a significant contribution and explained 16 per cent of the variance. Digit Span performance was predicted also by Home Stimulation—to an extent of 24.15 per cent. This is the first time that the Home Stimulation scores based on Richardson's questionnaire have

TABLE 7.5 : **Results of multiple R for siblings : Prediction of cognitive test performonce using social-familial variables (income, etc.)**

Predicted Variables	Criterion Variables	% of Variance Predicted
Progressive Matrices	Child's education	21.00
Figure Copying	Child's education	23.80
Memory for Designs	Child's education	36.58
Visual Short-term Memory	Child's education	36.58
Digit Span	Child's education	19.81
Free Recall	Child's education; Father's education	32.90

been found to be of some value in influencing the performance of children in cognitive tasks. In the sibling control group, the results are much more significant, and are in line with those of the previous two groups. The results are reported in Table 7.6.

TABLE 7.6 : **Results of multiple R for controls for siblings : Prediction of cognitive test performance using social-familial variables (income, etc.)**

Predicted Variables	Criterion Variables	% of Variance Predicted
Progressive Matrices	Child's education; Marital status*; Protein in diet	50.91
Figure Copying	Child's education	37.44
Memory for Designs	Mother's education Child's education	43.05
Color Naming	Child's education	14.16

* Both parents in house

In many studies the index children have been compared with their siblings. This was largely possible because the studies had used standardized test norm for age of the child. None of the cognitive tests we had used, except the Progressive Matrices, had standardized age norms available for them. But we reasoned that, if the index children as a group did not differ significantly in their mean age from the siblings taken as a group, perhaps we could do a simple comparison of the two groups on each of the tests for cognitive performance. We found that, although the index children were some five months younger than the siblings whose mean age was compared, this difference was not statistically significant. Thus, we did a series of *t*-tests which took into account the unequal variances (Welch's *t* prime adjustment of *t*-tests) between the cognitive test means of index and siblings. The only test on which the two groups were significantly different was in Figure Copying, the siblings doing better than the index children (p—.048). Thus, the siblings hardly do better in intellectual tasks than the index children who were hospitalized for severe malnutrition, except in one of the nine tests.

DISCUSSION

It is clear from the results that an episode of malnutrition does not make a unique contribution to the cognitive performance of the children. However, these findings have to be interpreted carefully. We know that the control children lived in the same depressing environment and were comparable to the index children in family characteristics. Furthermore, because of these biographical and environmental similarities, it is quite likely that the control children experienced sub-optimal nutrition which did not amount to an episode of malnutrition which required hospitalization. At least one problem seems to have been resolved by our study: that is, chronic undernutrition or sub-optimal nutrition seems to have the same effect on the cognitive development of a child as episodic malnutrition when the children are examined around the age of 9 or 10.

The present study, however, could be improved. If medical data on *all* children in the four groups could be collected, one would be able to compare the groups in terms of their health status. Perhaps, then, the relation between indices of health and cognitive competence could be investigated comprehensively. But one doubts that the major conclusion of the present study would have to be revised in the light of the medical data. Theoretically, one might have found that the control children were less healthy than the index, that they had suffered from infections and infestations to a significantly greater degree which had reduced their growth below the level of the index children. And these, in turn, had 'caused' a degree of cognitive incompetence which equalled the incompetence of the index children. Under these conditions, our major conclusion may be invalid.

It seems to us that a prospective study of the index cases and their cohorts, slightly different from the one in Mexico presently conducted by Cravioto (1972) would be much more satisfactory. Briefly, the study should monitor the development, both physical and cognitive, of index children following the occurrence of marasmus or kwashiorkor. The age of onset of the syndrome will be different—for instance, below ages 1, 2, 3, and 4. As these index children will be studied longitudinally, it will be possible to compare the biomedical and cognitive characteristics of 'ex-patients' with 'patients' at a particular age (e.g., the 2 yrs, 3 yrs and 4 yrs old children currently hospitalized with index children who had an episode of malnutrition at age 1, and are presently 2 yrs old etc.). For each age group of index children, cohorts will also be chosen; the cohorts would be from the same disadvantaged class and neighbourhood. In essence, the design will allow a combination of longitudinal and cross-sectional examination of the effect of malnutrition.

Returning to the main finding of the present study, we feel that it is not inconsistent with the current state of knowledge. Consider, for instance, the observations by Waterlow (1975) "... what matters in practice is the total environment of the child throughout the period of growth and development. It is not an episode of malnutrition in early life that leads to handicap". Further, support for Waterlow's position is obtained when we consider that middle class children suffering from a period of severe malnutrition recover fully and their cognitive development returns to normal (Winick, Meyer & Haris, 1975). It is also possible to infer from the study on the effect of famine in Holland (Stein, Susser, Saenger & Marolla, 1975) that maternal hunger and malnutrition during pregnancy do not leave a permanent mark on the intellectual development of the child when he is tested as an adult. The survivors of the Dutch famine, however, were hardly subjected to the disadvantaged life conditions of the Ceylonese children in our study. Thus, it is clearly the total environment of the disadvantaged child during the period of growth which depresses his intellectual performance. In the present study, all children were extremely disadvantaged—the index children, siblings and their controls.

Essentially, the conclusion of our research is a negative one, that children hospitalized for severe malnutrition, were not worse than other disadvantaged children in cognitive tests. If organic impairment occurred during severe malnutrition, it was not evident 5 to 6 years later in the performance of index children relative to their controls.

On the positive side, the results point to the importance of early education of disadvantaged children. Our research suggests that in spite of the depressed condition which is associated with undernutrition, the child's intellectual performance improves with school attendance. Education of the child, and to a certain extent, mother's education emerged as predictors of the child's performance on the cognitive tasks. School attendance facilitates the development of thinking through the use of language. Thus, any rehabilitation programme for the previously marasmic or kwashiorkor child as well as his chronically undernourished counterpart should provide for the stimulation of language and thought in addition to giving food supplements. A well-designed prospective study of the type mentioned in a preceding paragraph, should incorporate programme for language use for the preschooler, and bonuses to the family for sending the older child to school.

REFERENCES

Birch, H.G., and Gussow, J. *Disadvantaged children : Health and school failure*, New York : Harcourt, 1970.

Chase, H.P., and Martin, H.P. Undernutrition and child development. *New England Journal of Medicine*, 1970, 282, 933-930.

Cravioto, J., and DeLicardie, E. Environmental correlates of severe clinical malnutrition and language development in survivors from kwashiorkor or marasmus. In *Nutrition, the nervous system and behaviour*. Washington, D.C. : Pan American Health Organization, 1972.

Das, J.P., Kirby, J., and Jarman, R. Simultaneous and successive syntheses : An alternative model for cognitive abilities. *Psychological Bulletin*, 1975, **82**, 87-103.

Das, J.P., and Pivato, E. Malnutrition and cognitive functioning. In N.R. Elis (Ed.), *International review of research in mental retardation*, (Vol. **8**), New York : Academic Press, 1977.

Hertzig, H.E., Birch, H.G. Richardson, S.A., and Tizard, J. Intellectual level of school children severely malnourished during the first two years of life. *Pediatrics*, 1972, **49**, 814-823.

Hurwitz, I. Psychological testing in studies on malnutrition. In J.D. Lleyd-Still (Ed.) *Malnutrition and intellectual development*. Lancaster, England : MTP Press, 1976.

Jellife, D. *The assessment of the nutritional status of the community*. Geneva : WHO Monograph **53**, 1966.

Monokeberg, F. Malnutrition and mental capacity. In *Nutrition, the nervous system and behaviour*. Washington, D.C. : Pan American Health Organization, 1972.

Olson, R.E. (Ed.) *Protein-calrie malnutrition*. New York : Academic Press, 1975.

Richardson, S.A. Ecology of malnutrition : Non-nutritional factors influencing intellectual and behavioural development. In *Nutrition, the nervous system and behaviour*. Washington, D.C. : Pan American Health Organization, 1972.

Richardson, S.A. The relation of severe malnutrition in infancy to the intelligence of school children with differing life histories. *Pediatric Research*, 1976, **10**, 57-61.

Stein, Z., Susser, M., Saenger, G., and Marolla, F. *Famine and human development : The Dutch hunger winter of 1944/45*. New York : Oxford University Press, 1975.

Stoch, M.B., and Smythe, P.M. Does undernutrition during infancy inhibit brain and subsequent intellectual development ? *Archives of Diseases of Children*, 1963 **38**, 546-552.

Waterlow, J.C. Adaptation to low protein intakes. In R.E. Olson (Ed.) *Protein-calorie malnutrition*. New York : Academic Press, 1975.

Winick, M., Meyer, K.K., and Harris, R.C. Malnutrition and environmental enrichment by early adoption. *Science*, 1975, **190**, 1173-1175.

EIGHT

E. Annamalai

THE POVERTY OF LANGUAGE
A Linguistic Appraisal

INTRODUCTION

LANGUAGE is a unique symbolic system in that it is not homogenous. It is a set of non-discrete speech forms which are mutually intelligible to the extent of not affecting normal communication. This is only a working definition since the psychological notion of mutual intelligibility is neither a sufficient nor a necessary condition for defining the language, which is by and large defined socio-culturally. It is not sufficient by the fact that mutually intelligible varieties like *Hindi* and *Urdu* are considered distinct languages and it is not necessary by the fact that highly unintelligible varieties of *Chinese* are called one language. Nevertheless, some understanding of the nature of the speech forms or varieties of a language is essential to know the way language is realized in social contexts.

Barring the individual variations of speech, which are comparable to mannerisms, the three kinds of speech varieties are *dialect*, *style* and *register*. Each of these varieties is determined by extraneous factors outside the language. Dialect is determined by the geographical location and social group in which one is born. Thus, one has in Tamil, *Kanyakumari* dialect and *Brahmin* dialect, in American English, Eastern dialect and Negro dialect and so on. Style is determined by the type of interaction between the participants of the speech set, which is governed by the role relation, the situational context and the medium. Thus, one has casual and formal styles, spoken and written styles, and so on. Register is determined by the topic of the discourse like the legal register, scientific register, etc.

Linguists claim that all languages are equal, though different. Languages may differ in the size and diversification of their vocabulary, which reflect the linguistic community's socio-cultural development in its broadest sense including the technological development. It is true that in a technological culture the language with technological vocabulary is in an advantageous position compared to a language which does not already have that vocabulary, provided it is assumed that the technological culture is good and necessary for every one. Even then, the vocabulary is the easiest part of the language to acquire and a language can make up its vocabulary once it is put into use in the new domains. As far as the structure is concerned, from phonology to syntax, any language is as complex, as abstract, and as logical, as any other. The universality of abstract linguistic structures, and of linguistic rules operating on them being subjected to abstract conditions and its implication to the structure of linguistic rules operating on them being subjected to abstract conditions and its implication to the structure of human mind have been demonstrated by linguists in recent years (Chomsky, 1968). New types of structure, if at all any, developed when a language is extended to new functional domains are minimal unlike the vocabulary. The equality of language is, therefore, the prevailing general opinion of linguists. They maintain this position not only with reference to the weaker claim that any language is good for its needs, but also with reference to the stronger claim that a language is good for any of the needs, given the opportunity.

Recently, however, some anthropological linguists (Hymes, 1971) have suggested that differences in vocabulary and structures may indicate stages in the development of languages as they lead to differences in explicitness and elaboration and, thus, to "communicational limitation". This is difficult to demonstrate because of the difficulty in operationally defining and measuring these characteristics. Even if the hypothesis of inequality of languages is proved to be correct, it does not claim that any language is inherently deficient. The claim is simply that the languages are at different points of development, which is an on-going process, corresponding with the development of the society marked by elaboration of stratification and diversity of specialization.

The equality of languages holds true for varieties of a language also. No dialect, for example, is less complex, less abstract or less logical and, therefore, more deficient than any other dialect.

THE CONCEPT OF LINGUISTIC DEPRIVATION

The psychological theory of linguistic deficiency derives from the failure to appreciate this point stressed by linguists after intensive and systematic study of languages and their varieties. This failure is compounded by the lack of distinction between the different varieties of a language discussed above. Besides these two conceptual inadequacies, the empirical data brought about by psychologists to support their thesis are also grossly inadequate and unrepresentative. Data regarding the verbal behaviour of low socio-economic status (SES) groups—many of them are of American black children—were collected in test situations involving unequal relation between the interviewer and the subject and the low SES children may have reacted to the situation with verbal reservation as an expression of hostility and defence in an alien situation against the imposition of the interviewer, who is invariably a white and of high SES (Labov, 1970). Delay, shortness, lack of seriousness and commitment in the answers of low SES children discovered by the psychologists in such encounters may, therefore, be indicators of the mental reservations of the children rather than their verbal repertoire. Linguists, who have observed the verbal behaviour of the low SES children in their natural environment, have found ample evidence for their verbal spontaneity and richness. Labov (1970) has demonstrated it by contrasting the eliciting situations and techniques. The verbal games and competitions in which the American black children rival with each other in their ghetto as have been documented by many linguists (for example, Kochman, 1972) and they show that they are far from being non-verbal.

The naivety with which psychologists like Bereiter have passed judgments about grammaticality and logicality of expressions by the American black children is amazing to linguists. The black children say 'they mine' instead of 'they are mine', 'me like juice' instead of 'I like juice', etc., not because their speech lacks in logic or in grammar, but because it undergoes certain rules of the grammar of their dialect. The copula is absent in the first sentence due to a phonological rule, which abbreviates, the copula in the standard English ('they're mine') and deletes it in the black English. (Labov, 1970). If the superficial absence of copula is considered to be an example of illogical sentence, then many languages of the world like the Dravidian, which do not use the copula at all, must be considered illogical and their speakers defective in thinking. The oblique form is used as the subject in the second sentence instead of the nominal form not due to inability to make grammatical distinction or not due to logical failure of using the inanimate 'juice' as the subject of 'get' as Bereiter seems to believe, but it is a result of non-acquisition of phonological differences of a morpheme, which is a common feature in language acquisition (Labov, 1970). Every deficiency thus pointed out may be shown to be a result of a normal grammatical operation. It is no reflection on the intelligence of the speakers.

But, unfortunately, the linguistically naive interpretation of non-standard dialects have led to the theory of linguistic deprivation, which in its extreme formulation, assumes that the low SES group--the speakers of non-standard dialects—do not have a human language system at all and, therefore, no normal cognitive growth (Bereiter, *et al.*, 1966). The educational model which is derived from this thesis argues, therefore, that they should be compensated for this deficiency by giving them a language in their preschool years.

Notwithstanding the above criticism, it is true that there are differences between the standard dialect and the non-standard dialect and, since the standard dialect is used in school, the non-standard dialect speakers have genuine learning problems. The learning problems caused by dialect differences are linguistic problems. There are problems of communication between the teacher and the taught, of interference of the home dialect in reading and writing and of comprehension of the subjects written and taught in the standard dialect. These are problems similar to those of second language learners and the solution is in the pedagogical use of the home dialect in the class room as the first language of the learner is used in second language teaching. The various ways and proportions of the home dialect to be used have been discussed by linguists and educationists (Baratz & Shuy, 1969; Fasold & Shuy, 1970; Fox, 1972; Burling, 1973). It is not necessary to go into the details here except to point out that the common philosophy underlying the various teaching models is not compensatory education but bidialectal education.

Bernstein's argument

Bernstein, a sociologist, has proposed that there is difference of code between the speech of the working class and the middle class. Code is defined by the probability of syntactic choices. On the basis of whether the syntactic choices are restricted or elaborated two codes are identified and called restricted code and elaborated code, respectively. The elaborated code has a high proportion of subordination, complex verbal stems, passive voice, contingency forms, hedges, uncommon adjectives, adverbs and conjunctions and low proportion of personal pronouns, tag questions and metaphors, idioms, traditional phrases (Bernstein, 1971). The elaborated code makes full exploitation of the syntactic possibilities whereas the restricted code makes a limited use of them. The utterances in the restricted code are, therefore, highly predictable.

Bernstein's concept of code differences has undergone significant change in the course of his writings on the subject—a change attributed to "conceptual development of ideas" by the author (Bernstein, 1971) and to self-contradiction by his critics (Trudgill, 1974; Gazder 1975). In his earlier writings, Bernstein (1971) suggested that there are logical, social and psychological implications to the code differences. "A correlate of this linguistic form (i.e. the restricted code which was called the public language then) is a low level of conceptualisation—an orientation to a low order of causality, a disinterest in processes, a preference to be aroused by and respond to that which is immediately given . . . a tendency to accept and respond to an authority . . . (discouragement of) of the verbalisation of tender feeling." He brought forth radical modifications to this extreme position in his later writings (Bernstein, 1971) partly because of the misinterpretations of his ideas by educationists and partly because of the criticism by linguists. According to the modified concept of restricted and elaborated codes, they are merely two different speech forms or varieties conditioned by the context of social interaction. They are not indicators of the speaker's linguistic competence, but are ways of linguistic usage. Bernstein (1971) clarifies is "not concerned with language, but with speech, and concerned more specifically with the contextual constraints of speech". He, thus, agrees with Chomsky that linguistic competence is universal irrespective of the class or race of the speaker and that linguistic performance may be a variable conditioned by non-cognitive factors. He relates this notion of speech variety to his earlier notion of code by saying that for the working class children the restricted speech variety, which is characteristic of the regulative context, is the only available variety, since it is used in all socializing contexts like the regulative context, the instructional context, the imaginative context and the interpersonal context and, therefore, it is the code for them. Nevertheless, Bernstein (1971) himself admits that the working class children may also have access to and make use of the elaborate variety but to a very limited extent. The linguistic realizations are different in the four contexts for the middle class children and their code, therefore, is elaborate. It means that the middle class children also have access to and make use of the restricted speech variety but the extent is less.

The predominant use of the restricted code by the middle class, according to Bernstein (1971), is not directly related to the social class, but through the family type. The two types of family relationships are position centred and person centred. In the former, the status of the members of the family and the boundaries of authority between them are unambiguously defined; that is, the scope of changing the role relationship in the process of communication is limited and, therefore, the speech variety is restricted. In the latter, the status and boundary are ambivalent and "the role system would be continuously evolving, accommodating and assimilating the different interests and attributes of its members . . . the members would be making their roles rather than stepping into them" (Bernstein, 1971) and, therefore, there is elaboration of speech varieties. The working class family is typically position centred and the middle class family is typically person centred and, hence, the correlation of restricted and elaborated codes with social class.

The code differences now turn out to be nothing other than style differences (Trudgill, 1975; Labov, 1970). As defined earlier, the style differences are characterized by the relative frequency of certain syntactic structures, by their availability to all social and regional groups and by their dependence on functions. So are the code differences of Bernstein. The characteristics of the restricted code are those of the casual style and the characteristics of the elaborated code are those of the formal style. The former are true of the spoken style and the latter of the written style in a diglossic language like Tamil. The differences between the two codes or styles may be generalized, as Bernstein himself has done, to say that the restricted code or the casual style is context dependent and assumes shared knowledge and beliefs between the interlocuters. The elaborated code or the formal style, on. the other hand, is context independent, i.e., removed from the speech context including the participants and, therefore, is abstracted and is fully specified as to the information communicated. Hence, there is in this variety less of personal pronouns and tag questions whose purpose is to get confirmed the shared knowledge. The crucial difference then between the two varieties is that the elaborated code or the formal style has a high degree of autonomy (Bernstein, 1977).

The question that should be discussed now is whether there are any consequences of these differences of linguistic varieties to intelligence and to education and what they are. It was pointed out earlier that dialect differences do not have any bearing on intelligence, but they may contribute to specific linguistic problems of learning in school. This is generally agreed by all, by linguists as well as non-linguists, as regards the regional dialects. They differ, however, as regards the social dialects. The non-linguists believe that there is a correlation between intelligence and the social class to which the speaker belongs and that it can be explained by the linguistic differences. It follows that difference in intelligence has consequence to education. This position of the non-linguists regarding the social dialect is due to their confusion of dialect differences and style differences. Linguistically there is no evidence to distinguish qualitatively between regional and social dialects.

The style differences also do not, the linguists believe, have any relation to the intelligence of social groups. They may have consequences to education, provided Bernstein is right about the restricted style and the lower class children are socialized only through the restricted style when they come to school. But this is not so according to Bernstein himself, as already mentioned. To quote him (Bernstein,1971) :

> Because the code is restricted it does not mean that the users do not realize, at any time, elaborated speech variants, only that such variants will be used infrequently in the process of the socialization of the child in his family (p. 198).

But there are many caveats to the conclusions of Bernstein about the restricted speech form. They lack, to a large extent empirical verification (Trudgill, 1975). The empirical evidence given in his papers in most cases are constructed (as mentioned by Bernstein himself about two contrastive texts) or anecdotal (like the observation in a bus) or projected answers to subjective questions (for example, "mothers were asked what they might say if their child committed a series af misdemeanours". Even the systematic data were collected in artificial interview situations and their drawbacks were pointed out earlier. The last is true of the studies of low SES children by psychologists also, who have compounded the style and dialect differences. Not only the test situations but the IQ tests also are not neutral. "An indefinitely large number of factors can affect IQ without having any direct bearing on what we intuitively recognize as intelligence. Among such factors is command of language . . . grasp of the language variety in which an

IQ test is couched can affect the outcome of the test" (Macnamara, 1972, p. 70). Another factor is the content of the tests, which is biased to the middle class culture; the so-called culture-free tests are not adequately free. Some of the studies are biased by the personal commitment of the investigator to a particular theory and this bias is reflected in the selection made by the investigator from among the available studies. Jensen (1969), for example, frequently cites Heber's studies of 88 Negro mothers in Milwaukee, which was known to contain a large concentration of retarded children and proves his theory that "the preponderance of the evidence is . . . less consistent with a strictly environmental hypothesis than with the genetic hypothesis," which according to Heber is a gross misinterpretation of his findings (Labov, 1970). Another example is setting the cutting point for the deprived group as 'college or less' for the variable 'the educational aspirational level of the parent for the child' in their Deprivation Index by Whiteman and Deutsch (1968). It means that even if a Negro child's father says that he wants his son to go all the way through college, the child will fall into the 'deprived' class on this variable (Labov, 1969).

Even if the data collected in natural, systematic and objective fashion show the existence of different styles correlating with social class, there are still many questions unanswered about their correlation with intelligence. It is hard to imagine of many style differences how they bear upon intelligence. As Trudgill (1975) says "it is difficult to see anything other than stylistic variation in a contrast between, say, 'The man who was crossing the street was hit by a car' (which belongs to the elaborated code) and 'The man was crossing the street and a car hit him' (which belongs to the restricted code). But why should differences of this type have educational consequences? . . . how features like subordinate class and passive verbs will have the effect of the constraint of a restricted code . . . to depress potential linguistic ability, raise the relevance of the concrete and descriptive level of response and inhibit generalising ability" as claimed by Bernstein (pp. 149-150).

It is agreed by everyone that language plays a role in cognitive development. According to Jensen (1970), Level II or the cognitive learning, which is theoretically independent of

Level I or the associative learning, "is closely related to the development of language and particularly to the transition from the use of language merely as a form of social communication to its internalized use as a means of representing and interpreting one's own experiences to oneself, ordering events, anticipating, planning and solving problems" between the ages of five and six. But it does not follow that different languages lead to different cognitive developments, nor do the different varieties of a language. The latter is assumed to be true in spite of lack of empirical demonstration because of the theory of linguistic deficiency, which is wanting independent proof. The argument of relation between linguistic deficiency and cognitive deficiency is, thus, circular. The observed superiority of the elaborated style is in the vocabulary and it may be easily learnt in the school by the child of the restricted style, if there is any, provided it is introduced gradually starting with the vocabulary the child already has in his control. This is similar to the languages acquiring new vocabulary as part of their development, as mentioned earlier.

A question related to cognitive deficiency is about the identification of the cognitive skills such as those mentioned by Jensen above. It is the experience of the people who have lived and worked with the "culturally and linguistically deprived groups" that they have these skills and show them in domains different from those tested in standard tests. A rural boy, for example, interprets insect movement, anticipates rain and plans his agricultural operations; a boy of the primitive Jenu Kuruba tribe interprets animal smell or footprints, anticipates the coming of an elephant herd and plans his route. This shows that the fault is neither in the language nor in the children but is in the testing instrument.

The question particular to the Indian situation is whether Bernstein's correlation of family types to social class is true here. It is likely that, this dichotomy does not hold true in India. When there is no empirical verification of this hypothesis on Indian data it is misleading to carry over the findings from one culture to another without verification.

There is, however, no denying of the fact that language is a factor in educational problems of the lower class children. This is because of the differences between the home language dialect or style and the school language dialect or style. The school language dialect or style has no inherent superiority to be the medium of learning in school, but it is so because its speakers have the power to make it so. The middle class style used in the school has bad qualities. Labov (1970) gives a sample of middle class speech rated as very high on a scale of job suitability and equally high as a potential friend, and shows how it is verbose—"turgid, redundant, and empty". Bernstein (1971) points out that "a formal language (the elaborated code) is not necessarily a logical, impersonal, emotionally exiscerated language". He also makes this observation in regard to the creativity of its speakers. When the children were invited to tell a story about some doll like figures the working class children's stories were freer, longer and more imaginative than the stories of the middle class children. The latter children's stories were tighter, constrained within a strong narrative frame. It was as if these children were dominated by what they took to be the form of a narrative and the content was secondary. Bernstein says further that the constraint of form in the middle class children's speech may explain the less diversity in their responses of word association compared to the working class children's responses reported in a number of studies; the former are conditioned only by the form class of the stimulus word whereas the latter by form class as well as meaning. Nevertheless, because of the position it holds in school all children must learn the school language or variety. The question is how it should be done without hardship to the children who do not possess it already.

COMPENSATORY EDUCATION

The concept of compensatory education—with variations in middle and strategies called by the names, the Headstart programme, Intervention programme, Environment programme, Preschool education, etc. is based on the theory of linguistic deprivation which rests on conclusions untenable and unwarranted as discussed above about the linguistic and cognitive superiority of the school variety and about the linguistic cognitive inferiority of the other varieties. The same theory is extended to suggest compensatory education to the children who speak a different language like the tribal children who invariably belong to the low SES group. It may be pointed out here again, at the risk of being repetitive, that Bernstein himself, whose influence on the educational psychologists who advocate compensatory education is great, has disclaimed, in his critique of the concept of compensatory education (Bernstein, 1971), that "our research shows just this. That the social classes differ in terms of the contexts which evoke certain linguistic realizations. Mothers in the middle class, and it is important to add not all, relative to the working class (and again it is important to add not all, by any means) place greater emphasis upon the use of language in socializing the child. This does not mean that working class mothers are non-verbal . . . . They are not linguistically deprived, neither are their children" (p. 196). He has argued against the elimination of the working class speech through schooling from the beginning of his writings.

The compensatory education is bound to fail not only because it is based on an unfounded psychological theory of linguistic deprivation but also because it is based on the refusal of a universally accepted educational principle. The educational principle is that the education begins to build from the resources the child already possesses. The compensatory education goes against this principle by proposing to replace the child's linguistic resources with another linguistic system before education starts. Ethnically, it is undesirable since it is biased and imposes one linguistic system along with its value system over the speakers of the other. It perpetuates the elitist's vested interest in education by fixing the entry qualification to the advantage of those who are already in. The bias is revealed in the nomenclature 'deprived' and 'disadvantaged' to describe those outside the middle class, who are really 'rich' and 'advantaged' because, with the right type of education, they will have control of more languages and language varieties—those of home and of school. Even as a strategy for the ultimate noble goals, it is unsuitable, particularly for the developing countries where the people who are below the middle class outnumber those in the middle class many times and, therefore, the compensatory education will be not an education for the minority but an education for the majority.

The major failing of the compensatory education as a programme is its mistaken identification of the source of the problem. The problem is not in the child but is in the school. The compensatory education "is designed to repaii the child, rather than the school" (Labov, 1970). Failure in school is not caused by the child but by the school itself. It follows that the school should change to ensure that the child does not fail and not the child to change to ensure that he does not fail in the school.

The consequences of the theory and practice of compensatory education are also serious. The theory rationalizes the prejudices of the teachers, educational administrators and the public against the lower class children that they are unintelligent and illogical and justifies their using such labels against them whenever they respond in their speech variety in school. This establishes an unfavourable social relation, between the teacher and the taught, damages the 'self concept' of the child and is counter productive to the 'self-fulfilling prophecies' in the classroom (Rosenthal and Jacobson 1968) all of which contribute viciously to learning failure (Labov, 1970) By the practice of enriching the linguistic input, besides the pattern drills being tedious to the child, "a wedge is progressively driven between the child as a member of a family and community, and the child as a member of a school" (Bernstein, 1971).

It has led to two grave conclusions, the first is that the children must be compensated much earlier, and the second is that the children are incompensatable. Those who lend to the first conclusion have moved to focus attention on the "patterns of parental deficit" and proposed "educationally oriented day care for culturally deprived children between six months and three years of age .... (to) .... hopefully prevent the deceleration in rate of development which seems to occur in many deprived children around age of two to three years" (Caldwell, 1965). Those who are disposed towards the second conclusion have proposed the 'inevitable hypothesis' of genetic differences correlating with social class and race. Jensen (1970), for example, criticises compensatory education that "the recent emphasis in the literature on the disadvantaged has been almost exclusively on post natal social environmental factors, despite the fact that years ago intensive large scale researches found that this class of environmental factors accounts for relatively little (less than 20%) of the variance in intelligence and no subsequent research has contradicted this conclusion and arrives at his inevitable genetic hypothesis.

Once the theory of deprivation is abandoned, one need not come to these dismal and dangerous conclusions. Even if it is true that the elaborated style, to which the lower class children have only infrequent access, facilitates, being more context free and autonomous, reflexive thinking, which is a necessary process in learning, the method to help the poor children to acquire the elaborated style is by providing the right contexts for it, since the different speech forms are contextual realizations of the same code. These contexts may be provided in the school, which is the second agent of socialization and where at the ages between five and six the transition from the associative or Level I learning to the language mediated Level II or cognitive learning manifests most conspicuously (Jensen, 1970). The crucial point is that this transition must be allowed to take place naturally and without sudden interruption in the medium of the dialect of the lower class children by the gradual and alternative use of the standard dialect. The solution, thus, for the educational problems of the children who speak at home a non-school variety is bidialectal education, as it is bilingual education for the children whose home language, i.e., the language of the early childhood experience, is different from the school language.

REFERENCES

Allen, V.L. *Psychological factors in poverty*. New York : Academic Press, 1970.

Baratz, J.C., and R.W. Shuy (Eds.) *Teaching black children to read.* Washington : Centre for Applied Linguistics, 1969.

Barling, R. *English in Black and White.* New York : Holt, Rinehart and Winston, 1973.

Bereiter, C. et al. An academically oriented pre-school for culturally deprived children. In F.M. Hechingor (Ed.) *Pre-school education today*. New York : Doubleday, 1966.

Bereiter, C., and Englemann, S. *Teaching disadvantaged children in the pre-school*. Englewood Cliffs, New Jersey : Prentice Hall, Inc., 1966.

Bernstein, B. *Class, codes and control*, Vol. 1 : *Theoretical studies towards a sociology of language*. London : Routledge and Kegan Paul, 1971.

Bernstein, B. *Class, codes and control*, Vol. 2 : *Applied studies towards sociology of language*. London : Routledge and Kegan Paul, 1973.

Caldwell, N. What is the optimal learning environment for the young child *American Journal of Orthopsychiatry*, 1965, 37, No. 1.

Chomsky, N. *Language and mind*. New York : Harcourt, Brace and World, 1968, (Revised edition, 1972).

Deutsch, M., I. Katz, and A.R. Jensen (Eds.) *Social class, race and psychological development*. New York : Holt, Rinehart and Winston, 1968.

Fashold, R.W., and Shuy, R.W. *Teaching standard English in the inner city*. Washington : Center for Applied Linguistics, 1970.

Fishman, J. Bilingual education and the future of language teaching and language teaching and language learning in the United States. In A. Simoes, Jr. (Ed.) *The bilingual child : Research and analysis of existing educational themes*. New York : Academic Press, 1976.

Fox, R.P. *Essays on teaching English as a second language and as a second dialect*. Urbana : National Council of Teachers of English, 1978.

Gazder, G. Conversational analysis and conventional socio-linguistics. In J.M. Atkinson, and D.R. Watson (Eds.) *Ethnographics : Studies in ethnomethodology*. London : Martin Roberton and Co., 1975.

Gordon, E.W. Some theoretical and practical problems in compensatory education as antidote to poverty. In V.L. Allen (Ed.) *Psychological factors in poverty*, New York : Academic Press, 197J.

Halliday, M.A.K. Relevant models of language. *Educational Review*, 1969, 22, (No. 1).

Hess, R.D. The transmission of cognitive strategies in poor families : The socialization of apathy and under development. In V.L. Allen. (Ed.) *Psychological factors in poverty* : New York : Academic Press, 1970.

Hymes, D. Foreword to M. Swadesh', *The origin and diversification of languages*. Chicago : Aldine-Atherton, 1971.

Jensen, A.R. Social class and verbal learning. In M. Deutsch I. Katz, A.R. Jensen, (Fds.) *Social class, race and psychological development*. New York : Holt, Rinehart, and Winston, 1968.

Jensen, A.R. How can we boost IQ and scholastic achievement? *Harvard Educational Review*, 1969, 39, 1-123.

Jensen, A.R. Learning ability, intelligence and educability. In V.L. Allen, (Ed.) *Psychological factors in poverty*. New York : Academic Press, 1970.

Kochman, J. *Rappin and styin out : Communication in urban Black America*. Urbana : University of Illinois Press, 1972.

Labov, W. The logic on non-standard English. In F. Williams (Ed.) *Language and poverty*. Chicago : Markham, 1970.

Macnamara. Bilingualism and thought. In B. Spolsky (Ed.) *The language education of minority children.* Rowley : Newbury House, 1972.

Rosenthal, R., and Jacobson, L. Self-fulfilling prophesies in the classroom : Teachers' expectations as unintended determinate of pupils' intellectual competence. In M. Deutsch, I. Katz, A.R. Jensen, (Eds.) *Social class, race and psychological development*, New York : Holt, Rinehart and Winston, 1968.

Trudgill, F. Review of Bernstein. *Journal of Linguistics*, 1973, 11, No. 1.

Whiteman, M., and Deutsch, M. Social disadvantages as related to intellective and language development. In M. Deutsch, I. Katz, A.R. Jensen, (Eds.) *Social class, race and psychological development*. New York : Holt, Rinehart and Winston, 1968.

NINE

Shantilata Sahu

EFFECT OF SOCIAL DISADVANTAGE ON MEDIATIONAL ABILITIES*

THE Mediational theory of human conceptual development (Kendler & Kendler, 1967; Kendler & Kendler, 1968) states that there is a transition beginning in early childhood, from a sensory-motor level of functioning to a level mediated by symbolic representational responses. At the mediational level learned behaviour is assumed to depend on symbolic representation of the relevant information.

The deficiencies in mediation are of two types : production and control deficiencies. Production deficiencies refer to failure to produce appropriate symbolic responses to the relevant class of environmental events. Control deficiencies refer to the failure of potential mediators, once produced, to control behaviour. Kendler (1972) has observed that both types of mediational deficiencies occur at the kindergarten level and decline with increasing maturity. But Reese (1962) suggested that with a well-learned concept there is necessarily no deficiency in mediation as a function of age, but with a less well-established concept there is a deficiency at any age.

So far as the effect of social disadvantage upon cognition is concerned, there still exists an unresolved controversy among the researchers in the field. While some of them indicate the adverse effect of social disadvantage upon the growth and development of cognitive pattern and abilities (e.g., Haywood, 1967; Miller, 1970; Whiteman & Deutsch, 1968; Jensen, 1973;

*The research is a part of a project financially supported by the U.G.C.

Das, Jachuk & Panda, 1970; Rath, 1972; Rath, 1974; Sinha 1977; Tripathi & Misra, 1975) others refute such a stand (e.g., Zigler, 1970; Ginsburg, 1972; Zigler, Abelson & Seitz, 1973; Williams, 1974; Houston, 1970; Quay, 1974).

Since mediational abilities make up an integral part of general cognitive abilities, it can be hypothesised that social disadvantage adversely affects it. The present study aimed to assess if social disadvantage retards mediational abilities of primary school children. Two different types of mediation conditions (i e., semantic mediation and three stage-mediation) were taken into account.

METHOD

Sample

Two hundred and ten children took part in the study. Out of these 105 belonged to the disadvantaged group and 105 belonged to the advantaged group. These groups were further devided into three grades i.e. II, III and V. Thus, there were 35 *S*s in each of the six subgroups. Disadvantage was empirically determined through applying the Cultural Deprivation Index developed by Samant (1975). The socially advantaged children came from families with high income, highly educated father, high caste affiliation and resided in urban areas. Socially disadvantaged children came from families with low income, low parental education, low caste group affiliation and resided in rural areas. Taxable income was taken to be high income, which was Rs. 8,000 per annum in the state; graduation and above was taken to be high education. Brahmin, Karan, and Khandayat caste groups were taken to be high caste groups. Similarly, Rs. 250 per family per month was taken to be low income (a IV grade employee in the state starts with approximately Rs. 250 per month). Lower primary and below was taken to be low education. The scheduled castes were taken to be low caste groups. Thus, two contrasted groups of children with reference to social dimension were taken into account. They were reading in second, third and fifth grades.

In order to get reliable information about family income, father's education, and caste group affiliation, all students reading in second, third and fifth grades of selected schools were given printed forms and were requested to get the forms filled up by their parents or guardians. In case of illiterate parents the investigator interviewed the parents to get these informations.

Tests

Test of primary and semantic generalization

A composite test following Osgood (1952, 1968), was used to assess the primary generalization and semantic mediation abilities. At first the *S*s were required to associate a meaningful word to a 1″ × 1″ square colour patch, up to a criterion level of one perfect association. No trial limit was observed. Then primary generalizations, based upon perceptual similarities, to $1\frac{1}{2}'' \times \frac{1}{2}''$ rectangular colour patch and $\frac{1}{2}''$ radius circular colour patch were tested. Finally, semantic generalization based upon semantic mediation to the colour name was tested.

A pilot study showed that in order to keep difficulty level at the optimal point for *S*s from different grades, there should be two different colour patches to be associated with two meaningful words for grade-II *S*s, three different colour patches to be associated with three meaningful words for grade-III *S*s, and four different colour patches to be associated with four meaningful words for grade-V *S*s. Primary and semantic generalization tests were made for two, three and four stimuli for *S*s from the second, third, and fifth grades, respectively. Four meaningful words (i.e., *Oriya* equivalents of 'Good', 'Beautiful', 'Light' and 'Active') representing evaluative, potency and activity dimensions of meaning (Osgood, Suci & Tannenbaum, 1961) were chosen to be associated with four different primary colour patches (i.e. Red, Green, Yellow and Blue). Number of trials taken to associate meaningful words with the colour patches; primary generalizations to rectangular and circular colour patches; and semantic generalizations to corresponding colour names were recorded for each *S*.

Test of three-stage-mediation

Three-stage-mediation test was used to assess mediational abilities of children. It has been successfully used by a number of researchers on children as well as adults (e.g., Jenkins, 1963; Kjeldergaard, 1968; Shapiro & Palermo, 1968; Boat & Cliffton, 1968; Cook & Smothergill, 1971). This paradigm provides a convenient and powerful way to test the capacity for mediated association through a simple paradigm involving paired associate (PA) learning. In this study A-B, B-C, A-C chaining paradigm was used. In this three-stage-mediation test, through paired associate (PA) learning, nonsense syllables or meaningful words can be used in place of A, B and C elements. The *S* first associates A-B pair, then goes for B-C pairing and finally is tested on A-C pairing.

A pilot study showed that in order to keep difficulty level at the optimal point for all grades, it was necessary to have two pairs, three pairs and four pairs, respectively for the second, third and fifth graders, in each of the A-B, B-C and A-C lists. Meaningful stimulus words were inserted for A, B and C elements and care was taken to ensure that all the stimulus words were familiar to all the *S*s. Number of trials necessary to master each list (i.e. A-B, B-C and A-C lists) were recorded for each *S*. Thus, each *S* had three scores on the three-stage-mediation test. Some *S*s failed to develop associations in 3 different stages. They were rejected while analysing the scores on three-stage-mediation test.

RESULTS

Average number of trials taken to associate meaningful words with colour patches, in the tests of primary generalization and semantic mediation, were found out for each of the six subgroups. Mean comparison showed that the difference between socially advantaged and socially disadvantaged *S*s was significant only for second graders ($t=2.13$; $df=68$; $p<.05$), but not for third ($t=0.00$) and fifth graders ($t=0.86$, $df=68$; $p>.05$).

Table 9.1 presents the results of mean comparison of the scores made by advantaged and disadvantaged children on primary generalization and semantic mediation tasks by grade level.

TABLE 9.1 : Mean scores of advantaged and disadvantaged children on primary generalization and semantic mediation tasks at II, III, and V grade levels.

Grades	Social Dimension	Tasks: Primary Generation Rectangle	Tasks: Primary Generation Circle	Tasks: Semantic Mediation
	Advantaged	3.40	3.43	2.66
V	Disadvantaged	3.80	3.77	0.60
	t	1.87	1.59	3.88**
	Advantaged	2.80	2.80	1.49
III	Disadvantaged	2.26	1.85	0.26
	t	2.67*	4.01**	4.58**
	Advantaged	1.60	1.45	.94
II	Disadvantaged	0.97	0.77	.20
	t	3.35**	3.51**	4.04**

**$p<.01$

*$p<.05$

It is clear that so far as scores on primary generalization (to both Rectangle and Circle) are concerned, advantaged second and third graders scored significantly higher than their disadvantaged counterparts. This trend was absent among the fifth graders. But, so far as scores on semantic mediation were concerned, advantaged children scored significantly higher than their disadvantaged counterparts across all the grades.

In order to determine the effect of social disadvantage and stage of learning on three-stage mediation test separate 2×3 factorial analyses of variance, with two levels of social dimension (advantaged/disadvantaged) and three levels of stage of learning (first/second/third), were performed on scores made by children of each of the three grade levels. Since stage of learning was a within factor variable repeated measures design was followed. The results indicated significant main effect of disadvantage for grade V while the main effect of stage of learning was significant for all the three graders. The cell means and *F* ratios are shown in the Table 9.2.

TABLE 9.2 : **Means and standard deviations for three-stage-mediation test scores of second, third and fifth grader advantaged and disadvantaged *S*s.**

Grade	Social Dimension	Association Trials				
		Stage-I	Stage-II	Stage-III	F ratios	
		Mean	Mean	Mean	Social Dimension	Stages of Learning
	Advantaged	3.40	4.86	3.17		
V	Disadvantaged	2.88	4.03	2.69	5.81*	26.25**
	Advantaged	3.27	4.30	3.30		
III	Disadvantaged	3.34	4.77	2.73	<1	22.41**
	Advantaged	2.25	2.54	1.97		
II	Disadvantaged	2.40	3.57	2.40	3.66	9.25**

** $<p.01$

* $p<.05$

Note : None of the *F* ratios for the interaction effect was significant.

It is evident that the advantaged children scored higher than their disadvantaged counterparts, though the difference was significant only at the fifth grade level. In regard to the effect of the stage of learning the data revealed that for second and third graders second stage was most difficult followed by first and third stages. This order was slightly changed for the fifth graders in which second stage was most difficult followed by third and first stages. Interaction effects were not significant, but there was a trend present in this direction, in case of second and third graders. Table 9.2 shows that socially disadvantaged second and third graders took greater number of trials for paired associate learning over thrce different stages of learning than their advantaged counterparts. The only exception was stage three for the third grade which required slightly greater number of trials on the part of advantaged children as compared with disadvantaged children.

DISCUSSION

There was a significant difference between socially advantaged and disadvantaged second graders so far as number of trials taken to develop association in primary generalization and semantic mediation test was concerned. Socially advantaged second graders could reach the criterion level within lesser number of trials compared to their socially disadvantaged counterparts. But, this difference did not exist between socially advantaged third and fifth graders. This shows that even in the area of rote learning the socially advantaged group does better than the soically disadvantaged group at the lowest grade level. Thereafter the disadvantaged group performs at a par with the advantaged group.

Table 9.1 reveals that in the tests of primary generalization there exists a social class difference for second and third graders, with advantaged group performing better than their disadvantaged counterparts. But, semantic mediation results showed that the advantaged children performed consistently better than their disadvantaged counterparts over all the grade levels.

Developmental studies have shown that children utilise the immediate perceptual similarities for generalization purposes, only up to a certain developmental stage, but thereafter make a shift to other non-perceptual abstract bases of generalization. Greenfield, Reich and Olver (1966) observe that the shift from perceptual to non-perceptual bases of judging equivalence takes place at a relatively early age for city as compared to rural school children. Sigel and Olmsted (1970) conclude that the impoverished children as compared to the middle class children, lack experiences that focus on the unseen, on the significance of representation, their experiences tend to emphasize the here and now. And, the manner in which a child goes about abstracting equivalence reflects the nature of his society (Macoby & Modiano, 1966). Ability to label and classify, use hierarchical categorization, and ability to discriminate between relevant stimulus cues and dimensions has been found to be substandard among the disadvantaged (Miller, 1970). Hence, it is but obvious that the advantaged group performs consistently better than its disadvantaged counterparts, over all the grade levels, on the test of semantic mediation. Moreover, even on measures of primary generalization the disadvantaged groups lag behind the advantaged groups up to the third grade level.

Results about three-stage mediation test indicated that the effect of stages of learning was significant across all the three grades. However, the effect of disadvantage was significant only for the fifth graders. The interaction F ratios were below the significance level, but showed a trend in expected direction (Table 9.2).

The average number of trials taken to reach the criterion level showed that Stage-II learning was more difficult than both Stage-I and Stage-III learning, which accounts for consistently significant variance obtained for stages of learning for all the three grades. A tendency towards significant interaction seen for second and third graders indicated that though the overall social dimension variance was not significant, yet, the two social groups performed differently over the three different stages of learning. For A-B learning (i.e., Stage-I) both the social groups required almost equal number of trials, but for B-C learning (i.e., Stage-II) the disadvantaged groups have taken relatively larger number of trials; and again for A-C learning (Stage-III) both the groups, needed lesser trials. Hence, though the overall social dimension variance has been nullified, yet, the interaction variance showed a tendency towards significance. All the six subgroups showed mediation effects, i.e., facilitation for A-C learning was present. Berkowski and Wanschura (1974), after an extensive review of research in three-stage mediation in the retarded, came to the conclusion that there is clear evidence for mediated facilitation during the terminal stage of PA learning (i.e., Stage-III). The present results also showed that though the socially disadvantaged face some difficulty for

Stage-II learning at times, yet, both socially disadvantaged and advantaged groups did show mediational facilitation.

A significant social dimension effect without an accompanying interaction effect for the fifth graders on three-stage-mediation scores implies that socially disadvantaged fifth graders were better rote learners than their advantaged counterparts. This trend was not present over the other two grade levels.

Thus, it can be concluded that socially advantaged groups perform better than the socially disadvantaged groups up to a particular stage (i.e. up to the third grade level) in tests of primary generalization. But, on the tests of semantic mediation the socially advantaged groups perform consistently better than the socially disadvantaged groups across all the grade levels. In the test of three-stage-mediation both socially advantaged and disadvantaged groups show mediational facilitation effects.

REFERENCES

Berkowski, J.G. and Wanschura, P.B. Mediational processes in retarded. In N.R. Ellis (Ed.) *International review of research in mental retardation.* New York : Academic Press, 1974.

Boat, B.M., and Cliffton, C. Jr. Verbal mediation in four year old children. *Child Development*, 1968, 39, 505-514.

Cook, H., and Smothergill, D. Verbal mediation and satiation in young children. *Child Development*, 1971, 42, 1805-1812.

Das, J.P., Jachuck, K., and Panda, T.P. Cultural deprivation and cognitive growth. In H.C. Haywood (Ed) *Social-cultural aspects of mental retardation.* New York : Meredith Corpn., 1970.

Dreger, R., and Miller, K.S. Comparative psychological studies of Negroes and Whites in the United States : 1959-1965. *Psychological Bulletin Monograph Supplement*, 1968, 70, (part 2).

Ginsburg, H. *The myth of the deprived child.* Englewood Cliffs. New Jersey : Prentice-Hall, 1972.

Greenfield, P.M. Reich, L.C., and Olver, R.R. On culture and equivalence : II. In J.S. Bruner, R.R. Olver, and Greenfield (Eds.) *Studies in cognitive growth.* New York : John Wiley and Sons, 1966.

Haywood, H.C. Experiential factors in intellectual development : The concept of dynamic intelligence. In J. Zubin, and G. Jervis (Eds.) *Psychopathology of mental development*, (Vol. II) New York : Grune and Stratton, 1967.

Houston, S.H. Are-examination of some assumptions about the language of the disadvantaged child. *Child Development*, 1970, 41, 947-963.

Jenkins, J.J. Mediational association: Paradigms and situations. In C.N. Coffer, and B.S. Musgrave (Eds.) *Verbal behaviour and learning.* New York : McGraw-Hill, 1963.

Jensen, A.R. *Genetics and education.* New York : Harper and Row: 1973.

Kendler, T.S., and Kendler, H.H. Experimental analysis of inferential behaviour in children. In L.P. Lipsett and C.C. Spiker (Eds.) *Advances in child development and behaviour,* (Vol. 3), New York : Academic Press, 1967.

Kendler, H.H., and Kendler, T.S. Mediation and conceptual behaviour. In K.W. Spence, and J.T. Spence (Eds.) *Psychology of learning and motivation* (Vol. 2) New York : Academic Press, 1968.

Kendler, T.S. An ontogeny of mediational deficiency. *Child Development* 1972, **43**, 1-17.

Kjeldergaard, P.M. Transfer and mediation in verbal learning. In T.R. Dixon and D.L. Horton (Eds.) *Verbal behaviour and general behaviour theory.* Englewood Cliffs, N.J. : Prentice-Hall, 1968.

Macoby, M., and Modiano, N. On culture and equivalence. In J.S. Bruner, R.R. Olver and P.M. Greenfield (Eds.) *Studies in cognitive growth.* New York : John Wiley and Sons, 1966.

Miller, J. Cultural deprivation and its modification. In H.C. Haywood (Ed.) *Social-cultural aspects of mental retardation.* New York : Meredith Corpn., 1970.

Osgood, C.E. The nature and measurement of meaning. *Psychological Bulletin*, 1952, **49**, 197-237.

Osgood, C.E. Suci, G.J., and Tannenbaum, P.H. *The measurement of meaning.* Urbana : University of Illinois Press, 1961,

Osgood, C.E. *Method and theory in experimental psychology.* New York : Oxford University Press, 1968.

Quay, L.C. Language, dialect, age, and intelligence : Test performance in disadvantaged Black children. *Child Development*, 1974, **45**, 463-468.

Rath, R. *Cognitive growth and class-room learning of culturally deprived children in the primary schools.* Paper presented at the East-West Centre for Cross-Cultural Studies, Honolulu, 1972.

Rath, R. From social isolation to stagnation : A study of scheduled caste groups. *Social Action,* 1974, **24**, 101-116.

Samant, C. *Construction of the scale of cultural deprivation and its application.* Unpublished Master's Thesis, Department of Psychology, Utkal University, Bhubaneshwar, 1975.

Reese, H.W. Verbal mediation as a function of age level. *Psychological Bulletin*, 1962, **59**, 502-509.

Shapiro, S.I., and Palermo, D.S. Mediation in children's aural paired-associate learning. *Child Development*, 1968, **39**, 569-577.

Sigel, I.E. and Olmsted, P. The development of classification and representational competence. *Ontario Institute for Studies in Education Monograph*, 1970, **9**, 49-67.

Sinha, D. Some social disadvantages and development of certain perceptual skills. *Indian Journal of Psychology*, 1977, **52**, 115-132.

Tripathi, L.B., and Misra, G. Cognitive activities as a function of prolonged deprivation. *Psychological Studies*, 1975, **20**, 54-61.

Whiteman, M., and Deutsch, M. Social disadvantage as related to intellective and language development. In M. Deutsch, I. Katz., and A.R. Jensen (Eds.) *Social class, race and psychological development* : New York : Holt, Rinehart and Winston, 1968.

Williams, R.C. Scientific racism and I.Q. : The silent mugging of the black community. *Psychology Today*, May issue, 1974.

Zigler, E. The nature-nurture issue reconsidered. In H.C. Haywood (Ed.) *Social-cultural aspects of mental retardation*. New York : Appleton - Century-Crofts, 1970.

Zigler, E., Abelson, W.D., and Seitz, V. Motivational factors in the performance of economically disadvantaged children on the Peabody Picture Vocabulary Test. *Child Development*, 1973, **44**, 294-303.

TEN

Girishwar Misra

DEPRIVATION AND COGNITIVE COMPETENCE*

INTRODUCTION

THE present paper aims at analysing the current status of deprivation studies in relation to cognitive competence. It is also contended that a more refined empirical-approach is necessary for considering experiential factors, while determining the impact of deprivation on cognition. It is in this context that the concept of prolonged deprivation is introduced. Some empirical findings from a large study are also presented. The paper is divided into four sections. The first section attempts at defining the relevant concepts and gives a brief resumé of the major theoretical positions regarding cognitive functioning. The second section is devoted to a critical appraisal of the findings of existing deprivation studies. The third section is concerned with the analysis of the concept of prolonged deprivation and related findings. The fourth section provides conclusions and interpretations.

DELINEATION OF CONCEPTS

Deprivation

The term 'deprivation' has been generally used as an explanatory

* This paper was prepared while the author was at Psychology Department, Gorakhpur University, Gorakhpur. The research reported in this paper was supported by the Indian Council of Social Science Research under grant No. 1-173/74 (EA).

construct and also as an empirical variable to account for a number of behavioural properties in controlled laboratory as well as in natural settings. In sensory deprivation studies it refers to experimental manipulation involving reduction in either sensory input or motor output or both. Such experimental manipulations are generally made in one or two sense modalities or motor functions lasting over a few hours or days or weeks and in some cases for months, e.g., rearing of chimpanzees and rats in visually impoverished environmental conditions (e.g., Riesen, 1947). However, the exact procedure adopted and specification of referents show wide range of variability (Zubek, 1969).

In studies done in natural settings 'deprivation' has come to acquire a variety of connotations. It is used interchangeably with other terms such as cultural deprivation (Riessman, 1962; Wight, Gloniger, & Kneene, 1970; Das, 1973), social and cultural disadvantage (Havighurst, 1964; Sinha, 1977), psychological deprivation (Langmeier, 1972), and social deprivation (Tulkin, 1972). In order to illustrate the point further, let us examine some of the prevailing concepts of deprivation as found in current research usage.

According to Hunt (1964), cultural deprivation is "failure to provide an opportunity to have the experiences required for adequate development of the semi-autonomous, central processes demanded for acquiring skill in cognitive processes". Gordon (1965) has used deprivation to represent 'deficiencies in the stimulus conditions of the childhood'. Whiteman and Deutsch (1968) have considered social deprivation as 'a relative term referring exclusively to specific types of environmental factors'. According to them any environmental factor may be considered deprivational when that factor is associated with certain social groupings such as, socio-economic status (SES) or race, and when the environmental variable is associated with impaired performance. Jensen (1968) has laid emphasis on 'lacks in environmental inputs'. Tannenbaum (1969) has concluded that 'social deprivation may be characterized as a condition in which particular behavioural alternatives for achieving self fulfilment are absent'. According to Wight, *et al.* (1970) deprivation refers to 'deficiencies, both in experience and in the conditions of learning'. Langmeier (1972) has viewed deprivation as a general phenomenon and defined the same as 'insufficient satisfaction of basic needs for a prolonged period'.

Thus, it is clear that the term 'deprivation' has been used in several ways to denote deficient environmental conditions and impoverished experiences along different dimensions. However, the referents of deprivation are not clearly defined and in a majority of the studies only specific aspects of deprivation have been arbitrarily considered while in actual life-conditions various aspects of deprivation occur jointly. Also, there is a lack of precision in use of the concept of deprivation.

Cognition

The term 'cognition' has been used to refer to the process of apprehending environmental stimulations. According to Neisser (1967) cognition includes "all the processes by which the sensory input is transformed, reduced, elaborated, stored, recovered and used". As a generic term it encompasses all processes through which knowledge of an object is attained (Leeper, 1951). In the view of Kogan and Kogan (1970) cognition stands for "hypothetical psychological processes involved in explanation of overt verbal as well as motor behaviour along-with certain psychological reactions. It is a super-ordinate term subsuming the more familiar representational processes like imagery, perception, free association, through mediation, reasoning and problem solving". Cognitive competence, therefore, may be viewed as efficiency of individual's cognitive functioning. The level of cognitive competence, as Langer (1969) says, 'informs (sets the limits to and the potentials for) the range of 'individual's conduct'.

In psychological theorization environmental experiences have always been regarded as a crucial factor in cognitive functioning. However, it was Freud (1905) who, for the first time emphasized the paramount role early experiences play in the development of personality and character. Since the second world war, there has been tremendous growth of interest in studying the role of environmental factors in determining human behaviour; and a number of theoretical models have been proposed. On the basis of neuro-physiological results, Hebb (1953) proposed that environmental experiences are essential prerequisites for the growth of psychological functions. In his view there is no behaviour beyond the level of the reflex that could be considered essentially independent of learning. According to Piaget (1947) the "organism's interaction with environment, chiefly through motor actions, causes cognitive operations to emerge". Bruner (1959) has also emphasized the role of environmental factors when he says that "an impoverished environment produces an adult organism with reduced ability to discriminate, with stunted strategies for coping with round about solutions, with less taste for exploratory behaviour, and a notably reduced tendency to draw inferences that serve to cement the direct events of its environment". Hunt (1964) states that the belief in fixed intelligence is untenable and it is far from completely predetermined. According to him experiences are programmers of the human brain-computer, and learning may be based on intrinsic motivation which is inherent in information processing and action.

In general, it is accepted that the experiential base, derived from environment, is a crucial factor in the development and growth of cognitive processes, and variability in cognitive competence may be assumed to be attributable to variation in experiential input. The empirical data with regard to this position come from a variety of studies in which deprivation studies loom large. In the following section an attempt is made to review the findings of these studies with greater emphasis on human studies of deprivation in natural life settings.

II
BRIEF REVIEW OF LITERATURE

I Animal studies

The importance of sensory experience has been investigated by raising animals under conditions of reduced sensory input. In a number of studies it has been found that a prolonged period of patterned sensory stimulation is a prerequisite of perceptual growth (Riesen, 1947; Nissen, Chow & Semmes, 1951). Results obtained by Rosenzweig, Krech, Bennet and Diamond, 1968) Harlow (1961) and Levine (1956) also show irreversible effects of deprivation, and facilitation due to enrichment. Bronfenbrenner (1968) has concluded in his cross-species survey of the effects of early deprivation in mammals that the effect is related to the phylogenetic position of the organism. In recent analysis of the effects of environment on development of brain and behaviour Rosenzweig (1971) has indicated that the findings are highly specific to species and even to strain of animal, to the ages at which differential experience is given, and to the particular test used. Some of the reported effects are subject to different interpretations. In studies of both forest and urban rhesus monkeys in India, Singh (1966, 1969) found that formal tests of ability given to monkeys show no long-run effects of enriched experience above a natural base line. The restricted environment did not affect problem-solving once the monkeys were adapted to the test situation.

Studies by Krech, Rosenzweig and Bennet (1966) and Rosenzweig (1971) provide evidence of cerebral effects of differential environmental treatments. On several brain measures, enrichment of experience above the colony level leads to changes that are opposed in direction to those caused by impoverishment of experiences. But before accepting these findings, base line measures are needed and any generalization in this area must be made with great caution (Fuller, 1973). Recently Singh and Anandalakshmy (1976) have concluded from a careful review of the salient studies on rats, dogs and monkeys that there is no relationship between the type of environment and cognitive ability.

II Human studies

A. Studies of artificially created short term sensory deprivation

Having become dissatisfied with the early Hullian S-R analysis of behaviour, Hebb (1949) criticized the idea of an empty organism only to be made responsive to stimuli, and launched a series of laboratory experiments for investigating behavioural consequences of sensory deprivation. The results of these and other subsequent studies of human beings under artificially produced sensory deprivation and isolation (e.g., Bexton 1953; Brownfield, 1964) indicated that deprivation of stimulation causes disorganization of a number of cognitive processes. However, as Zubek (1969) has observed the procedural variations and inconsistent specification of referents pose difficulties in systematizing the results.

B. Institutionalization and clinical studies

Under the influence of psycho-analytic theory, considerable work has been done on effects of severe trauma or extreme deprivation of familial care. A number of clinical studies (Levy, 1943); (Ribble, 1943) have shown that inadequate mothering is a major factor in the etiology of emotional disturbances. These early findings were extended by institutionalization studies (e.g., Goldfarb, 1945; Spitz, 1946; Yarrow, 1961; Provence & Lipton, 1962; Dennis & Najarian, 1957). In general, these studies provide evidence that being deprived of normal experiences has a marked and sometimes prolonged effect upon physical as well as intellectual development. In a 15 and 20 year follow up study, Dennis (1973) found that even those children who were adopted showed some developmental retardation in maturity. Those who remained in institutions showed marked retardation throughout life. Similarly, in a 25 year follow through of Skeels's studies by Skodak, it was found that almost all of those who received early attention had been maintaining themselves effectively in life on their own, whereas most of those who had not received such stimulation became public charges (Skeels, 1966). Recently, children living in orphanages (Sinha & Shukla, 1974), foster homes (Talmadge, Hayden & Schiff, 1969) and other child-care centres (Langmeier & Matejeck, 1970) have been studied, and significant relationships between conditions of deficient stimulation and retardation in cognitive competence have been noticed.

C. Deprivation in natural settings

In the last two decades, a phenomenal increase in the number of studies showing variation in a variety of cognitive and motivational processes along the dimensions of social class, race, ethnic group, caste and SES has been noticed in developed as well as developing countries. The results about cognitive effects of deprivation are summarized as follows.

Intelligence : It has been found that IQ as measured through tests of intelligence varies as a function of SES, social class and residential area (e.g., Whiteman, Brown & Deutsch, 1967; Salpatek, 1971; Tripathi, 1970; Chopra, 1970; Pandey, 1970; Singh, 1976). Furthermore there is evidence that some differences hold within ethnic groups (Kennedy, Van de Reit

& White, 1963; Pettigrew,1964). Prolonged living under conditions of poverty also results in a steady decline of the IQ (Jordan, 1963; Jones, 1954). However, children below approximately 2 years of age do not show IQ differences along social class and SES variables (Bayley, 1965). It is only afterwards that the differences become prominent.

Verbal ability : Studies of vocabulary and verbal ability have shown that disadvantaged children clearly appear lower (e.g., Templin, 1957; John & Goldstein, 1964; Jensen, 1968; Bernstein, 1960; John & Goldstein, 1964; Rath, 1975) on these factors as compared to the privileged ones. There is also evidence that the middle class children have better verbal reasoning abilities than lower class children (e.g., Marjoribanks, 1972; Kellaghan & MacNamara, 1972). The problem-solving strategies also differ as a function of SES and social class (Bresnahan & Shapiro, 1972).

Perceptual and conceptual processes : Lack of efficiency in depth perception, perceptual differentiation, categorization, identification, conceptualization and other cognitive processes have been found in deprived groups (e.g., Bailie, 1972; Sinha & Shukla, 1974; Covington, 1967; Cox, 1969; Rath & Dash, 1972; Das, Jachuk & Panda, 1970; Das, 1973; Longly, 1972; Kohn & Rosman, 1973; Stodoloski & Lesser, 1967; Sinha, 1977; Verma & Sinha, 1977).

Memory : There is some evidence that middle class children have better memory than lower class children (Glassman, 1968; Schultz, Charness, & Boreman, 1973). In studies of recall Misra and Shukla (1979) found a significant difference in memory of high and low deprived children.

The above mentioned studies bring out several issues which need careful consideration before taking the risk of broad generalizations.

(*i*) In a majority of the studies deprivation has been manipulated through subject selection from dichotomous groups along dimensions such as SES, class, caste, culture, and social discrimination, cultural deprivation, and social disadvantage etc. have been viewed to be basic determinants or causal agents of the poor performance. It is needless to emphasize that more often than not the empirical or quantifiable referents of these terms are not equally shared by various investigators. Thus, the manipulation of independent variable, i.e., deprivation, has not been done in proper order. For instance, in many studies it was assumed on apriori grounds that the socio-cultural environment of high and low castes are different (e.g., Rath, 1975; Sinha, 1977; Das, 1973). But in none of these studies relevant deprivational variables have been specified along which the samples varied or differed.

(*ii*) The effects of social class and other such variables are not independent of the test characteristics in several studies. As a result some psychologists have opined that the differences may be accounted for in terms of factors such as familiarity with test materials, rapport with testers, and subjects' motivation etc. For instance, Price Williams (1962) failed to find any significant difference due to cultural differences when he used indigenous materials in the study of concept formation. Similar results have been observed by Heney and Kooper (1973) and Scaropani, Suziedelis and Shore (1973) with regard to conceptualization. Zigler and Butterfield (1968) tested children under standard and optimizing conditions and found an increase of 10 points in IQ scores. In a recent review of verbal communication styles Higgins (1976) found that there is little support for hypothesized relationship between social class and communication style.

(*iii*) Some psychologists feel that the tests employed in studies measure *performance* and do not reveal differences in *competence*. One of the chief spokesmen of this view is Ginsberg (1972). He grants that children from poverty-environments score lower on standard tests and that they do badly in school, but he does not take this as evidence that they are fundamentally less skilled or less competent. Instead, he takes it as evidence that the tests have not measured the poor child's competence. He strongly argues that the tests measure performance, and the school measures performance;

they do not necessarily tap the child's competence or fundamental ability.

(*iv*) It has also been argued that the differences in performance between the deprived and the privileged occur due to the fact that poor children are simply genetically less bright. As Jensen (1969) suggests about 80% of the variance is accounted for in terms of heredity. Jencks (1972) gives a more conservative estimate of 45% though there is considerable agreement that the contribution is substantial. On the other hand, Bee (1974) has argued that the demonstrable environmental influences appear to account for virtually all the variance and there is little reason to emphasize a genetic explanation.

(*v*) In studies of deprivation in natural life settings little attention has been paid to the measurement aspect of deprivation. Attempts at identification and quantification of deprivation may be grouped under four categories i.e., (i) consideration of residential area, (ii) institutionalization, (iii) membership of some social/cultural/economic group, and (iv) use of indices of deprivation. However, putting individuals in deprived or non-deprived groups according to the first three approaches can not be considered sufficient for assessing the degree of deprivation in its entirety. The indices of deprivation developed so far (Davis, 1968; Munsey, 1971; Whiteman & Deutsch, 1968; Rath & Samant, 1975) are also criticized on more than one ground. Particularly the coverage of deprivational variables is partial and narrow, and such variables have not been adequately articulated in terms of their empirical referents.

It seems that the major problems in explaining the effects of deprivation, particularly in natural life settings, arise from limited degree of specificity of the terms and lack of correspondence between them and their empirical referents. As a consequence, related phenomena have often not been measured in any systematic manner. In a majority of the studies, deprivational variables have been treated at the nominal level. Also, the emphasis of researchers has not been on discovering the mechanisms operative in creating deficiencies or sufficiencies in the development of cognitive or other psychological processes. It appears that various social groupings, such as, caste, ethnic origin, culture or class, are significant for studying deprivation because they provide varied opportunities for acquiring different sensory and other experiences. These categories characterize special vocations, life-activities, religious practices, entertainment patterns, and family relationships and are usually linked with low or high economic opportunities and resources. As a result, individuals belonging to such groups in their formative years come to acquire specific experiences. These experiential variations may be considered as the direct determinants of the extent to which an individual comes to acquire cognitive competence. The caste or other social group in itself can not be regarded as antecedental to cognitive functioning. Unless the patterns of experiential variations are shown to be functionally related to psychological processes, no adequate explanation of the vast array of data generated by studies on caste and social class can be offered. Viewed, thus, it seems reasonable to assume that if one is able to index these experiences, measure them separately for each individual, and then correlate them with specified psychological function, a better and more meaningful explanation can be put forward. It is in this context that the concept of 'prolonged deprivation' is proposed.

III
A STUDY OF PROLONGED DEPRIVATION

The concept of prolonged deprivation

A close scrutiny of the experiential opportunities which people enjoy in their personal as well as community life, makes it evident that members of a particular social group or community get varying degrees of opportunities to acquire experiences. Social-cultural life in any group or community can be meaningfully conceptualized as a dimension at one end of which lie those who have all the psychological, physical, social, economic and other facilities for fulfilment of their biogenic as well as sociogenic needs leading to maximum amount of varied experiences in life, while on the other end may lie those who are materialistically, socially and psychologically handicapped to the maximum possible degree in fulfilment of their needs and acquisition of diverse experiences. Thus, people grow with differential experiential input which accumulates and works as a basis for cognitive functioning. Another point which is intrinsic to the idea of accumulated experiential input of an individual is the temporal aspect of deprivation. Even in experimental manipulation of sensory and/or motor deprivation it is necessary to specify and control the duration of deprivational treatment. Therefore, it is imperative that the temporal aspect of deprivation in natural setting should be given recognition and weightage, not only in conceptualization, but also in the measurement of deprivation. In view of the fact that variety and extent of experiential input is an outcome of relatively longer periods in a natural setting, an epithet 'Prolonged' has been added to the term 'deprivation' and it is called 'Prolonged Deprivation'.

The concept of prolonged deprivation as proposed here is based on a wide range of environmental and interactional variables constituting the basic sources of experiences to the living organism. It may be viewed as having numerous empirical referents. Any attempt at studying deprivation must specify as many operations and sources of deprivation as are possible and must differentiate these from the spectrum of life in a particular society. Thus, it is a multidimensional phenomenon manifest over (a time) duration. The dimensions can be identified and delimited. However, at the present state of psychological knowledge and methodological know-how, it is not feasible to conceptually differentiate and these continue empirically to examine their differential contributions to the individual's psychological make up. It is, therefore, reasonable to propose that deprivation should be treated globally and should include all aspects of experiential inputs of an individual in a specified natural setting for determining its level.

In order to measure the degree of prolonged deprivation a scale named Prolonged Deprivation Scale (PDS) has been developed (Misra & Tripathi, 1977b). This scale utilizes the techniques of interview, observation and rating for measurement of deprivation. Special attention has been given to make the measurement more realistic and meaningful. The scale consisting of 96 five-point rating scales includes almost all important aspects of deprivation such as physical, social, economic, educational, cultural and psychological etc. It has been standardized on a large sample from eastern Uttar Pradesh (Misra & Tripathi, 1977a).

Prolonged deprivation and cognitive competence

With the help of PDS, deprivation level of a large sample of mainly rural and partly urban young men of the age group of 15 to 25 years was determined and a number of cognitive functions were investigated. On the basis of scores on PDS the sample was divided into three deprivation groups i.e. high deprivation (HD) (scoring above Q3), medium deprivation (MD) (scoring in between 37.50th percentile and 62.50th percentile) and low deprivation (LD) (scoring up to Q1). The mean age values for these groups were 18.62, 18.20 and 18.98 years, respectively.

The measures of cognitive competence included the tasks of pictorial depth perception, perceptual identification, categorization of concrete (wooden) shapes, categorization of pictures, Cattell's Culture Fair Test (CFT), as a measure of complex conceptualization, correct recalls made on I,V,X trials of learning words and nonsense syllables, number of correct solutions on a verbal reasoning task, and total amount of deviation from true vertical in 8 trials on a portable Rod and Frame Test (RFT). In addition Kohs' Block Design Test (BDT) was used to determine intellective performance.

The data obtained from the present study were analyzed with a view to determining the extent to which scores on PDS were correlated with scores on various cognitive measures. Secondly, an attempt was made to see whether change in degree of prolonged deprivation results in corresponding change in performance on cognitive tasks. For this purpose, performance of the LD, MD and HD groups was analysed. In addition to these general analyses performance of *S*s individually matched in terms of age and intelligence test (BDT) scores were studied (for details see, Tripathi & Misra, 1975; 1976; Misra & Tripathi, 1980).

The correlational analysis indicated that in the general

as well as matched samples scores on all the tasks yielded significant negative correlations with PDS scores except the RFT scores which yielded a non-significant relationship. On the tasks of verbal reasoning and categorization of concrete shapes obtained correlations were significant at .05 level. On other tasks obtained correlations were significant at .01 level. The results obtained in the case of matched sample confirmed the pattern of relationship observed in the case of general sample. The results of cross-comparisons of the mean scores of three deprivation groups are shown in Table 10.1.

It is evident that the performance of the LD group is characterized with relatively higher degree of cognitive competence as compared to the HD group. It has also scored higher than MD group on conceptualization (CFT) and verbal reasoning tasks. On other tasks the differences were non-significant, though the mean scores of MD group were consistently lower than those of the LD group. With regard to differences between HD and MD groups it was found that the MD group did significantly better on majority of the tasks except perceptual identification, categorization and verbal reasoning. In general, similar results were borne out in the case of matched samples. It was found that even when the HD and LD groups were matched on intelligence and age the former displayed significantly lower level of performance on most of the cognitive measures.

Caste factor and cognitive functions

One of the significant findings of the present study relates to the role of caste factor in determining cognitive competence. The nature of 'caste' is so complex and ill-defined that it is very difficult to determine the actual denotation of this term, particularly while considering it as an antecedent or correlate of some cognitive or personality variable. Despite this fact social and behavioural scientists have frequently used it in their researches and its importance has been widely acknowledged. Our results demonstrated that birth in a specific caste is not accompanied by specific level of cognitive competence, rather it is the cumulative experiential base which makes a person cognitively more or less competent. It was noted that approximately the same amount of difference was present between

TABLE 10.1 : **Mean scores of high, medium and low deprived groups on cognitive tasks**

Cognitive Tasks	General Sample			Matched Sample		
	Low	Medium	High	Low	Medium	High
Kohs' Block Design Test	55.20 a	50.60 b	47.60 c	—	—	—
Depth perception	7.90 a	6.87 b	6.37 b	8.37 a	7.37 a	4.87 b
Perceptual identification	19.19 a	15.57 b	13.85 c	16.07 a	14.78 ab	13.37 b
Categorization of concrete objects	2.38 a	2.07 b	1.56 c	2.25 a	1.88 b	1.46 c
Categorization of pictures	6.67 a	5.97 b	5.71 b	7.05 a	5.77 b	5.28 b
Culture Fair Test	17.70 a	13.99 b	13.70 b	16.96 a	13.84 b	12.64 b
Learning score on I trial (words)	7.00 a	6.41 a	5.36 b	7.37 a	6.25 ab	5.33 b
Learning score on V trial (words)	10.15 a	10.21 a	8.36 b	10.72 a	10.52 a	9.00 b

Learning score on X trial (words)	12.80	11.62	10.67	12.91	12.51	11.32
	a	b	c	a	a	b
Learning score on I trial	1.66	1.68	1.22	1.72	2.14	1.47
(Nonsense syllables)	a	a	b	a	a	b
Learning score on V trial	3.88	3.86	2.43	1.85	2.03	1.17
(Nonsense syllables)	a	a	b	a	a	b
Learning score on X trial	6.14	5.82	6.14	5.97	5.65	3.66
(Nonsense syllables)	a	a	b	a	a	b
Verbal reasoning	14.70	13.04	12.72	14.90	12.75	12.50
	a	b	b	a	b	b
Rod and Frame Test	65.60	71.30	51.58	44.25	58.22	54.62
	a	a	b	a	a	b

Note : Similar subscripts do not differ significantly.

performance of high and low deprived subjects when they were individually matched in terms of age, intelligence test scores as well as caste, as was found in the case of general sample. This clearly demonstrates that caste membership is not basic determiner of one's competence. Supportive evidence to this effect was found in an earlier study of the author (Tripathi & Misra, 1975). In that study, the possible role of caste factor was checked by analysing the data of medium deprivation group. This group was composed of the subjects of both high and low castes. These subjects were grouped in high and low caste categories and mean performance scores were compared. All the resulting *t* values were found to be non-significant and the obtained results failed to support the argument that differences in test scores were merely caste functions.

It seems that caste in itself is of very little significance so far as an individual's cognitive growth is concerned. However, in our existing social network, caste still operates as a powerful factor and proves to be an effective variable in restricting the variety of life experiences. More often than not, caste differences reflect variations along the social, cultural, educational, economic and other aspects of experiences. This further supports our reasoning that variations along cognitive functions can and should be better accounted for in terms of a more realistic and proximal factor, such as, experiential deprivation and not in terms of caste or other distal variables, such as, area of residence, SES and ethnicity etc.

Evidence of higher level of competence in highly deprived subjects

The results of the study also showed that the generalization that deprivation leads to deficient performance on a number of cognitive tasks was true only for the group. However, when we tried to apply this generalization to individual cases it broke down. A close perusal of the profiles of performance of individual subjects showed that some of the subjects falling within the category of high deprived group displayed the level of performance which was at times better than the average performance of low deprived group. Furthermore, it was also observed that some subjects of low deprived group displayed a very low level of competence on a number of tasks. These findings may be explained in terms of genetic differences. It can be argued that higher level of performance of highly deprived subjects may be due to the fact that these subjects were equipped with more efficient central nervous system and biological potentialities giving rise to greater competence even on the basis of meagre experiential content. The other possibility is that these highly deprived subjects may not have been deprived in certain critical experiences. Unfortunately, the present data tells nothing about the relative contribution of genetic factors and the analysis of deprivation was made in terms of a global score and not in terms of specific experiential domains. It is felt that efforts should be made to identify competent and talented children living in deprived conditions and making provisions to provide the necessary opportunity for their fullest growth of potentials.

Performance at medium deprivation level

The performance of MD group on all the tasks was higher than HD group and lower than LD group. However, on majority of the tasks the differences between MD and LD groups were non-significant. This may mean that deprivation is a threshold phenomenon, the effect of which depends upon its relationship with the optimum value of experiential input. If experiential inputs are below that point the performance is likely to deteriorate. In contrast, increase in the experiential inputs beyond threshold value may not lead to marked gain in performance. This situation tends to suggest that there is no straightforward linear relationship between deprivation and performance. The methodological implication of this finding is that the extreme group strategy in deprivation research is insufficient. From the point of view of intervention the results suggest that effort should be made to maintain the provision of optimal stimulation and experiences rather than a very high degree of enrichment.

IV
CONCLUSIONS

In the light of researches reviewed here it is apparent that there is much diversity in data and interpretations of deprivational effects on cognition. As an independent variable deprivation has been manipulated in several ways ranging from few hours' confinement to reduced stimulation, to unspecified living in unstimulating natural life conditions. On the other hand, the dependent variable of cognition has also been investigated from several angles through a variety of tasks varying in complexity and other attributes. In general, researchers have been more attracted by SES, social class, rural-urban differentials, culture, caste and other distal environmental variables and have often failed to recognize or have overlooked some known facts about psychological processes involved in deprivation. Consequently the progress in understanding the mechanisms through which deprivation operates in accelerating or retarding cognitive functioning has rather been slow and roughened with controversies. Varying conceptual and methodological orientations of researchers, as well as academic and socio-political interests, have also hampered the growth of deprivation studies.

Behaviour does not take place in vacuum but in some environment which not only elicits it but also sets limits on its magnitude, modification and differentiation. Environmental factors as assets and or liabilities interact with the biological and experiential make up of the organism. Substantial correlations obtained between cognitive functions and prolonged deprivation support this general contention. On majority of the cognitive tasks highly deprived group differed significantly from the low deprivation group. Such findings are unambiguous in the case of the general sample as well as the matched sample. The medium deprivation group too showed differential cognitive functions. This group scored significantly higher than highly deprived group on the tasks of verbal reasoning, categorization, and complex conceptualization task (CFT). On the other hand, differences between MD and LD groups on the tasks of verbal learning, perceptual identification and depth perception, were non-significant, though the mean scores of the latter group were greater than those obtained by the MD group.

At this point, a bit of speculation appears to be in order for understanding the mechanisms which account for the differential cognitive functioning of various deprivation groups.

Cognitive structures are built with the bricks of 'representations' or mediational processes. In other words, representations of objects, events and relations may be considered as cognitive units which are acquired through experiences stored in memory and retrieved on demand. Cognitive competence means more systematic and durable storage with selective and adequate retrieval capacity. Deprivation or lack of it, as is intuitively clear, is a necessary condition for acquisition of cognitive units. It seems that acquisition, storage and retrieval capacities are subject to enhancement through intensive experiences. This contention seems to be supported by studies within the framework of learning set theory (Harlow, 1959). Deprivation can be directly interlinked with necessary sensory input, its facilitation or inhibition in representational storage and retrieval in response to extroceptive stimulations and interactions with the environment. The data obtained in our study suggest that these three aspects of cognitive competence are largely determined by the degree of deprivation at the experiential level.

In the present study, a global measure of deprivation was used. It can not be denied, however, that deprivation of specific experiences has differential effects on behaviour. Deprivation areas need to be specified and made measurable for isolating and determining their differential effects on cognition. The results of the study discussed indicate that prolonged experiential deprivation may lead to impoverished growth of cognitive functions and suggest that experiential enrichment is essential for fuller psychological growth. But it is also true that we are still a long way away from being able to specify precisely the specific features of environment that promote or retard the cognitive growth. It is clear, however, that the various aspects of environmental stimulation are important and that these aspects differ from highly deprived to less deprived groups.

The conceptual model of the study involved a unidirectional approach emphasizing environmental effects upon organism while the relationship between environment and organism is bidirectional or reciprocal (Endler & Magnusson, 1976). It seems that an adequate understanding of deprivational effects requires refined treatment of environmental variables and their mode of interaction with organismic characteristics. Future research has to be focused on this aspect of the problem.

In addition, attempts are also required to develop effective intervention strategies on the basis of deprivational background rather than membership of specific caste or cultural group. Focus on maximum utilization of existing potentials by treating individuals in terms of their own distinct abilities and achievements is also wanted. This involves assessment of potentials as well as adequate provision of opportunities for a diversity of conditions suited to the diversity of individual abilities and needs. Finally, it may be pointed out that deprivational effects are not limited to cognition only. They have motivational consequences also which, in turn, may influence cognitive performance (see Pandey & Tripathi's paper in this volume). Therefore, analysis of motivational concomitants of deprivation should be given due consideration while investigating cognitive effects of deprivation.

REFERENCES

Bailie, D.A. The effect of single and combined pictorial cues on the perception of depth by children age five and six from two SES groups. *Dissertation Abstracts International*, 1972, **4**, (A), 1911.

Bayley, N. Comparisons of mental and motor test scores for ages 1-15 months by sex, birth order, race and geographical location, and education of parents. *Child Development*, 1965, **36**, 379-411.

Bernstein, B. Language and social class. *British Journal of Psychology*, 1960, **11**, 271-276.

Bexton, W.H. *Some effects of perceptual isolation in human subjects.* Unpublished Doctoral Dissertation, McGill University, Montreal, 1953.

Bresnahan, J.L., & Shapiro, M. Learning strategies in children from different socio-economic levels. In H.W. Reese (Ed.) *Advances in child development and behaviour.* (Vol. 7) New York : Academic Press, 1972.

Bronfenbrenner, U., Early deprivation in mammals : A cross-species analysis. In G. Newton and S. Levine (Eds.) *Early experience and behaviour*. Illinois : Thomas, 1968.

Brownfield, C.A., Sensory deprivation : A comprehensive survey. *Psychologia*, 1964, **1**, 63-93.

Bruner, J.A., The cognitive consequences of early sensory deprivation. *Psychosomatic Medicine*, 1959, **21**, 89-95.

Cazden, C.B. Subcultural differences in child language : An interdisciplinary approach. *Merril Palmer Quarterly*, 1966, **12**, 185-219.

Chopra, S.L. Socio-economic background and educational opportunity in India. *Journal of Educational Psychology*, 1970, **27**, 365-369.

Covington, M.V., Stimulus deprivation as a function of social class membership. *Child Development*, 1967, **38**, 602-607.

Cox, C.A. Remediating visual perceptual skills in lower socio-economic children. *Dissertation Abstracts International*, 1966, **30**, (6-A), 2327.

Das, J.P. Cultural deprivation and cognitive competence. In N.R. Ellis (Ed.) *International review of research in mental retardation.* (Vol. 6) New York : Academic Press, 1973.

Das, J.P. Jachuck, K., Panda, T.P. Caste, cultural deprivation and cognitive growth, In H.C. Haywood (Ed.) *Social cultural aspects of mental retardation.* New York : Appleton Century Crofts, 1970.

Davis, R.E., Social deprivation and cognitive functioning in lower class children. *Dissertation Abstracts International*, 1968, **29**, (11-B), 1105-1106.

Dennis, W. *Children of the Creche*. New York : Appleton Century Crofts, 1973.

Dennis, W., and Najarian, P. Infant development under environmental handicap. *Psychological Monographs*, 1957, **71**, (Whole No. 436).

Endler, N.S., Magnusson, D. *Interactional psychology of personality*. New York : John Wiley and Sons, 1976.

Freud, S. *The psychopathology of everyday life*. In A.A. Brill (Trans., and Ed) *The basic writings of Sigmund Freud.* New York : Modern Library, 1938.

(*Three contributions to the theory of sex*, originally published 1905).

Fuller, J.L. Genetics and vulnerability to experiential deprivation : *Proceedings of American Association for Advance of Science*, 1973, pp. 113-124. (Personal Communication).

Ginsberg, H. *The myth of the deprived child*. New Jersey : Prentice-Hall, 1972.

Glassman, L.D. *A social-class comparison of conceptual processes in children's free recall.* Unpublished Doctoral Dissertation, University of California, Berkeley, 1968.

Goldon, E.A. Review of compensatory education. *American Journal of Orthopsychiatry*, 1965, **35**, 640-651.

Goldfarb, W. Psychological privation in infancy and subsequent adjustment. *American Journal of Orthopsychiatry*, 1945, **15**, 247-255.

Haney, J.H. and Kooper, F.H. A developmental comparison of social class and verbal ability influences on Piagetian tasks. *Journal of Genetic Psychology*, 1973, **122**, 235-245.

Harlow, H.F. Learning set and error factor theory. In S. Koch (Ed.) *Psychology : A study of science* (Vol. 2) New York : McGraw-Hill, 1959.

Harlow, H.F. The development of affectional patterns in infant monkeys. In B.M. Foss (Ed.) *Determinants of infant behaviour.* New York : John Wiley & Sons, 1961.

Havighurst, R.J. Who are the socially disadvantaged ? *Journal of Negro Education*, 1964, **33**, 210-217.

Haywood, H.C. Experiential factors in intellectual development : The concept of dynamic intelligence. In J. Zubin and G. Jervis (Eds.) *Psychopathology of mental development*. New York : Grune, 1967.

Higgins, E.T. Social class differences in verbal communicative accuracy : A question of 'which question' ? *Psychological Bulletin*, 1976, **83**, 695-714.

Hebb, D.O. *Organization of behavior.* New York : John Wiley & Sons, 1949.

Hebb, D.O. Heredity and environment in mammalian behaviour. *British Journal of Animal Psychology*, 1953, **1**, 43-47.

Hunt, J. McV. The psychological basis for using preschool enrichment as an antidote for cultural deprivation. *Merrill-Palmer Quarterly*, 1964, **10**, 209-243.

Jencks, C. *Inequality : A reassessment of the effects of family and schooling in America.* New York : Basic Books, 1972.

Jensen, A.R. How much can we boost IG and scholastic achievement ? *Harvard Educational Review*, 1969, **39**, 1-123.

Jensen, A.R. Social class and verbal learning, In M. Deutsch, I. Katz, and A.R. Jensen (Eds.) *Social class, race and psychological, development*, New York : Holt, Rinehart and Winston, 1968.

John, V.P., and Goldstein, L.S. The social context of language acquisition. *Merrill-Palmer Quarterly*. 1964, **10**, 265-275.

Jones, N.E. The environment and mental development. In L. Carmichael, (Ed.) *Manual of child psychology*, New York : John Wiley & Sons, 1954.

Jordan, A.M. Parental occupations and children's intelligence scores. *Journal of Applied Psychology*, 1933, **17**, 103-119.

Kellaghan, T., and MacNamara, J. Family correlates of verbal reasoning ability. *Developmental Psychology*, 1972, **7**, 49-53.

Kennedy, W.Z., Van de Reit, V., and White, J.C., Jr. A normative sample of intelligence and achievement of Negro elementary school children in the south eastern United States. *Monographs of the Society for Research in Child Development*, 1963, **28**, (6).

Kirk, G.E., and Hunt, J. Mcv. Social class and preschool language skill : I. Introduction. *Genetic Psychology Monographs*, 1975, **91**, 281-298.

Kogan, J., and Kogan, N. Individual variation in cognitive processes. In P.H. Mussen (Ed.) *Carmichael's manual of child psychology*. (Vol. 1) New York : John Wiley & Sons, 1970.

Kohn, M., and Rosman, B.L. Cognitive functioning in five year old boys as related to socio-emotional background and demographic variables. *Development Psychology*, 1973, **8** 277-294.

Krech, D., Rosenzwieg, M.R., & Bennett. E. Environmental impoverishment, social isolation and changes in brain chemistry and anatomy. *Psychology and Behavior*, 1966, **1**, 99-104.

Langer, J. Disequilibrium as source of development. In P.H Mussen et al. (Eds.) *Trends and issues in developmental psychology.* New York : Holt, Rinehart & Winston, 1969.

Langmeier, J., & MateJeck, Z. Mental development of children in families and in infants homes. *Social Science and Me dicine*, 1970, 4, 569-577.

Leeper, R. Cognitive processes. In S.S. Stevens (Ed.) *Handbook of experimental psychology.* New York : John Wiley & Sons, 1951.

Levine, S.A. A further study of infantile handling and avoidance learning. *Journal of Personality*, 1956, 25, 70-80.

Levy, D. *Maternal overprotection.* New York : Columbia University Press, 1943.

Longley, J.F. Classification behaviours of mentally retarded lower socio-economic status and middle socio-economic status elementary children. *Dissertation Abstracts International*, 1972, 32.

Marjoribanks, K. Environment, social class and mental abilities. *Journal of Educational Psychology*, 1972, 63, 103-109.

Misra, G., and Tripathi, L.B. The concept of prolonged deprivation and its measurement. *Indian Journal of Behaviour*, 1977, 1, 48-60 (a).

Misra, G., and Tripathi, L.B. *Manual of prolonged deprivation scale.* Agra : National Psychological Corporation, 1977 (b).

Misra, G., and Tripathi, L.B. *Psychological consequences of prolonged deprivation.* Agra : National Psychological Corporation. 1980.

Misra, G., and Shukla, A. Experiential deprivation and development of serial memory. *Psychologia*, 1979, 22, 155-163.

Munsey, W.L. Development of an index of cultural deprivation independent of ethnic group membership. *International Dissertation Abstracts*, 1971, 32, 3050.

Neisser, U. *Cognitive psychology.* New York : Appleton Century Crofts, 1967.

Nissen. H.W., Chow, K.L., and Semmes, J. Effects of restricted opportunity for tactual, kinesthetic and manipulative experiences on the behaviour of a chimpanzee. *American Journal of Psychology*, 1951, 64, 485-507.

Pandey, R.N. *Differences in mental ability among social classes.* Unpublished Doctoral Thesis, Gorakhpur University, Gorakhpur, 1970.

Pettigrew, T.F. *A profile of the Negro American.* Princeton, New Jersey : D. Van Nostrand, 1964.

Piaget, J. *The psychology of intelligence.* (M. Piercy and D.E. Berlyne, Trans.) London : Routledge and Kegan Paul, 1947.

Price-Williams, D.R. Abstract and concrete modes of classification in Nigeria. *British Journal of Educational Psychology*, 1962, 32, 50-61.

Provence, S., and Lipton, R. *Infants in institutions.* New York : International University Press, 1962.

Rath, R., and Dash, A.S. *Cognitive growth and class room learning of naturally deprived children in the primary schools.* Paper presented at the East West Centre for Cross Cultural studies, Honolulu, 1972.

Rath, R. *Teaching and learning problems of disadvantaged children*, Unpublished Manuscript, Psychology Department, Utkal University, Bhubaneshwar, 1975.

Rath, R. Samant. *Cultural deprivation index.* Unpublished Manuscript, Psychology Department, Utkal University, Bhubaneshwar, 1975.

Rieson, A.H. The development of visual perception in man and chimpanzee. *Science*, 1947, **106**, 107-108.

Ribble, M.A. *Rights of infants.* New York : Columbia University Press, 1943.

Rosenzweig, M. Krech, D., Bennett, E., and Diamond, M. Modifying brain chemistry and anatomy by enrichment or impoverishment of experience. In G. Newton, and S. Levine (Eds.) *Early experience and behaviour.* Ill : Charles, 1968.

Rosenzweig, M.R. Effects of environment on development of brain and of behaviour. In E. Tabach (Ed.) *The biopsychology of development*, New York : Academic Press, 1971.

Scarr-Salpatek, S. Race, social class, and IQ. *Science*, 1971, **174**, 1285-1295.

Scaropani, P.J., Suziedelis, A., and Shore, M.F. Conceptual ability in black and white children of different social classes : An experimental test of Jensen's hypothesis : *American Journal of Orthopsychiatry*, 1973, **43**, 541-553.

Shultz, T.R., Charness, M., and Berman, S. Effects of age, social class and suggestion on free recall. *Developmental Psychology*, 1973, **8**, 57-61.

Singh, A.K. *Social disadvantage, intelligence and academic achievement.* Paper presented at the 14th annual conference of the Indian Academy of Applied Psychology, Indian Institute of Technology, Kharagpur, 1976.

Singh, S.D. Effect of human environment on cognitive behaviour in the rhesus monkey. *Journal of Comparative Psychology*, 1966, **61**, 280-283.

Singh, S.D. Urban monkeys. *Scientific American*, 1969, **221**, 108-115.

Singh, S.D. and Anandalakshmy, S. *Environmental determinants of cognitive ability : Facts and fallacies.* Paper presented at the international seminar on Psychology of Cognition, Delhi University, Delhi, 1976.

Sinha, D., Shukla, P. Deprivation and development of skill for pictorial depth perception. *Journal of Cross-Cultural Psychology*, 1974, **5**, 434-450.

Sinha, D. Social disadvantages and development of certain perceptual skills. *Indian Journal of Psychology*, 1977, **52**, 115-132.

Skeels, H.M. Adult status of children with contrasting early life experiences. *Monographs of the Society for Research in Child Development*, 1966, **31**, (Serial No. 105).

Spitz, R.A. Analytic depression. In *The psychoanalytic study of the child.* (Vol. 2,) New York : International University Press, 1946.

Stodolosky, S.S., and Lesser, G. Learning patterns in the disadvantaged. *Harvard Educational Review*, 1967, **37**, 546-553.

Talmadge, M., Hayden, B.S., and Schiff, D. Longitudinal analysis of intellectual and educational achievement change in culturally deprived, emotionally disturbed boys. *Perceptual and Motor Skills*. 1969, **29**, 435-440.

Tannenbaum, A.J. Some non-intellectual concomitants of social deprivation. *Israel Annals of Psychiatry and Related Disciplines*, 1969, **7**, 9-30.

Templin, M.C. *Certain language skills in children : Their development and interrelationships*. Minneapolis : Minnesota University Press, 1957.

Tripathi, R.B. The influence of rural-urban background on test score. *Journal of Gujarat Research Society*, 1970, **32**, 125-28.

Tripathi, L.B., and Misra, G. Cognitive activities as a function of prolonged deprivation. *Psychological Studies*, 1975, **21**, 54-61.

Tripathi, L.B., and Misra, G. Some cognitive processes as functions of prolonged deprivation. *Indian Journal of Psychology*, 1976, **51**, 129-143.

Verma, L., and Sinha, M.M. Effect of SES on perceptual differentiation contingent upon induced frustration in children. *Indian Psychological Review*, 1977, **15**, 27-35.

Tulkin, S.R. An analysis of the concept of cultural deprivation. *Developmental Psychology*, 1972, **6**, 326-339.

Wight, D.W., Gloniger, M.F., and Kneene, P.J. Cultural deprivation : Operational definition in terms of language development. *American Journal of Orthopsychiatry*, 1979, **40**, 77-86.

Whiteman, M.B., Brown, B.R., and Deutsch, M. Some effects of social class and race on children's language and intellectual abilities. In M. Deutsch and Associates. *The disadvantaged child*. New York : Basic Books, 1967.

Whiteman, M.B., and Deutsch, M. Social disadvantage as related to intellective and language development. In M. Deutsch, I. Katz, and A.R. Jensen (Eds.) *Social class, race and psychological development*. New York : Holt, Rinehart and Winston, 1968.

Yarrow, L.J. Maternal deprivation : Toward an empirical and conceptual reevaluation. *Psychological Bulletin*, 1961, **58**, 459-490.

Zigler, E., and Butterfield, E.C. Motivational aspects of changes in IQ test performance of culturally deprived nursery school children. *Child Development*, 1968, **39**, 1-14.

Zubek, J.P. *Sensory deprivation : Fifteen years of research*. New York : Appleton-Century-Crofts, 1969.

ELEVEN

Durganand Sinha

SOME SOCIAL DISADVANTAGES AND DEVELOPMENT OF CERTAIN PERCEPTUAL SKILLS

INTRODUCTION

SOCIO-ECONOMIC disadvantages suffered by certain groups tend to have a detrimental effect not only on the general development of the individual but are reflected on the level of cognition and perceptual skills possessed by him. Following Luria's (1971, p. 262) observation on cognitive activities as "a social phenomenon in origin, and as processes formed during the course of mastery of general human experience", it has been pointed that the perceptual skills of the individuals are shaped by the experiences through which a group passes and are reflected in its level of functioning of the psychological processes. Cross-cultural studies of certain kinds of illusions (Segall, Campbell & Herskovits, 1963), depth perception (Hudson, 1960) and interpretation of pictorial materials (Hudson, 1967; Deregowski, 1968; Jahoda, 1970) have amply demonstrated that the ecological and cultural environments in which people live, influence their visual habits. Difficulties experienced by non-western people in interpreting pictures and photographs have emphasized the importance of the nature of environment in which these groups live in the development of appropriate skills. Deficiencies in the environment, either due to physical factors or induced through socio-economic disadvantages, have their impact

Largely based on papers presented at the IPA International Symposium on Cognition, Delhi University, March 26-27, 1976, and subsequently published in the *Indian Journal of Psychology*, 1977, 52, 115-132.

through failure in providing the necessary experiential base essential for the development of the skill in question. Hudson (1960), for example, has observed that while his subject had no difficulty with identification of individual pictorial items, he found interpretation of entire picture difficult. While emphasizing the practical importance of understanding pictorially conveyed messages, he (Hudson, 1967) observed that only about one quarter of his 300 African mineworkers could grasp the gist of the safety posters especially intended for them. He concluded that cultural and specific educational experiences were relevant determinants of three dimensional perception. Similar observations can be made about our family planning and other promotional posters and pictorial materials. Deregowski and Serpell (1972) found that their African subjects encountered more difficulty to sort pictures than depicted objects. A number of studies conducted in India have demonstrated the importance of cultural and economic deprivations on cognitive and perceptual growth. Das, Jachuck and Panda (1970) have observed that on intelligence test, poor Harijan children obtained the lowest scores whereas the rich Brahman children the highest. On the basis of a series of studies, Das (1973) has reported that in India, high caste and economic prosperity independently enhance cognitive competence. Sinha and Shukla (1974) studying the impact of familial deprivation on the acquisition of skill to interpret different pictorial depth cues found the "deprived" children deficient.

The nature of environment provides the necessary sensory inputs, stimulation and experiential base for the development of perceptual skills of various kinds. Enrichment or deficiency of the environment produces differentials in the development. The study reported here, which is a part of a larger project investigating the impact on the acquisition of certain perceptual skills due to differing ecologies of urban, rural, and tribal children, is specifically concerned with the influence of stimulation from certain kinds of socio-cultural environment, as emanating from contrasting caste-statuses and qualities of schooling, on the development of skill to interpret pictures and arrange them in proper sequence. In the light of the general findings in this area, it was hypothesized that both social disadvantages suffered due to inferior caste-status and poor quality of schooling would produce a general detrimental influence on the development of the perceptual skills in question. Further, it was expected that the combined effects of social disadvantages and poor schooling will be very marked, while, on the other hand, exposure to proper schooling facilities will eradicate some of the deficiencies in the level of functioning of the scheduled caste children.

METHOD

Design

In the light of the above, differentials in development of skills to interpret pictures and sequential perception as influenced by caste-status and quality of schooling were specifically taken up for study. Thus, there were three variables under investigation, namely, age, caste-status and quality of schooling. Though there is controversy regarding the exact age at which skills for pictorial perception begin to develop, and the age by which they come to full fruition, there is a general consensus that below the age of four, the skills, if they exist at all, are rudimentary and by the age of ten or so they develop to a very appreciable extent (Shukla & Sinha, 1974). There is also evidence that under very adverse conditions of environment and education, many of the skills for pictorial perception remain at a low level even in adults.

Sample

Keeping this in view three age-groups within the period of 4 to 10 years were taken, namely, 4-5, 7-8, and 9-10 years. For each age-range boys belonging to scheduled caste (SC) and non-scheduled caste (NSC) groups from superior and ordinary schools were drawn, according to $3 \times 2 \times 2$ factorial design, with 20 subjects in each sub-group, i.e., a total of 240 subjects. There were 80 subjects in each age-range equally divided into 20 subjects in each of the four sub-groups formed according to two caste-statuses and two categories of schooling, There were equal numbers of caste-Hindu and scheduled caste boys in each age-group, and from both inferior and superior schools.

Schools were categorized into two types on the basis of educational and other facilities available in the institutions.

Schools which provided adequate audio-visual aids, toys, playgrounds and facilities for recreational activities, conveyance facilities, had trained personnel, and adequate accommodation were classed as *superior* schools. They also charged fees, which were considerable, and generally children from well-to-do and upper middle, and middle class families enrolled in these institutions. Most of the nursery schools and the primary sections of good institutions belonged to this category. On the other hand, schools which lacked most of the above facilities were classed as *ordinary* schools. They were located generally in the congested areas of the city, had inadequate accommodation both for teaching and recreational purposes, and possessed hardly any audio-visual aids. They were mostly managed by the municipal corporation, and did not charge any fees. As a result, children from poorer homes and of those who could hardly afford the cost of education flocked to these institutions. Thus, while categorizing quality of schooling, poverty and other variables emanating from population congestion, inadequate housing and civic amenities entered inevitably. Therefore, in the sample design both scheduled and non-scheduled caste children were included from both the categories of schools to cancel out the possible effects of these factors.

A list of all the boys conforming to the sample requirements was prepared with the help of the school register in each category of institution and 20 subjects were randomly selected for test administration. It may be observed that while it was easy to obtain adequate number of non-scheduled caste subjects, there were very few scheduled caste boys according to our sampling requirements in any one institution of the superior category. Therefore, in order to get the requisite quota of subjects, a number of schools of each category had to be selected. To counteract the possible influence of institutions, both scheduled and non-scheduled caste boys were selected for testing from each school.

Material and procedure

Two pictorial tasks were presented to the subjects : the first was designated, the *Pictorial Interpretation* and the second, *Sequential Perception*. The former consisted of three achromatic 13 × 9.5 cm. pictures: (i) *Cat and the Rat*, (ii) *Two Warriors and a Lady*, and (iii) *Man and the Monkeys*. Each picture was so drawn that certain objects depicted in it could not be visible to some of the characters in the picture due to the *interposition* of other objects between them or being not in the field of vision. However, all these objects in the picture were easily perceived by the subject. The subject's task was to indicate whether an object, "hidden" for a particular character in the picture by some larger intervening object or placed outside his field of vision, was visible to him or not. This subject could give the correct answer only if he understood interposition and relative positioning of the objects in the picture.

The child was first asked to identify various objects depicted in each picture which were all familiar and representational. Except for some children in the lowest age-group, not much difficulty was encountered in identifying them. In any case, special care was taken to get the *crucial* objects, regarding which questions were asked, identified by every subject. Whenever any difficulty was encountered, the experimenter helped the child to identify the objects. Only when the process of object-identification was complete, the subject was asked questions like "can the rat see the cat?" or "can the cat see the box?" As the questions were being put, the objects concerned were pointed to by the experimenter. The answers given by the subject ("yes" or "no"; "perceptible" or "not perceptible") were noted, and he was requested to explain why the object concerned could not be perceived. In order to break the response-set, similar questions regarding perceptible objects were interspersed, but they were ignored in scoring. A score of one was given for each correct response. There being five *crucial* questions for the first picture and three and four respectively for the other two, a maximum score of twelve was possible on the entire task with the minimum score of zero.

Sequential Perception consisted of three tests, each consisting of four pictures which, when placed in proper sequence, depicted a simple story. They were : (i) *Cat and the Two Clever Rats*, (ii) *The Hunter and the Deer*, and (iii) *Boy and the Dog on a Rainy Day*. The four pictures were placed in a jumbled way before the subject and the subject was first required to identify the objects depicted. Care was taken that in no case did the first picture of the sequence come in the beginning. The subject was told that when placed in proper sequence, a story would emerge, and he was required to find out the proper sequence, placing the four pictures accordingly and then narrating the story contained therein. Before administering the main test, there was a practice set depicting a school-boy preparing and going to his school. In the practice trial, irrespective of the manner in which he placed the pictures, he was asked to narrate what was happening in them. After the subject had narrated whatever he could make out of the sequence in which he had put the pictures, the experimenter would place the pictures in the *proper* sequence and ask the subject to narrate the story. If he encountered any difficulty, the experimenter narrated the story and again jumbled the pictures and asked him to re-arrange them in proper sequence. Only when the experimenter was satisfied that the subject had understood the task, and what was required of him, did he proceed with the actual test series.

Both these tasks were administered individually to the subjects after establishing proper rapport. They were presented as a game and the child was told that he would be shown many pictures. The tasks elicited considerable interest in most of the children tested.

In Sequential Perception, test administration was done in four phases, and if the subject succeeded in an earlier phase, it was not necessary to continue with the next phase. Only in case of failures, the phases were gone through one after the other. In the first phase, the pictures were jumbled and placed before the subject and he was allowed two minutes to arrange them in proper order. Even if he failed, he was requested to narrate what was happening, and the number of cards put in proper order were noted. If he successfully placed all the four cards, he was asked to narrate the story, and the next series was taken up. If he failed to get the sequence correct, the experimenter went on to the third phase, where the first and the last cards were put in their places and the subject was required to put the remaining two in their proper sequence, and narrate the story. If he failed, the experimenter passed on to the last phase where the story was narrated to the subject, and he was required to put the four pictures according to their proper sequence so that they matched with the story. A maximum of two minutes was allowed to the subject for each phase, and the number of cards put correctly in each case was noted.

Scores were allotted according to the phase on which the child succeeded, viz., 4 for the first, and 3, 2, 1 respectively for the three succeeding phases. If he failed even on the fourth phase, he was given zero. Thus, on the Sequential Perception task, a maximum of 4 and a minimum of zero score was possible on each set, making a maximum possible score of 12 on the entire test. The stories depicted were also graded on the basis of their coherence and relevance, and coded accordingly.

Before passing on to the analysis of the results it is to be observed that the two perceptual tasks used were different in their complexity. While the Pictorial Interpretation simply required understanding of certain pictorial cues, the other, viz., the Sequential Perception demanded not only the capacity to describe and understand the details depicted in the four pictures, but also to discover the links between adjacent pictures and understand correctly what was happening, place them in proper order accordingly, and then extract a story. It involved more by way of language skill. In other words, it required the transformation of information from visual to verbal modality, and to that extent the test could be considered as much more complex than the Pictorial Interpretation.

RESULTS

The mean scores obtained by all the subjects of the three age-groups irrespective of caste status and type of schools are given in Table 11.1. There is an increase in score with age on

ABEE 11.1 : **Mean scores of the three age-groups of subjects on perceptual tasks**

Age-Groups	*N*	Pictorial Interpretation	Sequential Perception
4-5 years	80	6.35	4.08
7-8 years	80	8.86	5.60
9-10 years	80	9.55	6.96

both the tasks indicating a distinct developmental trend. Using analysis of variance with 3 (Age) × 2 (Castes) × 2 (Schools) factorial design on the scores obtained, the main effect of age was found to be highly significant on both the measures ($F=37.07$ and 24.50 for Pictorial Interpretation and Sequential Perceptions respectively; $df=2$, 228). It is to be observed that while the level of performance on the Pictorial Interpretation task went up considerably with increase in age, reaching an average of 9.55 with the possible maximum score of 12, improvement on the Sequential Perception with age, though statistically significant ($F=24.50$, $df=2$, 228), was not there to the same extent. The average score of the oldest age-group in this case was just a little more than half of the maximum possible score on the measure. It indicated that of the two perceptual skills concerned, the capacity to interpret pictorial cues was acquired earlier and reached a higher level of proficiency than to understand and interpret a series of pictures and place them in proper order so that a coherent story emerged from the sequence—a skill which remained at a rudimentary level even up to the age of ten years.

The results obtained on analysis of variance indicated that not only the main effect of age was significant, but also that of the quality of schooling and caste status on both the tasks (Tables 11.2 and 11.3). *F*-ratios for all interactions were

TABLE 11.2 : **Summary of 3×2×2 factorial analysis of variance of the scores on pictorial interpretation task**

Source	*df*	MS	*F*
A (Age)	2	221.336	37.07**
B (School)	1	210.938	35.33**
C (Caste)	1	33.102	5.04*
AB	2	7.236	1.21
AC	2	0.629	0.11
BC	1	19.836	3.32
ABC	2	7.811	1.31
Within	228	5.970	

** $p < .01$
* $p < .05$

TABLE 11.3 : **Summary 3×2×2 factorial analysis of variance of the scores on Sequential Perception task**

Source	*df*	MS	*F*
A (Age)	2	162.654	24.50**
B (School)	1	88.816	13.38**
C (Caste)	1	141.066	21.25**
AB	2	1.527	0.23
AC	2	1.953	0.29
BC	1	0.066	0.01
ABC	2	10.779	1.62
Within	228	6.640	

** $p < .01$

statistically not significant. Therefore, not only was there a definite developmental trend in the performance, but the factors of caste and quality of schooling operated as independent variables. In each of the three age-groups, subjects from superior schools and belonging to the caste-Hindu group displayed a significantly higher level of performance on the two tasks in comparison with those from ordinary schools and the scheduled castes.

Cross-comparisons of the sub-groups at different age-ranges belonging to the scheduled (SC) and non-scheduled castes (NSC) from superior and ordinary schools were made for the two measures (Tables 11.4 and 11.5). Though the NSC children tended to score higher in all except one case in comparison to their counterparts of the same age level in both the categories of schools. On both the measures, the differences were small. Duncan's multiple range test was employed to compare individual means of various sub-groups. On Pictorial Interpretation the test revealed the following differences to be statistically significant :

(1) In the age-group 4-5, the scores of children from superior schools, irrespective of caste-status, were significantly higher than those of the scheduled caste group from ordinary schools;

(2) Non-scheduled caste children from ordinary schools

TABLE 11.4 : **Mean scores of sub-groups on Pictorial Interpretation task**

Age-Groups	Superior Schools NSC		Superior Schools SC			Ordinary Schools NSC		Ordinary Schools SC		
	Mean	SD	Mean	SD	Diff.	Mean	SD	Mean	SD	Diff.
4-5 years	7.45	3.14	7.75	3.18	—0.30	6.15	2.91	4.05	1.91	2.10
7-8 years	9.70	2.66	9.60	2.28	0.10	8.45	2.06	7.20	2.33	1.25
9-10 years	10.50	1.28	9.90	1.74	0.60	9.15	2.56	8.65	2.54	0.50

TABLE 11.5 : **Mean scores of sub-groups on Sequential Perception task**

Age-Groups	Superior Schools NSC		Superior Schools SC			Ordinary schools NSC		Ordinary schools SC		
	Mean	SD	Mean	SD	Diff.	Mean	SD	Mean	SD	Diff.
4-5 years	4.90	2.67	4.20	2.65	0.70	4.45	2.76	2.80	2.79	1.65
7-8 years	6.95	2.50	5.50	2.65	1.45	6.00	2.25	3.95	2.72	2.05
9-10 years	8.95	1.93	6.40	3.15	2.55	6.60	2.19	5.80	2.42	0.80

scored significantly higher than the scheduled castes from the same schools;

(3) With the age-group 7-8 years, both the groups from superior schools had higher scores than scheduled caste children from ordinary schools;

(4) In the age-group 9-10, non-scheduled caste children from superior schools were significantly higher than scheduled caste children from ordinary schools.

On the Sequential Perception it was found that :

(i) Non-scheduled caste children of 4-5 years from superior schools scored significantly higher than their scheduled caste counterparts from ordinary schools.

(ii) In 7-8 year-old groups, non-scheduled caste children from both superior and ordinary schools were significantly higher than scheduled caste children from ordinary schools.

(iii) For the 9-10 years-old children, those from superior schools not only scored significantly higher than both the groups of children from ordinary schools, but were also higher than their scheduled caste counterparts from the same set of schools.

In short, nature of schooling seemed to be operating as a powerful influence in the sense that not only the non-scheduled caste boys but in many instances the scheduled caste children hailing from better quality schools tended to perform better on both the simple and complex types of perceptual tasks than their counterparts from ordinary schools. To that extent at least, getting better schooling facilities was neutralizing some of the disadvantages suffered due to inferior socio-cultural status. Further, the extent of differences between the non-scheduled and scheduled caste groups revealed that the handicap experienced by the latter was comparatively greater on more complex tasks which required language skill.

The nature and extent of differences in scores between those of the scheduled and non-scheduled caste groups in the two categories of schools on both the measures are worth noting. In the ordinary schools, the differences in performance were all in favour of the non-scheduled caste groups, and tended to be much larger in lower age-groups. With age, the differences tended to get levelled off. On the other hand, in superior schools, the reverse seemed to be the case. The differences, if at all, at the lower age-level were minimal, and with increase in age, they went on getting more and more accentuated revealing what may be descriptively designated as a "broomstick effect". In fact, in one instance at least, i.e., on the Pictorial Interpretation measure, difference in the lowest age-group was slightly in favour of the scheduled caste group. But with increasing age, not only there was a reversal, but the difference in favour of non-scheduled over the scheduled caste went on getting larger and larger revealing a distinct "broomstick effect".

DISCUSSION

The main hypotheses of the invesigation were generally supported by the findings. Disadvantages due to socio-cultural status of belonging to the scheduled castes and inferior quality of schooling had a detrimental influence on the development of the two perceptual skills under study. The effect was much greater on the more complex of the two tasks, which not only required interpretation of pictorial cues but also a degree of verbal skill. Secondly, though caste status was a significant variable, its influence was comparatively less perceptible on the simpler of the two perceptual tasks. Thirdly, quality of schooling that the child received was a powerful factor in the sense that the level of performance on both non-scheduled and scheduled caste children was significanly higher in the superior schools than their counterparts from the ordinary schools. But differences were more marked between two groups of scheduled caste children from superior and ordinary schools than between respective non-scheduled caste children from the two categories of schools. It indicated the importance of better quality of education received by the children in levelling off at least some of the deficiencies in perceptual skill induced by certain socio-economic disadvantages suffered from scheduled caste status.

It is to be noted that in superior schools, the initial disadvantage in performance due to scheduled caste status was insignificant on the youngest age-group. In fact, on the simpler of the two tasks, there was a slight advantage in favour of scheduled caste children of 4-5 years (Table 11.4), indicating that such children who joined better institutions had not shown initially the effects of the disadvantages of the "surrounding" layer of ecology. However, among the older groups, the trend was reversed, and the non-scheduled caste children performed better than their scheduled caste counterparts. The discrepancy in performance in favour of non-scheduled caste went on getting accentuated with age. Though the "broomstick effect", i.e., differential between two caste-groups being minimal initially but getting progressively accentuated with advance in age, was present on both the tasks, it was much more marked on the complex one, and only on the performance of children from the superior schools (Tables 11.4 and 11.5). In other words, on a complex task requiring linguistic skill, the underprivileged children were getting increasingly behind the more privileged children with advance in age. And this tendency was specially visible in children from superior schools. That is, despite the quality of schooling, with advancing years the scheduled caste/non-scheduled caste differential in performance was getting increasingly more marked. This phenomenon can be ascribed to greater social discrimination and isolation experienced by older scheduled caste children in better institutions. With advance in age, children become more conscious of their caste status. The caste-Hindu boys aften ridicule and make fun of scheduled caste children, informally isolate them, and thereby engender a feeling of social inferiority and deprivation which prevent them from taking full advantage of the facilities provided by the school. This is particularly true of superior institutions which admit students from more privileged homes. It not only neutralizes the influence of better facilities of the institution, but tends to accentuate the effects of social disadvantage on the performance on both the simple and the complex tasks. To this extent, the hypothesis that exposure to better school facilities will tend to eradicate some of the deficiencies in the level of functioning of the scheduled caste children was not borne out by the results. If social discrimination prevails, educational facilities by themselves are not able to have the beneficial influence in developing various perceptual and cognitive skills in the school environment.

The findings are in general agreement with those of Das and Singha (1975) whose "overall results suggest that rich Brahmin children were clearly superior to all other children" and that "the least disadvantaged children performed best on a majority of cognitive tasks". The results emphasise the vital role of differences in ecology—both the "upper layer" and the "surrounding layer" (Bronfenbrenner, 1974) as underlying the lower level of performance of the scheduled caste children on the two perceptual tasks. The differences between the non-scheduled and scheduled caste groups tended to persist and as a variable caste had a major effect. Even though children came from similar categories of schools which in a way indicated that economic differential were not too overwhelming between the two groups, the difference in performance persisted, though not always to a significant level. The finding tends to indicate that even though the caste-Hindus and scheduled caste children may have similar economic circumstances, the latter still operate under grave social disadvantages retarding their perceptual growth. As Das and Singha (1975) rightly observe, the social-cultural atmosphere in which caste-Hindus live even though poor would be still superior to scheduled caste children of similar economic level.

It may be observed that in the ordinary schools, despite the initial disadvantage reflected in lower level performance of the scheduled caste children at the lowest age-level, as the children grew up and progressed in schools, differences between the caste groups got reduced with increasing age. Schooling seemed to be neutralizing the disadvantages of caste-status. This was especially true on the Pictorial Interpretation task (Table 11.4). On the other task demanding more complex perceptual and linguistic skills, the result was different, and the performance of the non-scheduled caste children remained at a significantly higher level for almost all the age-groups and in both categories of schools. Being underprivileged proved to be a greater handicap on complex tasks where besides interpretation of pictorial cues, a degree of linguistic skill was demanded.

Lower perceptual competence of disadvantaged minority groups can be attributed to many factors, viz., genetic, nutritional, lack of stimulating experience, social motivation and cultural values. The present study focused only on two of the factors : social disadvantages emanating from scheduled caste status, and differences in quality of schooling. On the basis of the present study, it is not possible to brush aside the genetic factors entirely, nor is there any support for its significant operation on the performance on the tasks concerned. Small and insignificant differences in the performances of the two groups especially on the simpler perceptual task would minimise the genetic basis as determining the competence of children in this sphere. The author believes that it is the socio-economic and cultural disadvantages and discriminations suffered by the scheduled castes for generations and over centuries that are far more important as factors underlying lower perceptual competence than genetic, nutritional or any other factor *per se*. Being discriminated against for centuries, and exploited by the higher castes as menials and landless labour and relegated to "dirty" occupations, traditionally considered unclean, and forced to live segregated in unhealthy environment, they were never allowed to enjoy or share the socio-cultural life of the caste-Hindu society. These discriminations have been legally abolished. But traditions die hard, and they still suffer from many socio-economic and cultural disadvantages. Added to these is the general lack of interest and apathy on the part of a large majority of scheduled caste parents towards educating their children who keep them at home to supplement their meagre family income. All these factors add up to such ecological disadvantages that their lower perceptual competence is not to be surprised at.

Many scholars working on perceptual skills have emphasized their importance for general educational and promotional programmes (Jahoda, 1970). Pictorial materials, both singly and in sequence, are used for test book illustrations, and for posters employed for promoting scientific agriculture, health, family planning and other types of promotional activities. These pictures, many of them being in sequence, have to be understood, and messages to be conveyed should reach the people for whom they are intended. The present investigation highlights some of the factors that retard the development of such skills especially among the so-called "weaker sections of society" for whom these messages are generally intended and are important. It demonstrates that though both caste status and quality of schooling have a vital role, merely providing superior school facilities to the underprivileged will not by itself reduce their deficiencies. On the other hand, it may operate as a detrimental influence by accentuating the differences between the privileged and unprivileged groups with advance in age. It brings out pointedly the importance of adequate and carefully designed educational programmes and facilities needed for the development of appropriate perceptual skills so that the effects of initial environmental disadvantages are in due course largely neutralized. In conclusion, the present study emphasizes in general the importance of physical and cultural environment of the child, in other words, his ecology, in the development of skills required to perform some perceptual tasks competently. The factors of caste and schooling operate in a complex manner in affecting the perceptual competence of children.

REFERENCES

Bronfenbrenner, U., Development Research, public policy, and ecology of childhood. *Child Development*, 1974, **45**, 1-5.

Das, J.P., Cultural deprivation and cognitive competence. In N.R. Ellis (Ed.) *International review of research in mental retardation*, (Vol. **6**) New York : Academic Press, 1973.

Das, J.P., Jachuck, K., & Panda, T. Cultural deprivation and cognitive growth. In H.C. Haywood (Ed.) *Socio-cultural aspects of mental retardation*. New York : Appleton-Century-Crofts, 1970.

Das, J.P., & Singha, P.S., Caste, class, and cognitive competence. *Indian Educational Review*, 1975, **10**, 1-8.

Deregowski, J.B., Pictorial recognition in subjects from relatively pictureless environment. *African Social Research*, 1968, **5**, 356-364.

Deregowski, J.B., & Serpell, R., Performance on sorting task. *International Journal of Psychology*, 1972, **6**, 273-281.

Hudson, W. Pictorial depth perception in sub-cultural groups in South Africa. *Journal of Social Psychology*, 1960, **52**, 183-208.

Hudson, W. The study of the problem of pictorial perception among unaccultured groups. *International Journal of Psychology*, 1967, **2**, 89-107.

Jahoda, G. A cross-cultural perspective in psychology. *Advance Science*, 1970, 27, 1-14.

Luria, A.R. Towards the problem of the historical nature of psychological processes. *International Journal of Psychology*, 1971, **6**, 259-272.

Segall, M.H., Campbell, D.T., & Herskovits, M.J., Cultural differences in perception of geometric illusions. *Science*, 1963, **139**, 769-771.

Shukla, P., & Sinha, D. A developmental study of the relative efficacy of different pictorial cues in depth perception. *Indian Journal of Psychology*, 1974, **49**, 220-230.

Sinha, D., & Shukla, P. Deprivation and development of skill for pictorial depth perception. *Journal of Cross-Cultural Psychology*, 1974, 5, 434-450.

Whiteman, M., & Deutsch, M. Social disadvantage as related to intellective and language development. In M. Deutsch, I. Katz, & A.R. Jensen (Eds.) *Social class, race and psychological development*, New York : Holt, Rinehart & Winston, 1968.

TWELVE

Durganand Sinha and *Girishwar Misra*

DEPRIVATION AND ITS MOTIVATIONAL AND PERSONALITY CORRELATES

INTRODUCTION

IN PSYCHOLOGICAL theorization the concept of motivation is posited to explain dynamic properties of behaviour, such as, arousal, persistence, vigour and goal-orientation. The differentials along these properties have led to conceptualization of 'need' which has been conceived basically as a deficiency of something vital to the organism. Apart from biological needs, a set of psychological needs derived from viscerogenic needs have been posited which though not crucial to human existence have long-range implications. Cross-cultural comparisons of need pattern (Aronoff, 1967), as well as, studies on social learning and child-rearing, indicate that as compared to biological needs, psychological needs are more susceptible to learning influences resulting in greater amount of inter-individual and inter-group variations in their strength (Hunt, 1960). Considering the inter-relationship of these two sets of needs, Maslow (1954) has proposed his famous theory of hierarchy and prepotency of needs. According to this theory, needs not only develop in a sequential manner, but one of the basic conditions for the emergence of psychological and higher order needs is the satisfaction of lower order biological needs.

Viewed in this light, 'deprivation' assumes a decisive role in shaping need pattern of the individual. Since satisfaction of motivational demands depends upon accessibility to resources available within the environment, deprivation can be assumed to shape and channelize our motives in significant ways. As a matter of fact, deprivation has been conceived of as a precondition or source of drive. There is convincing evidence from animal studies that drive level increases with degree of deprivation up to a certain point beyond which increase in deprivation level results in inanition and becomes disruptive (Bolles, 1975). However, this analogy is not applicable to psychological or growth needs which originate largely from individual's interaction with social stimuli in which case lack of stimulation or appropriate experiences is likely to restrict the emergence and growth of these needs (McClelland, 1961).

Thus, deprivation seems to have different consequences for biological and psychological needs. In line with Maslow's (1954) theory, it can be predicted that under conditions of deprivation biological needs would predominate over higher order needs. However, the findings in this context have not always been clearcut and free from contradictions indicating thereby the highly complex nature of the phenomenon.

Evidence from clinical studies

The effects of deprivation and isolation have been extensively investigated in studies of children reared in institutions (e.g., Bowlby, 1951; Yarrow, 1961; Rutter, 1972). Early studies (e.g. Levy, 1937; Skeels & Dye, 1939; Ribble, 1943; Bowlby, 1940; Goldfarb, 1955) have tried to understand aberrant child behaviour patterns as a function of deficient conditions of stimulation in early childhood. Children, who have spent their early years in an institutional environment, display more behaviour problems, more aggression and greater demand for attention. The whole pattern of behaviour is termed as the 'syndrome of distress' consisting of protest, despair and detachment (Rutter, 1972). The results have been explained by extending homeostatic drive model. Thus, Levy (1937) used the phrase 'primary affect hunger' and Spitz (1949) talked about 'emotionally starved' children. Recent studies have focused on specific process variables and environmental factors which lead to development of pathological or deviant personality. In this connection, Langmeier (1972) has identified four main aspects of deprivation occurring in institutionalized children: lack of stimulation, lack of cognitive structure, lack of specific attachment, and lack of individualization. As compared to normal family-reared children, institutionalized children show an immature personality pattern with enhanced, undifferentiated social interest or with trends towards social provocation and aggression. However, there are considerable differences in reactions to deprived living conditions and it is difficult to propose any 'deprivation syndrome'.

Animal studies

Researches on animals raised in atypical environments reveal that they develop some abnormalities. In these studies, specific aspects of the environment have been manipulated: complete or partial visual deprivation for different periods of time, social isolation, and provision of cloth-covered or mobile mother-surrogates (Riesen, 1961; Harlow, 1953). Harlow (1971) found that if infant monkeys were subjected to partial deprivation in which they were allowed to see but not interact with other monkeys permanent inadequacies in social and sexual development would result. Experiments on puppies reared in 'restricted' environment and released after seven and a half month and period showed that when put in unfamiliar situations while the normally reared puppies displayed exploratory activity, the others exhibited "freezing" behaviour. Apart from other behavioural differences, the restricted dogs when given a "fighting for a bone test" showed a tendency to share the bone in contrast to battling normal pets. They were also more indifferent and lower in activity (Clarke *et al.*, 1951).

The studies of 'drive-deprivation' in which an organism is prevented from normal gratification of hunger, sucking, or of secondary drives show that early drive-deprivation not only leads to a general increase in drive level but more particularly with respect to the specific need previously deprived. Whether the increased drive due to early deprivation produces a facilitating or inhibiting effect on a given behaviour pattern depends on how well organized the pattern was before deprivation. It has been found that high drive and an unorganized behaviour pattern before deprivation lead to frustration manifested by anxiety, inhibition of exploratory and manipulatory behaviour, fear and aggressiveness when faced with learning the behaviour in future (Bronfenbrenner, 1968).

In learning experiments, deprivation procedure of various

sorts have been used to motivate animals. The studies, as Bartoshuk (1971) has pointed out, do show that deprivation operations probably selectively favour the occurrence of relevant consummatory responses, and this bias probably increases as deprivation increases.

SOCIO-CULTURAL DEPRIVATION AND MOTIVATION

Although motivational variables are of considerable importance in understanding the mechanisms through which deprivation exerts its influence on cognitive and intellective performance, more attention has been given to differences in the cognitive development of deprived and non-deprived groups. Data on motivational and personality characteristics of the deprived are meagre and there is also less agreement on the effects of deprivation. However, there is evidence to suggest that environmental factors are of great significance in facilitating or inhibiting given needs, in conceiving the goals as well as in determining the extent to which one's needs are gratified. Support for this assumption comes from the studies on different aspects of socio-cultural disadvantage/deprivation, though divergence in criteria used create obvious problems of interpretation of the findings.

Achievement motive

Some evidence for the effects of deprivation can be derived from the extensive cross-cultural studies by McClelland (1961) and others on achievement motive and its correlates, i.e., socio-economic status (SES), ethnicity and parent-child relationship. In different socio-cultural settings of Africa (Morsback, 1969), Brazil (Angelini, 1970), United States (Rosen, 1962; McClelland, 1961) and Nigeria (LeVine, 1966), it has been observed that individuals belonging to lower social stratum display low degree of achievement concern. It has also been observed that SES is positively related to need for achievement (*nAch*) (Nygard, 1969). Rosen (1956) and Veroff, Atakinson, Feld and Gurin (1960) found persons of lower educational and occupational levels as having lower *nAch* scores. McClelland (1961) ascribes it to matricentric structure of the family and persistence of child-rearing practices that had their origin in slavery. The absence of one or both parents has also been found to be associated with low achievement (Santrock & Wohlford, 1970). Lott and Lott (1963) have reported that Whites have reliably stronger *nAch* than the Negroes. Irwin Katz (1970) observed that poor students engaged in more self-criticism were less favourable in their self evaluations than the well-to-do students. Among the poorer Negro boys, it was not the absence of standards of evaluation that was associated with academic failures, but absence of clear external cues which made it difficult to accept their performance as adequate. Their standards were so rigid and stringent as to be utterly dysfunctional. As Katz (1970) observed, what they had internalized was a most effective mechanism for self-discouragement.

The findings on the relationship between social class and *nAch* imply the role of deprivation in development of this need. Srivastava and Tiwari (1967) reported that highest *nAch* score was present in the middle class, second in the upper class and the lowest in the lower class. Desai and Trivedi (1972) however, found father's SES as not related to children's *nAch* scores. On the other hand, Chaudhury (1971) observed positive relationship between *nAch* and social class. Reviewing the relevant literature Mehta and Mehta (1974) observed that the evidence on the relationship between social class and *nAch* is "not very conclusive". However, there seems to be a tendency in favour of a positive relationship between social and economic prosperity and *nAch*. In a recent study, Ojha and Jha (1979) noted that middle class SES, nuclear family system and enterpreneurial occupations were associated with high achievement motivation, while upper and lower class SES, joint family system and bureaucratic occupations were associated with low *nAch*.

Gokulnathan (1970) and Gokulnathan and Mehta (1972) have reported higher *nAch* in tribal than non-tribal students and in girls than boys. Mehta (1969) has noted a curvilinear relationship between *nAch* and father's education. Werner and Murlidharan (1970) found that adequately nourished nursery school children scored higher on *nAch* than their inadequately nourished counterparts. However, this effect was true in the case of boys only. Majority of girls were low in *nAch*. Misra and Tripathi (1978a) observed that low deprived group exhibited significantly higher level of achievement striving than medium and highly deprived groups. Correlational analysis of data revealed a significant negative relationship between prolonged deprivation and achievement motive. Analysing the development of achievement motive in relation to prolonged deprivation, parental attitudes towards independence training, demands for mastery and independence and restrictions on independence-activities, a significant effect of deprivation level on the strength of achievement motive was found by Tiwari and Misra (1977). The low deprivation group was highest in *nAch* and medium deprivation group appeared lowest. Strong parental attitude in favour of independence was accompanied by high *nAch*. The parents of low *nAch* subjects evinced independence attitude. Parents of high *nAch* subjects made demands for independence and mastery more frequently. So far as restrictions were concerned the results indicated that parents of high *nAch* group reported highest percentage of restrictions at the age of 12 years and above. Other groups reported significantly higher percentage of restrictions before the age of 5 years. The evidence seems to suggest that early demands and late restrictions are characteristic features of parents of high *nAch* subjects. These findings have been replicated and extended in a subsequent study by Tiwari (1979). Investigating the development of achievement motive on groups of subjects ranging from 7 to 24 years, negative relationship with prolonged deprivation was observed. Deprivation seemed to interfere in certain crucial respects.

Sinha (1969) initiated a number of studies analyzing differentials among farmers from highly developed and undeveloped villages on a number of indices of motivation. Many of the findings throw light on the motivational characteristics of low economic status farmers. Sinha and Chaubey (1972) observed the middle SES group in highly developed villages to take intermediate risk more often than either the low or high SES groups. In the undeveloped villages, however, the upper and upper-middle class groups showed greater preference for intermediate risk-taking. High level of aspiration was found in the middle class groups and in some cases in the upper and upper-middle classes. Younger subjects from developed villages understimated their chances of success on the tasks more frequently than their counterparts from poorly developed villages (Chaubey, 1974). The general trend of findings of Sinha and his colleagues indicated that poverty among villagers was associated with extreme caution, reluctance to take risk and stagnant motivation.

Level of aspiration

Level of aspiration is a crucial aspect of individual's motivation, since it determines his effort towards attaining goals as well as the degree of his adjustment. It has been observed that well adjusted persons tend to have veridical estimate of themselves in relation to demands of the environment and hence have a fairly realistic level of aspiration. Maladjusted persons, on the other hand, tend to be unrealistic in goal-setting. The empirical evidence concerning the relationship between deprivation variables and level of aspiration tends to suggest that deprived groups are characterized by low level of aspiration. Aspirations of upper class and middle class students are higher than those of lower class. Western studies have indicated that deprived groups lack optimism. As Katz (1970) observes, they are socialized to "self imposed failure". In certain cases, however, they may show a compensatory reaction leading to very high aspirations (Dreger & Miller, 1970). Further, majority of the students showing higher educational and occupational aspirations belong to higher status groups while those having low aspirations come from low status families.

In Indian setting, Rath (1972, 1974a) has not only observed low aspiration levels for income, occupation, and education for poor tribal students in comparison to those of higher caste, but there was very high and significantly positive correlation between very low educational, economic, and job aspirations of the parents and school-going children of the low caste and tribal groups. He (Rath, 1973) contended that "aspirations of children are nothing but the internalized projections of similar aspirations of their parents". With low motivation, teaching and learning situations become dull, children finding increasing difficulty in coping with the school and tend to drop out. He points that "as there is no push from home and no pull from the school, the child adopts the normal behaviour of escape from such a painful and constrained situation"

Misra and Tripathi (1978b) have investigated aspirations

about social status in relation to prolonged deprivation. Aspired status of high deprived group was lowest as compared to low and medium deprived groups. Comparison of ratings for present status with aspired status revealed maximum discrepancy in the case of high deprived group followed by medium and low deprived groups, respectively. Considered in temporal perspective, these results suggest that while aspirations of high deprived groups are lower than the other two groups, they are not realistic thereby providing a source of frustration.

In the context of the extent of development in certain villages, Sinha (1969) also obtained similar results, i.e., farmers hailing from very backward or poor villages reflected comparatively lower aspiration level on different counts. Those from highly developed villages were significantly higher in their aspiration for land, income, housing, changes in farming and household possessions. Further, on a performance test of level of aspiration, those from undeveloped villages had lower overall aspiration, smaller goal discrepancy index, and displayed static aspiration level, extreme caution and absence of risk-taking. A follow-up after five years (Sinha, 1974) revealed downward trend in aspirational level, and decline in optimism in viewing the future. In other words, there was among the economically backward a lowering of expectancy in viewing the future even though the country as a whole had shown certain degree of prosperity.

Anxiety

Against the background of the findings that upper class individuals are better adjusted and emotionally stable, and positive relationship between low SES and abnormality (Shanmugam, 1957), high incidence of anxiety in the deprived can be posited. The results, however, are not conclusive. Studies of Durrett (1965), Mohanty (1967), and Gokulnathan (1971) reveal that various indices of SES are not related to anxiety. On the other hand Nijhawan (1972), Murlidharan and Sharma (1971) have reported that lower class people display higher level of anxiety. Scheduled caste students have been observed to be more anxious than caste Hindu students (Sharma, 1971). Misra and Tripathi (1978) have reported significant positive relationship between trait and state anxiety and prolonged deprivation—a finding also confirmed by Tiwari (1979).

Personality

It has been argued that impoverished conditions of life produce a kind of personality pattern that results in various kinds of inadequacies in behaviour thereby accentuating the problem of poverty. The roots are traced to parental interactions and the general process of socialization which the child in the impoverished environment undergoes. As Hess (1970) puts it, the mother-child interaction among the lower class can be described as "socialization of apathy and underachievement". It is suggested that the in-school and out-of-school problems of the disadvantaged lie in personality difficulties. Levy (1966) refers to the remarks of a young teacher in a Harlem school : "what impressed me most was the fact that my children (9-10 years old) are already cynical and disillusioned about school and life in general. They are hostile, rebellious, and bitter . . .". This picture is fairly typical of the lower economic levels. In a less impoverished neighbourhood, it is found that teachers complain less about children's open hostility and rebelliousness, and more about their covert withdrawal into apathy, inattention, and laziness. It has been observed that lower class individuals suffer from different types of conflicts with the result that they gradually become more and more socially aloof and deviant.

In India, Rath (1974b) has analyzed the relationship between social conditions personality dimensions. He argues that the bio-social needs of the people are integrated with the external social demands. The latter are gradualized by internalized and the former are steadily socialized in course of socio-cultural adjustments. He hypothesized that the upper and lower caste groups would show significant differences in personality make-up. Comparing six groups on measures of neuroticism and insecurity, the low caste groups were found to have higher incidence of neuroticism. They also manifested greater sense of insecurity. Rath concluded that the personality dimensions are the functional resultants of the existing social conditions.

Comparing groups representing the two extremes of caste hierarchy, i.e., Brahmin (advantaged) and Harijan (disadvantaged) groups, Dhapola (1977) found them to be similar on the more prominent needs as measured by EPPS. However, on the needs of exhibition and change, Brahmins were significantly higher than Harijans. On TAT protocols Harijans were significantly high on achievement, deference, intraception and abasement, while Brahmins were higher on affiliation and succorance.

Combining income, sex, rural-urban residence and caste or ethnic status to provide the index of social disadvantage, Singh, (1977) found that (i) the tribals, the females and the rural were more traditional in their attitudes, more religious and more moral as compared to non-tribals, males and urban persons, (ii) the differences between various caste/ethnic groups were more concentrated in the female sample, presumably, because they were less exposed to the levelling effects of a heterogenous society, and (iii) the degree of social disadvantage was negatively related to modernity of social and religious attitudes and positively with moral attitudes. As for the personality variable, results indicated that (i) while there were no significant caste/ethnic differences on authoritarianism, rigidity and alienation, all the sub-groups scored above the midpoint of the scale. There was also no difference in conformity; (ii) the tribals were clearly more extrovert and anxious than the non-tribals—the tribal Christians being the most extrovert. The rural female tribal Hindu was the most anxious. On the whole, tribals had less positive self-image than the non-tribals indicating their lower position in the society and (iii) there were some sex and rural-urban differences. The females were more conforming, anxious, intelligent and less extrovert and alienated. The males were more rigid, authoritarian, conforming, and anxious. They were less extrovert, intelligent, had a lower self-image and were alienated.

In general, these findings suggest that the personality characteristics of advantaged and disadvantaged groups differ in some aspects. As Hess (1970) has observed "the consequences of lower class life is a cluster of attitudes that express low self-esteem, a sense of inefficacy, and passivity . . . . These are not as much stable personality traits as they are adaptive responses to frustration and unpredictability, to being acted upon, to being forced to wait for someone in authority to act" (p. 467).

Self-concept
Psychologists have shown considerable interest in the study of relationship between deprivation and self-concept. Disadvantaged children have been found to possess negative self-images (Witty, 1967; Tannenbaum, 1969). Whiteman and Deutsch (1968) not only observed the more deprived to have lower and more negative self-concept, but self-concept differences were also significantly related to reading scores.

A few studies have not found negative self-image to be a necessary correlate of deprivation. Soares and Soares (1971) observed the self-perceptions of disadvantaged children to be more positive on all measures (self concept, ideal concept, reflected self-classmate, reflected self-teacher, reflected self-parent) than of the advantaged children.

Studies conducted in India have also yielded conflicting results. Sharma (1975) has observed a positive relationship between self-concept and increase in SES level. Rath and Sircar (1960) comparing three upper and three lower caste groups found that the scheduled caste groups tend to ascribe to themselves more unfavourable traits. Rath (1974b) concluded that the widely prevalent social attitudes found among the upper caste people towards the low caste people seem to be psychologically internalized in the case of low caste groups. Similarly, Dhapola (1977) noted inadequacies in self system, social extension of self, interpersonal attitudes among Harijans in comparison to Brahmins. But their self-concept was as positive and variegated as that of the Brahmins. Misra and Tripathi (1980) also observed the self-perception to be positive irrespective of the level of deprivation. Though the medium deprivation group scored highest followed by high and low deprivation groups, none of the comparisons yielded significant differences. Negative correlation between prolonged deprivation scores and self perception ratings indicated that as the deprivation level decreased the self-concept became more favourable.

Motivational orientation
Pareek (1970) defining poverty mainly in terms of deprivation and helplessness has elaborated the motivational pattern induced by poverty. Apart from orientation to helplessness and feeling of powerlessness, he suggests a paradigm of culture of

poverty, i.e., poverty as structural component produces a three-fold motivational pattern characterised by low need for achievement, low need for extension, and high need for dependency. He contends that dependency motivation is expressed through lack of initiative, avoidance syndrome (shifting responsibility to others, exaggerating obstacles), excessive fear of failure, seeking favours of superiors, overconformity, and aggressive rejection of authority. Conditions of poverty produce a specific pattern of motivation and, through the relevant process of socialization an expectancy that can be called the frame of powerlessness is generated. The specific motivational pattern and expectancy of powerlessness produce behaviour seen among the culturally deprived.

Within the general framework of Maslow's (1954) theory, Misra and Tripathi (1978) expected that those in a state of prolonged experiential deprivation would be weaker in higher order sociogenic needs. But comparison on power, affiliation and approval needs did not reveal significant differences among low, medium and high deprived groups.

The underprivileged and deprived groups have been also viewed as having passive orientation, and more inclined to believe that external forces and agencies exclusively control the rewards they receive which is reflected in negative relationship between SES and external locus of control. Das and Panda (1971) found the high caste children to be more internal and Harijan children more external in attribution of failure in academic situations. Analysing coping strategies of underprivileged first generation University students, Sinha (1980) noted them to have a strong tendency to refer success to external factors like kindness of teachers, God and so on. They did not ascribe it to their own effort and, thereon failed to take adequate pride in their accomplishment and experience a sense of fulfilment which would be reinforcing to their behaviour. The mediating mechanism that they adopted of ascribing success to external agencies frequently led to superstitious behaviour, perpetuation of fatalistic outlook and produced superstitious ritualism, i.e., performing the same rites before undertaking a big task. It also sometimes led to ingratiation of the significant others.

[illegible]

[illegible] in the place [illegible] [illegible]

[illegible] the middle [illegible]

[illegible] a great number of [illegible]

[illegible]

[illegible]

(Meade, 1966), and reporting pessimistic attitudes (Teahan, 1958). In some studies, the general assumption that the poor have shorter time perspective has been disputed. However, till more direct evidence to the contrary is reported, the conclusion appears warranted that participants in the sub-culture of poverty are unwilling and unable to defer or plan for the future (Sarbin, 1970).

Ushasree (1980) contends that socially disadvantaged children do not internalize the motivation to achieve academically and have not learned to work for delayed gratification of needs. They have difficulty in working towards distant goals and display lower academic adjustments than the non-disadvantaged pupils. Greater capacity of the middle class children to delay rewards may be attributed to the ability to look further into the future than the lower class children.

Assuming that people of low status have less information about how goals may be attained and how fears may be encountered, it has been argued that lower status people may become resigned to their fate and leave things happening. Social class also determines the kind of future-related concerns, i.e., hopes and fears. Investigating the impact of social status on future orientation, Trommsdorff and Lamm (1975) observed that persons of high status named significantly more concerns (hopes and fears) and had a greater number of different categories of concerns than persons of low status. They also had a more extended future orientation than low status persons.

Learning-motivation and incentive system

Differentials in learning-motivation and incentive systems have been analysed in relation to class and racial differences and effectiveness of various kinds of reward, tangible against symbolic, immediate versus delayed and so on. From a developmental angle Zigler and Kanzer (1962) postulated the dependence of early learning on immediate need-gratification. In latter stages, social reinforcers like praise, attention and affection become increasingly effective, which in turn become less important motivationally than mere information that one's response is correct. Within this framework, it was observed that with poor children tangible reinforcers were more effective than verbal ones. In other words, lower class children had not made the usual developmental progression with regard to the reinforcers. Using a similar framework, Terall, Durkin and Wiesley (1959) observed that learning among middle-class children was somewhat better with neutral incentive, and the lower-class children's performance was significantly better with material reward. Zigler and deLabry (1962) obtained similar results. Further, examining class differentials for two types of verbal reinforcement viz., praise and disapproval, Rosenhan (1966) has shown that under conditions of approval, the performance of lower-class white and Negro children substantially improved. The lower-class white and Negro performed more poorly under conditions of disapproval. However, Unikel and his associates (1969) have found social and tangible reward as equally effective in different SES groups.

Sharma (1981) has also found concrete reward to be more effective on deprived children. Studying differentials in digit symbol substitution under concrete, symbolic and no reward conditions, there was no difference between the deprived and non-deprived children when no reward was provided. However, deprivation and nature of reward were significant effects. The deprived children performed significantly better under concrete reward while there was no difference under symbolic reward. It is, however, to be noted that the scores of deprived children were higher than their non-deprived counterparts under all the three reward conditions.

In conclusion, diverse facets of motivation and personality characteristics of the deprived child have been analysed. While the findings are useful and interesting by themselves, they appear inchoate and scattered, and there is urgent need for integrating them to present a coherent picture of how living under conditions of socio-economic disadvantage shapes the personality of the child. On the basis of the existing evidence, the question whether there is a distinct personality and motivational syndrome associated with the deprived remains undecided.

REFERENCES

Agarwal, A., and Tripathi, K.K. Temporal orientation and deprivation. *Journal of Psychological Researches*, 1980, 24, 144-152.

Angelini, A.L., Bitencourt, L., Jose, F., and Rosamilha, N. Motivo de realizacao edesenvolvimento economico. *Revista Intermericana depsicologia*, 1970, 4, 33-41.

Aronoff, J. *Psychological needs and cultural system.* Princeton, New Jersey : D. Van Nostrand, 1967.

Bartoshuk, A.K. Motivation. In Kling and Riggs (Eds.) *Woodworth and Scholsberg's experimental psychology*. New York : Holt, Rinehart and Winston, 1971.

Bolles, R.C. *Theory of motivation.* New York : Harper and Row Publishers, 1975.

Bowloy, J. The influence of early environment in the development of neurosis and neurotic character. *International Journal of Psychoanalysis*, 1940, 21, 154-178.

Bowloy, J. Maternal-care and mental health. *Bulletin of the World Health Organization*, 1951, 3, 355-534.

Bronfenbrenner, U. Early deprivation in mammals : A cross-species analysis. In G. Newton, & S. Levine (Eds.) *Early experience and behaviour.* Illinois : Thomas, Springfield, 1968.

Chaube, N.P. *Motivational dimensions of rural development.* Allahabad : Chaitanya Publications, 1974.

Chaudhury, N. *The relationship between achievement motivation, anxiety, intelligence, sex, social class and vocational aspirations.* Unpublished Doctoral Dissertation, Punjab University, Chandigarh, 1971.

Clarke, R.S. *et al.* Individual differences on dogs : Preliminary report on the effects of early deprivation. *Canadian Journal of Psychology*, 1951, 5, 150-156.

Das, U.C., and Panda, K.C. *Effects of certain non-intellective variables on cognitive performance.* Unpublished Manuscript. Regional College of Bhubaneshwar, Bhubaneshwar, 1977.

Desai, D.B., and Trivedi, R.S. *Achivement motivation development in high school pupils.* Unpublished Manuscript. Sardar Patel Univèrsity, Ballabh Vidyanagar, 1972.

Dhapola, T.S. *A study of personality make-up of Harijan students.* Unpublished Manuscript. Kashi Vidyapeeth, Varanasi, 1977.

Dreger, R.M., and Miller, K.S. Comparative psychological studies of Negros and Whites in the United States, 1959-1965. *Psychological Bulletin Monograph Supplement*, 1968, 70.

Durrett, M. Normative data on the children's manifest anxiety scale for Marathi speaking Indian children of different income levels. *Indian Journal of Psychology*, 1965, 40, 1-6.

Goldfarb, W. Emotional and intellectual consequences of psychological deprivation infancy : A re-evaluation. In P.H. Hoch and J. Zubein

(Eds.) *Psychopathology of children.* New York : Grune and Stratton, 1955.

Gokulnathan, P.P. Social class and educational achievement in relation to achievement motivation measured by an objective test. *Indian Journal of Psychology*, 1970, **45**, 67-74.

Gokulnathan, P.P., and Mehta, P. Achievement motive in tribal and non-tribal Assamese secondary school adolescents. *Indian Educational Review*, 1972, **7**, 67-90.

Harlow, H.F. Mice, monkeys men and motives. *Psychological Review*, 1953, **60**, 23-32.

Harlow, H.F. *Learning to love.* San Fransisco : Albino, 1971.

Hess, R.D. The transition of cognitive strategies in poor : The socialization of apathy and underachievement. In V.L. Allen (Ed.) *Psychological factors in poverty.* New York : Academic Press, 1970.

Hunt, J. McVick. Experience and the development of motivation : Some reinterpretation. *Child Development*, 1960, **34**, 489-504.

Katz, I. A new approach to the study of school motivation in minority group children. In V.L. Allen (Ed.) *Psychological factors in poverty.* New York : Academic Press, 1970.

Langmeier, J. Personalities of deprived childred. In Monks, F.J. (Ed.) *Determinants of behavioural development*, New York : Academic Press, 1972.

Lerhan, L.L. Time orientation and social class. *Journal of Abnormal and Social Psychology*, 1952, **47**, 589-592.

Levy, D.M. Primary effect hunger. *American Journal of Psychiatry*. 1973, **94**, 643-652.

Levy, B. An urban teacher speaks out. In S.W. Webster (Ed.) *The disadvantaged learner.* San Fransisco : Chandler, 1966.

Levine, R. *Dreams and deeds : Achievement motivation in Nigeria.* Chicago : University of Chicago Press, 1966.

Lott, A.J. and Lott, B.E. *Negro and White youth.* New York : Holt, Rinehart and Winston, 1963.

Maslow, A.H. *Motivation and personality.* New York : Harper and Row, Publishers, 1954.

McClelland, D.C. The achieving society. Princeton, New Jersey : D. Van Nostrand, 1961.

Meade, R.D. Time estimates as affected by motivational level, goal distance and rate of progress. *Journal of Experimental Psychology*, 1959, **58**, 275-279.

Meade, R.D. Achievement motivation, achievement and psychological time. *Journal of Personality and Social Psychology*, 1966, **4**, 577-580.

Mehta, P. *The achievement in high school boys.* New Delhi : National Council of Educational Research and Training, 1969.

Mehta, P. and Mehta, N. Achievement motive research in India. *Indian Journal of Psychology*, 1974, **49**, 320-336.

Miller, J.O. *Cultural deprivation and its modification : Effects of intervention.* New York : Appleton-Century-Crofts, 1970.

Misra, G. and Tripathi, L.B. Prolonged deprivation and motivation. *Journal of Psychological Researches*, 1978, **22**, 171-179 (a).

Misra, G., and Tripathi, L.B. Prolonged deprivation and status perception. *Indian Journal of Social Work*, 1978, **39**, 113-121 (b).

Misra, G., and Tripathi, L.B. *Psychological consequences of prolonged deprivation.* Agra : National Psychological Corporation, 1980.

Morsback, H. A cross-cultural study of achievement motivation and achievement values in two South African groups. *Journal of Social Psychology*, 1969, **79**, 267-288.

Mohanty, G.S. Parental socio-economic status of college students as a variable in neuroticism, anxiety and hostility. *Journal of Psychological Researches*, 1967, **11**, 102-105.

Murlidharan, R., Sharma, A. Manifest anxiety in Indian children. *Indian Educational Review*, 1971, **6**, 67-68.

Nijhawan, H.K. *Anxiety in school children.* New Delhi : Wiley Eastern, 1972.

Nygard, R. Motive to approach success and motive to avoid failure in boys from different social groups. *Scandinavian Journal of Educational Research*, 1969, **4**, 222-232.

Ojha, H., and Jha, P.K. A study of achievement motive a function of social class, family system and family occupation. *Psychologia*, 1979, **22**, 57-63.

Pareek, U. Poverty and motivation : Figure and ground. In V.L. Allen (Ed.) *Psychological factors in poverty.* New York : Academic Press, 1970.

Rath, R. *Cognitive growth and classroom learning of deprived children in the primary schools.* Paper presented at the East-West Centre for Cross-cultural Studies, Honolulu, 1972.

Rath, R. *Teaching-learning problems of primary school children : A challenge to Indian psychologists and educationists.* Presidential address, 14th Annual conference of the Indian Academy of Applied Psychology, University of Calcutta, December, 27-29, 1973.

Rath, R. *Teaching and learning problem of the disadvantaged tribal children.* Presidential Address, 12th Annual Conference of the Indian Academy of Applied Psychology, Utkal University, Bhubaneshwar, December, 28-30, 1974 (a).

Rath, R. *Psychological aspects of social change.* New Delhi : Allied Publishers 1974 (b).

Rath, R. and Sircar, N.C., Intercaste relationship as reflected in the study of attitudes and opinions of six Hindu caste groups. *The Journal of Social Psychology*, 1960, **51**, 3-25.

Ribble, M.A. *The rights of infants.* New York : Columbia University Press, 1943.

Rosen. B.C. The achievement syndrome. *American Sociological Review*, 1956, 21, 203-211.

Rosen, B.C. Race, socialization and the achievement motivation in Brazil. *American Sociological Review*, 1962, 27, 612-624.

Reisen, A.H. Stimulation as a requirement for growth and function in behavioural development. In D.W. Fiske and S.R. Maddi (Eds.) *Functions of varied experience*. Homewood, Illinois : Dorsey, 1961.

Rosenhan, D.L. Effects of social class and race on responsiveness to approval and disapproval. *Journal of Personality and Social Psychology*, 1966, 4, 253-259.

Rutter, M. *Maternal deprivation reassessed*. Harmondsworth, Middlesex: Penguin Books Limited, 1972.

Santrock, J.W., and Wohlford, P. Effects of father absence : Influence of the reason for and the onset of absence. *Proceedings of the Annual Convention of American Psychological Association*, 1970, 5, 265-266.

Sarbin, T.R. The culture of poverty, social identity and cognitive outcome In V.L. Allen (Ed.) *Psychological factors in poverty*, New York : Academic Press, 1970.

Shanmugam, T.E., Effect of low socio-economic status on emotional instability. *Journal Psychological Researches*, 1957, 1, 60-67.

Sharma, S. Self acceptance and socio-economic status. *Journal of Education and Psychology*, 1975, 32, 205-208.

Sharma, S. Parental occupation and anxiety. *Recent Trends in Education* 1971, 2, 21-24.

Sharma, M. *An experimental study of the effect of types of reward in performance of deprived and non-deprived children*. Unpublished Long Experimental Report for Master's Course, Department of Psychology, Allahabad University, Allahabad, 1981.

Simmel, E. Time estimation in hospitalized patients as a function of goal distance and magnitude of reward. *Perceptual and Motor Skills*, 1963, 17, 91-97.

Singh, A.K. *Social disadvantage, attitude and personality*. Unpublished Manuscript Psychology Department, Ranchi University, Ranchi, 1977.

Sinha, D. *Indian villages in transition : A motivational analysis*. New Delhi : Associated Publishers, 1969.

Sinha, D. *Motivation and rural development : Two studies on Indian farmers*. Calcutta : Minerva Associates, 1974.

Sinha, [D. Some cognitive and motivational concomitants of poverty. *Social Change*, 1980, 10, 3-8.

Sinha, D., and Chaubey, N.P. Achievement motive and rural economic development. *International Journal of Psychology*, 1972, 7, 267-272.

Skeels, H.M. and Dye, H.B. A study of the effects of differential stimulation on mentally retarded children. *Proceedings of the American Association of Mental Deficiency*, 1939, 39, 114-136.

Soares, A.T., and Soares, L.M. Comparative differences in the self-perceptions of disadvantaged and advantaged students. *Journal of School Psychology*, 1971, **9**, 424-429.

Spitz, R.A. The role of ecological factors in emotional development in infancy. *Child Development*, 1947, **20**, 145-156.

Srivastava, P.K., and Tiwari, M.L. Socio-economic stratification and need achievement. *Psychological Studies*, 1967, **12**, 9-16.

Tannenbaum, A.J. Some non-intellectual concomitants of social deprivation. *Israel Annals of Psychiatry and Related Disciplines*, 1969, **7**, 9-31.

Teahan, J.E. Future time perspective optimism and academic achievement. *Journal of Abnormal Social Psychology*, 1968, **57**, 379-380.

Terrell, G. Js., Durkin, D., and Wiesley, M. Social class and nature of the incentive in discrimination learning. *Journal of Abnormal Social Psychology*, 1959, **59**, 270-272.

Tiwari, A.N. *An empirical study of the development of achievement motive as a function of prolonged deprivation.* Unpublished Doctoral Dissertation, Gorakhpur University, Gorakhpur, 1979.

Tiwari, A.N., and Misra, G. A. study of achievement motive in relation to prolonged deprivation, *Psychologia*, 1977, **20**, 172-189.

Trommosdorff, G. and Lamm, H. An analysis of future orientation and some of its social determinants. In J.T. Fraser, and N. Lawrence (Eds.) *The study of time.* (Vol. 2). New York, Heidelberg : Springer, 1975.

Unlike, I.P., Strain, G.S. and Adams, H.E. Learning of lower socio-economic status children as a function of social and tangible reward. *Developmental Psychology*, 1969, **5**, 553-555.

Ushasree, S. Social disadvantage, academic adjustment and scholastic achievement, *Social change*, 1980, **10**, 25-30.

Veroff, J., Atkinson, J.W., Feld, S., and Gurin, G. The use of thematic apperception to assess motivation in a nation-wide interview study. *Psychological Monographs*, 1960, **74**, No. 12 (Whole No. 449).

Werner, O.E., and Murlidharan, R. Nutrition, cognitive status and achievement motivation of New Delhi nursery school children. *Journal of Cross-Cultural Psychology*, 1970, **1**, 271-281.

Witty, P.A. (Ed.) The educationally retarded and disadvantaged. In Sixty six year book of education, Part I. Chicago, Illinois : National Society for the Study of Education, 1967.

Whiteman, M., and Deutsch, M. Social disadvantages as related to intellective and language development. In M. Deutsch, I. Katz, and A.R., Jensen (Eds.) *Social class, race and psychological development*. New York : Holt, Rinehart and Winston, 1968.

Yarrow, L.J. Maternal deprivation : Toward an empirical and conceptual re-evaluation. *Psychological Bulletin*, 1961, **58**, 459-490.

Yarrow, L.J. Enrichment and deprivation : Towards a conceptual and empirical differentiation of the early environment. In F.J., Monks *et al.* (Eds.) *Determinants of behavioural development*, New York : Academic Press, 1972.

Zigler, E., and deLabry, J. Concept-switching in middle-class, lower-class and retarded children. *Journal of Abonormal Social Psychology*, 1962; **65**, 267-273.

Zigler, E., and Kanzer, P. The effectiveness of two classes of verbal reinforces on the performance of middle and lower-class children. *Journal of Personality*, **30**, 157-163.

Zigler, E., and deLabry, J. Concept-switching in middle-class, lower-class and retarded children. *Journal of Abnormal and Social Psychology*, 1962, 65, 267-273.

Zigler, E., and Kanzer, P. The effectiveness of two classes of verbal reinforcers on the performance of middle and lower-class children. *Journal of Personality*, 1962, 30, 157-163.

THIRTEEN

Namita Pande and *R.C. Tripathi*

SCHEDULED CASTE CHILDREN IN HIGH CASTE SCHOOL
Some Motivational Consequences

INTRODUCTION

EDUCATION of the socially disadvantaged has received a great deal of attention from the educators and policy makers in the Western countries but not so much in our own country. Integration of schools is sought not only on the grounds that discrimination is abhorrent but because such an experience is thought to be educative to both Black and White children. School integration in the U.S. has been sought through bussing of children studying in racially segregated schools from one corner of the city to another. There is evidence to suggest that Black students from the segregated schools do not feel quite at home in the integrated settings. Williams (1968) points out that the concerns and affective reservations of the Blacks pertain to peer-acceptance, fairness of White teachers, and achievement in the class room. These very few empirical studies bring out what the integrated school experience does to the motivations of the Black students. Deutsch (1960) however, notes that the teachers of Negro students often reinforce negative self-images of their students through words and deeds. Little wonder why Negro students then score lower on standardized achievement and aptitude tests in comparison to their White counterparts. However, evidence on this matter is equivocal. Higgins and Sivers (1958) and Anastasi and D'Angelo (1952) found that in the integrated schools no significant differences existed among the racial groups with respect to I.Q.

whereas, in a segregated setting Black I.Q. was significantly lower than Whites on Binet or Otis tests.

The situation in India is somewhat different. There are no racially segregated schools. We do have, however, schools run by ethnic minorities such as Christians, Muslims, Harijans and the like. When a student belonging to an ethnic minority moves from a minority institution to an institution run by high caste Hindus, we probably have a parallel with the American situation. The climate of the school for such a student may be said to be similar to what a Black student gets in a White school.

The school climate for the disadvantaged groups of students is qualitatively different than for the advantaged students. In a school situation where advantaged students are put together with the disadvantaged, a feeling of self depreciation is generated. As Freire (1970) holds, "self depreciation is another characteristic of the oppressed, which derive from their internalization of the opinion the oppressors have of them. So often do they hear that they are good for nothing and are incapable of learning anything that they are sick, lazy and unproductive that in the end they become convinced of their own unfitness".

School climate, and by this, we refer to structuring of social relationships within the school situation has significant implications for the learning and motivation of children. Schools are important socializing agencies. Therefore, their role in the development of self-concept of students is quite significant. The positive self-concept is what sustains actions. Intuitively, it appears to us that schools run by ethnic minorities should be able to develop positive self-concept of students belonging to the minority groups. Such climate ought not to have only positive motivational consequences but should show up in case of various cognitive abilities too.

The relationship between academic motivation and achievement of the socially deprived has also been explained in terms of deficient cognitive functioning, negative self-perception and impoverished environmental conditions ensuing from a low SES. Such explanations are followed by a plea to concentrate more upon the early experiences of the deprived. But what is to become of those children who are already in school in which the developed mental patterns cannot be reversed. Little attention has been given on types of intervention by which the deprived child could be helped to perform well in school. Moreover, the types of relationship between cognitive abilities, pre-school environmental conditions and achievement is not always consistent. There are empirical evidences to show that many children with I.Q. in the retarded range (i.e., below 10) cope adequately in ordinary schools (Rutter, Tizard & Whitemore, 1970) and many children in special schools for subnormals have a normal I.Q. Father's educational attainment and occupational status exert only a modest influence on achievement in reading and mathematics (Hauser, 1971). Apart from these, with Negro students, it has been found that several disadvantaged students achieved significantly well despite their environmental disabilities. Further, that academic achievement of these students could not, in all cases, be attributed to intelligence.

We have emphasized above the process variables of the school in terms of which the actual learning context could be conceptualized. The importance of the school as a system cannot be overlooked if we are interested in the development of learning process of school children. In this paper, we will limit our interest to motivation and academic achievement of the socially deprived scheduled caste students in school. In doing so, we would focus primarily upon one major variable of the educational organization its climate.

The concept of climate

To understand the scheduled caste motivation in school, we opt for defining the educational climate of the school organization as a global perception held by the scheduled caste child about his organizational environment rather than a set of organizational attributes which could be identified separately from the individual's perceptions and measured by a variety of methods. We believe following Schneider and Hall (1972) that these global perceptions reflect an interaction between personal and organizational characteristics in which the individual by forming perceptions, acts as an information processor using inputs from (a) the events and the characteristics of the organization and (b) characteristics (e.g., needs and values) of the perceiver.

Many studies have tried to invesigate the relationship between environmental variables and student achievement at college or university level (e.g., Knapp & Goodrich, 1952; Knapp & Greenbaum, 1953; Holland, 1957, Stern, 1962; Pace, 1963). Sharma (1969) administered Halpin and Crofts Organizational Climate Descriptive Questionnaire and found it to be positively related to the achievement of boys. Kumar (1975) found that in schools with open climate pupils tended to show better personal and social adjustment. Climate of an organization has also been found to relate positively with self-acceptance Ross, 1973; House, 1973), pupil morale (Smith, 1973) and verbal participation (Kleinfeld, 1973).

Educational climate for the scheduled caste

Taking the educational climate as a potent factor for the motivation of the deprived scheduled caste group, we can assess the effectiveness with which our educational institutions provide for the educational needs of the scheduled caste. We have reasons to believe that the scheduled caste child fits very little with what the school wants and expects out of him. Like in the West, Indian schools also represent middle class values. In this respect, the analysis of Lightfoot (1971) is also applicable to the Indian setting. He says, "since middle class culture dominates our schools, the elaborate code of communication (formal language), the dominant value pattern (competition, punctuality, hard work, cleanliness etc.) and the external demands of ability grouping for special education (middle class standardized test) as well as the instructional programmes and techniques children are exposed to, testifies to the recognition that the children of the lower class will in all likelihood, become increasingly disadvantaged in the present school environment" (Lightfoot, 1971). As a result of this, a vicious circle is set into motion. Often a lower caste child enters the school less equipped because as DeCecco (1968) maintains he comes from a pre-school environment which fails to develop entering behaviour necessary to begin his formal education. In the school, he is exposed to a middle class culture with which adjustment is difficult. This lack of fit is further pronounced by an indifferent, if not hostile climate and results in his lack of motivation. The less motivated he is, the less likely he is to attain desired academic standard which provides a further confirmation of his inherent incapabilities. He eventually drops out or this process results in premature school termination (Rath, 1976).

The concept of climate supportiveness

One of the significant dimensions of educational climate is climate supportiveness. By climate supportiveness we refer to a positive affect which members have towards an organization and its functioning. Feelings of supportiveness or unsupportiveness can be considered as attitudinal dispositions for the academic and non-academic pursuits in the school.

The factors responsible for the perception of the school climate as supportive could be both, inherent in the perceiving individual and also in the specific features of his environment. Factors peculiar to the individual that influence perception of school climate are his value structure, personality and needs. An important environmental factor related to the perception of a lack of support is the behaviour of teachers and peers. Teacher expectancy and peer group acceptance have been particularly found significant in determining the supportiveness of the perceived climate. These concepts, therefore, need to be discussed in some detail.

Teacher expectancy

The concept 'expectancy effect' as determinant of educational achievement has received much attention, beginning with Rosenthal and Jacobson's studies (Rosenthal, 1973).

Briefly said there exists a growing amount of evidence that teachers slot children into different categories the same way people performing different roles are slotted. It is found that teachers expecting good performance from students give more feedback, create warmer socio-emotional mood, teach more material that is difficult and give enough time to their pupils to respond. (Rosenthal, 1973). Teacher's praise and approval enhances self-regard (Hess & Maehr, 1965) perhaps by changing attributional patterns (Dweck & Reppucci, 1973; Weiner, Frezier, Kukla, Reed, Rest and Rosenbaum, 1971) and give rise to high academic achievement (Shaw, Edison & Bell, 1960; Brookover, Paterson & Thomas, 1962). However, what is particularly significant to note is that teacher's expectations relate positively to the motivation and achievement of the students belonging to deprived groups. Coleman (1966) has indicated that the correlation of pupil achievement and the behaviour of teachers and fellow pupils is higher for Black than that for Whites. Yee (1968) demonstrated that teachers' attitudes are more influential in setting attitudes for lower class children than the middle class. A number of studies have shown that the achievement of the minority group is depressed because their teachers do not expect them to perform well (Clark, 1965). Negro academic achievement has often been found to be a little raised in Black schools because the Black teachers are less pesimistic in their evaluation of Black students (Gottleib, 1964) and they share, with their students, a similarity in racial or ethnic background.

Peer group acceptance

The child's teacher is not the only source of his evaluation. His peers may also exert an independent influence. Peer-group implies a more or less enduring association of individuals who enjoy a parity of status in atleast some common motive or interest. Peer-group characteristics have been found to be closely related to attainment (Coleman, 1966). It is said that socio-emotional aspects of peer-group appear to take precedence over the other influences in school in shaping pupils' motivation to learn. Students coming from lower castes find little support from their peers who generally come from high or middle caste groups. There is evidence to show that educational context does not alter the attitudes of students towards different caste-groups. Shankar (1966) found that the cognitive component of the attitudes of Hindu students towards Harijans did not become less unfavourable because of education.

The review of the studies presented so far makes it clear that the perception of the school climate as unsupportive in the case of students coming from such disadvantaged groups as Harijans may be due to the expectations and behaviours of their teachers and peers. This explains the minority group preference to stay at a minority institution. An important study in this respect was conducted by Bolner and Vedlitz (1971) which demonstrated the preference of Black high school students attending Black colleges to continue attending the same instead of integrating into the mainstream, not because of fear of physical or social harm but because of their feeling of the school as 'their own'. It is often been found that the integrated schools tend to lower the self-concept of the lower class children (French, 1972). Further, the segregation and aspiration of Negro youth is not always negatively related as would commonly be expected.

II

SOME MOTIVATIONAL CONSEQUENCES OF STUDYING IN A HIGH CASTE RUN SCHOOL FOR SCHEDULED CASTE STUDENTS

To understand the relationship between the perception of climate supportiveness and motivational patterns of the scheduled caste group as outlined above, report of an empirical study (Tripathi & Pande, 1976) is presented. The purpose of this study was to assess the motivational outcomes of scheduled caste students when they study in a minority institution as opposed to a school run by high caste people.

The sample of the study consisted of 108 male school students studying in the sixth, eighth and tenth grades and belonging to two different institutions, one, a Hindu majority institution and the other, an institution run by a local Harijan Ashram and deemed to be a minority institution. The total sample of 108 students was selected from the two schools, 54 students coming from each. These 54 subjects were further selected from different grades. Twenty subjects were drawn from the tenth grade, 20 from the eighth and 14 from the sixth grade in each school. In each grade, half of the subjects belonged to the scheduled and half to the non-scheduled castes. The students of both the castes were matched on intelligence. Thus, the study involved a $2 \times 2 \times 2$ factorial design. The first factor was the nature of the institution and had two levels as predominantly majority run and minority institutions. The second factor was caste which was spilt into scheduled and non-scheduled castes. The third factor, grade had three levels—sixth, eighth and tenth.

The scale to measure climate supportiveness consisted of three dimensions, the perceived teacher expectations by the students, perception of peer-group acceptance and the home environment of the student. Realizing that the home environment should emphasize the value of educational achievement for supportive climate to influence student motivation, home environment was considered an important dimension of climate supportiveness. The perception of climate as supportive was predicted to relate with the motivational variables such as the academic self-concept, need for achievement, fear of failure, and level of aspiration measured in terms of goal-setting behaviour.

Results to a large extent confirmed our expectations. It was found that the climate of the minority school was perceived more supportive than the climate of the majority school. Further, non-scheduled caste students perceived their school climate as more supportive than scheduled caste students. Table 13.1 shows that scheduled caste students found the climate of minority school supportive to a greater degree in comparison to the majority school. No such difference was obtained for non-scheduled caste students.

Besides perception of school climate, the main effects due to school and caste and interaction effect between school and caste were also found significant for need for achievement and academic self-concept. Non-scheduled caste students from the majority school showed higher need for achievement and a more positive academic self-concept than those scheduled caste students belonging to the minority school. Table 13.2 shows that non-scheduled caste students had very little difference in their mean need-achievement score, in the majority and minority schools but the mean score for the scheduled caste students in the majority school was considerably lower than their score in the minority school. Similarly, the academic self-concept of the scheduled caste students was markedly low in the majority school than in the minority school. No such difference was observed for non-scheduled caste students. Such main effects due to caste and interaction effect due to school and caste were not obtained for fear of failure. Table 13.2 also shows that in the majority school scheduled caste students had higher fear of

TABLE 13.1 : **The main effects of school, caste, grade and their interactions on climate supportiveness, need for achievement, fear of failure and academic self-concept**

Source	df	Climate Supportiveness		Need for Achievement		Fear of Failure		Academic Self-Concept	
		MS	F	MS	F	MS	F	MS	F
School	1	8.84	19.64**	4.56	9.50**	2.40	6.86*	4.32	16.00**
Caste	1	10.27	22.82**	4.31	8.90**	0.75	2.15	2.08	7.70**
Grade	2	1.31	2.91	0.98	2.03	2.84	8.11**	0.19	0.69
School X Caste	1	13.44	29.86**	2.81	5.85*	0.80	2.28	3.20	11.80**
Caste X Grade	2	3.07	6.81*	0.76	1.57	0.56	1.60	0.66	2.40
School X Grade	2	3.93	8.72**	0.32	0.66	3.40	9.71**	0.85	3.14
School X Caste X Grade	2	0.46	1.02	0.19	039	1.35	3.84*	0.13	0.45
Corrected Error	96	0.45		0.48		0.35		0.27	

{*Source* : Tripathi & Pande, 1976)

$^{**}p<.01$

$^{*}p<.05$

failure than the non-scheduled caste students, though, this difference was not statistically significant. Fear of failure increased in the eighth grade for both scheduled and non-scheduled caste students and then declined in the tenth grade.

Goal discrepancy was taken as the measure of level of aspiration. Since the scale in this case was not linear or monotonic, ANOVA was not applied. Instead, in the two schools, students were categorized under two categories, namely those falling below Q 1 and above Q 3, both comprising students showing unrealistic aspirations. It was found that in the majority school 20 out of 27 scheduled caste students had unrealistic aspirations as against only 7 non-scheduled caste students. The χ^2 value was highly significant ($\chi^2=11.32$; $p<.001$). In the minority school the split for the scheduled caste students was 12 and 15 for realistic and unrealistic aspirations as against 15 and 12 for the non-scheduled caste students. χ^2 value of .64 ($p= .44$) indicated no difference in the distributions.

Table 13.2 which presents means on the four dependent variables of the scheduled and non-scheduled caste students belonging to the low schools reveals a very interesting pattern. It shows a progressive decline in scores for climate supportiveness, need for achievement and academic self-concept for the scheduled caste studying in the majority school. Perception of climate supportiveness for the scheduled caste students decreased with each grade in the majority school. No such trend was observed for the non-scheduled caste students. Similarly need for achievement of the scheduled caste students studying in the majority school dropped and academic self concept became progressively more negative as they ascended to higher grades except in case of need for achievement in Grade VIII. Also the level of aspiration became more unrealistic with succeeding grades. The phenomenon was also observed by Sinha (1977) in a study which investigated development of perceptual skills of the scheduled and non-scheduled caste students in the English and the regional language schools. It further confirmed that, in general, studying in the majority-run school had negative motivational consequences for the scheduled caste students.

TABLE 13.2 : **Mean of climate supportiveness, need for achievement, fear of failure, academic self-concept and level of aspiration by school, caste and grade**

	MAJORITY Non-Scheduled Caste			INSTITUTION Scheduled Caste			MINORITY Non-Scheduled Caste			INSTITUTION Scheduled Caste		
	VI	VIII	X	VI	VIII	X	VI	VIII	X	VI	VIII	X
Climate Supportive-ness	13.0	13.6	12.6	11.6	9.3	6.4	11.2	13.4	15.4	12.7	13.3	12.8
Need for Achievement	7.3	8.1	8.1	5.8	6.6	4.6	7.0	8.7	8.6	7.6	8.2	7.8
Fear of Failure	2.8	6.3	2.6	5.2	6.2	3.2	4.0	3.7	2.6	2.8	3.3	4.5
Academic Self-Concept	6.3	6.4	5.7	5.4	3.9	3.5	5.5	6.5	6.9	6.5	6.9	6.1
Level of Aspiration	9.6	9.2	8.7	7.6	8.7	10.4	3.2	5.5	3.5	10.5	3.5	7.5

(*Source* : Tripathi & Pande, 1976)

III

A MODEL OF THE SCHEDULED CASTE UNDER ACHIEVEMENT

The findings of the study described in the earlier section clearly indicated that scheduled caste children find the climate of schools run by the high caste generally unsupportive. Furthermore, for scheduled caste students, although these findings are based on only one case, we have reason to believe that they will generally be true of other schools as well. There is extensive evidence that academic achievement of the scheduled caste children generally tends to be much lower than that of the non-scheduled caste students. It is commonly observed that in various competitive examinations, the mean of qualifying marks for the scheduled caste candidates is much lower than that of the non-scheduled caste candidates. Two parallel sets of studies explain the under-achievement of the scheduled caste children in schools. The first set of studies emphasize the role of cognitive abilities, whereas the second set of studies emphasize motivational variables. Differences in cognitive abilities between the upper caste and scheduled caste children have been reported in the studies by Rath, Dash and Dash (1970), Sinha (1976) and Tripthi and Misra (1975). Similarly, significant differences in motivational levels between the scheduled caste and tribal children and upper caste children are also obtained in the studies done by Rath, Dash and Dash (1979). We have already discussed studies which show that child's home and school environments influence his motivation intimately and consequently his school attainment. It is our contention that the question of under achievement of the scheduled caste in schools has to be considered by taking all these factors into consideration. Figure 13.1 presents a model to explain academic under achievement of children belonging to disadvantaged social groups, such as, the scheduled caste

The model as presented below has been conceptualized as a dynamic model. It postulates that an unsupportive educational climate which may result from forces operating in the home and educational environment of the child is likely to influence academic motivation of the child negatively. Poor

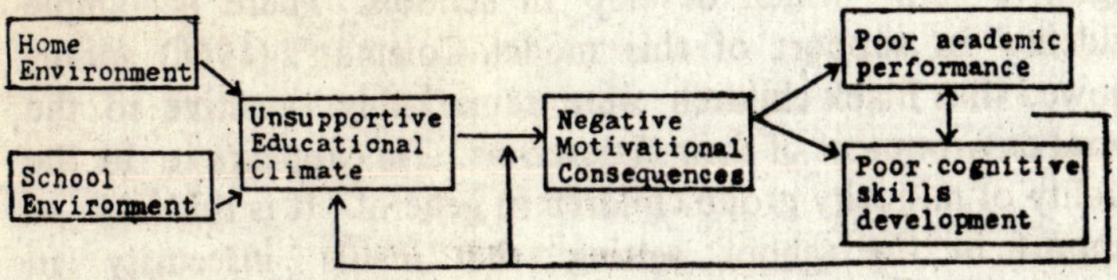

FIG. 13.1 : *A model of underachievement of disadvantaged children*

academic motivation will not allow for the acquisition and development of various cognitive skills which are required for effective school performance. Also because of poor motivation, the cognitive skills which have already been acquired are unlikely to find full utilization in school. Poor performance in school will further influence the academic motivations negatively. The self concept of such a child is likely to become more negative; fear of failure will further go up; and persistence is likely to come down. Poor performance of child will also reinforce the negative evaluations of his teachers, peers and his own parents and thus, result in an increasingly unsupportive climate for him. Initially, what may start out as mildly unsupportive educational climate for a disadvantaged child is likely to become more and more negative for him as the years go by. As the pressures of school become more and more severe and as the child finds himself unable to cope with the cognitive and motivational demands of the school, he is likely to take the first exit available to him, either by dropping out from the school or by accepting some lowly placed job.

The difference in the model proposed above and other models of academic attainment of the disadvantaged students lies in emphasizing the primacy of motivational variables and the role they play in the acquisition of certain cognitive skills. It is generally assumed that scheduled caste and upper caste children differ with respect to various cognitive skills to begin with and poor cognitive skills are responsible for their under attainment. The study reported in Section II and another study by Sinha (1977) provide ample proof that these differences widen with each year spent in school. It is, therefore, contended that the educational climate may actually be the precursor of cognitive skills which develop in schools. There is ample evidence in support of this model. Coleman's (1966) survey showed that Black children were remarkably sensitive to the social environment of their classrooms. This appears to be the quality of minority group children in general. It is this lack of support in the school setting that instils insecurity in disadvantaged children. Pffeifer (1976) found that students who had negative perception of the university climate also estimated their probability of success as low. It can, therefore, be reasonably assumed that such individuals will also be lower with respect to tendency to achieve success. The crucial factor, however, which contributes to the perception of unsupportive climate has to do with the expectations of teachers (or teacher-expectancy). Numerous studies have shown that teacher expectancy and academic motivations are closely interrelated. Once a child belonging to the disadvantaged group starts perceiving that he is being evaluated negatively by his teachers, it becomes difficult for him to emotionally identify with his teachers or, for that matter, with his peers. In the case of scheduled caste or a child belonging to a disadvantaged group, there is total absence of a model in school, someone he can relate to or identify with. Generally, there are few teachers belonging to his own caste group who can provide support to him. He is left to his own devices to cope with various problems he may face in the school situation. His own teachers show disinterest in solving his problems and only intensify his feelings of anxiety, threat, and poor self-worth.

Just as there is evidence that unsupportive educational climate produces negative motivational consequences for a child, there is also evidence that negative motivation influences academic achievement negatively. The evidence in this connection is so preponderant that it will not serve any purpose to review it here. As a matter of fact, Green and Faroqhar (1965) have reported that the scores on a test of motivation were better predictors of the achievement of Black students than their scores on verbal aptitude.

The model also postulates that negative motivational outcomes in case of students belonging to tbe disadvantaged group will affect cognitive skills negatively. This may happen in two ways. Firstly, it is possible that because of the poor motivational level, disadvantaged students may not feel enthusiastic enough to perform to their capacities on tests of cognitive skills. Zigler, Abelson and Seitz (1973) found that on Peabody Picture Vocabulary Test exceptionally low scores that were obtained in case of economically disadvantaged children were more due to motivational factors, such as, presence of an unsupportive experimenter than due to linguistic deficits. Another reason is that acquisition of any skill depends upon proper motivation. In the absence of such motivation one cannot expect proper development and acquisition on cognitive skills required for good scholastic performance. A study by Chitnis (1977) supports this contention. She found that the percentage of dropout and irregular attendance at school is higher in case of scheduled caste children. Thus, the disadvantaged students, particularly the one belonging to the scheduled caste, faces a double bind situation. Since the majority of educational institutions are run by the high caste for the high caste (even the governmental institutions are no exception), a student perforce has to go to these schools. However, when he enters such schools, he is faced with an unsupportive educational climate which 'kills' his motivational level and thereby creates a situation in which be learns very little. If he goes to schools run for him by the government or other agencies, he runs the risk of being stigmatized. The education of disadvantaged group, thus, poses a major challenge before the Indian educators.

REFERENCES

Anastasi, A., and D'Angelo, R.Y. A comparison of Negro and White preschool children in language development and Goodenough Draw-a-Man IQ. *Journal of Genetic Psychology*, 1952, 81, 147-165.

Bolner, J., and Vedlitz, A. The affinity of Negro pupils for segregated schools : Obstacles to desegregation. *Journal of Negro Education*, 1971, 40, 313-321.

Brookover, W.B., Paterson, A., and Thomas, S. *Self-concept of ability and school achievement*. East Lansing : Office of Research and Publications, Michigan State University, 1956.

Chitnis, S. *A long way to go : A report on survey of scheduled caste high school students and college students in fifteen states of India.* (Mimeographed) Centre for Social Studies, Surat, India, 1977.

Clark, K.B. *Dark ghetto : Dilemma of social power.* New York : Harper and Row Publishers, 1965.

Coleman, J.S. *Equality of educational opportunity.* Washington, D.C. : U.S. Printing Press, 1966.

DeCeceo, J.P. *The psychology of learning and instruction.* Englewood Cliffs, N.J. : Prentice-Hall Inc., 1968.

Deutsch, M. *Minority group and class status as related to social and personal factors in scholastic achievement.* (Monograph No. 2) New York : Society for Applied Anthropology Monograph, 1960.

Dweck, C.S., and Reppucci, N.S. Learned helplessness and reinforcement responsibility in children. *Journal of Personality and Social Psychology*, 1973, **25**, 109-116.

Freire, P. *Pedagogy of the oppressed.* London : Penguin, 1970.

French, J.T. Educational desegregation and selected self-concept factors of lower class Black children. *Dissertation Abstracts International*, 1972, **33**, (5-A), 2167.

Gotteleib, D. Teaching and students : The view of Negro and White teachers. *Sociology and Education*, 1964, **37**, 345-353.

Green, R., and Faroqhar, W.W. Negro academic motivation and scholastic achievement. *Journal of Educational Psychology*, 1965, **56**, 241-243.

Hauser, Rober, M. *Socio-economic background and educational performance*, Washington : American Sociological Association, 1971.

Hess, H. I., and Maehr, M.L. Two experiments on the concept of self and the reaction of others. *Journal of Personality and Social Psychology*, 1965, **1**, 100-105.

Higgins, C., and Sivers, C.H. A comparison of Stanford Binet and Colored Raven's Progressive Matrices IQs for children with low socio-economic status. *Journal of Consulting Psychology*, 1958, **20**, 265-268.

Holland, J.L. Undergraduate origin of American scientist. *Science*, 1957, **126**, 433-437.

House P.A. The learning environment as a predictor of the academic self-concept of ninth grade mathematics students. *Dissertation Abstracts International*, 1973, **34**, 2460

Kleinfeld, J.S. Classroom climate and the verbal participation of Indian and Eskimo students in integrated classrooms. *Journal of Educational Research*, 1973, **67**, 51-52.

Knapp, R.H. and Goodrich, W.B. *Collegiate origins of American scientists.* Chicago : University of Chicago Press, 1952.

Knapp, R.H., and Greenbaum, J.J. *The younger American scholar : His collegiate origins.* Chicago : University of Chicago Press, 1953.

Kumar, K. Social climate in school and characteristics in pupils. *Indian Journal of Clinical Psychology, 1975, 2, 163-172.*

Lightfoot, A. The potency of social class in determining educational inequalities. In A. Lightfoot (Ed.) *Inquires into the social foundations of education*. Chicago : Rand McNally and Company, 1971.

Pace, C. R. *CUES : College and university environment scales : Technical Manual*. Princeton, New Jersey : Educational Testing Service, 1963.

Pffeifer, M.C. Jr. Relationship between scholastic aptitude, perception of university climate and college success for Black and White student. *Journal of Applied Psychology*, 1976, 61, 341-347.

Rath, R. "Personality and behavioural problems of the disadvantaged." Unpublished manuscript. Department of Psychology, Utkal University, 1976.

Rath R., Dash, A.S., and Dash, U.N. *Cognitive abilities and school achievements of socially disadvantaged children in primary schools*. Bombay : Allied Publishers Private Ltd., 1979.

Rosenthal, R. The Pygmalion effect lives. *Psychology Today*, 1973, 7, 56-63.

Ross, J.D. A study of the effect of learning environment on selected factors related to self-concept of school children. *Dissertation Abstracts International*, 1973, 33, 6600.

Rutter, M. Tizard, J., and Whitemore, K. (Eds.) *Education, health and behaviour*. New York : Longmans, 1970.

Schneider, B., and Hall, D.T. Toward specifying the concept of work climate : A study of Roman Catholic diocesan priests. *Journal of Applied Psychology*, 1972, 56, 447-455.

Shankar, P. Education and caste Hindu attitudes of Harijans. *Psychologia*, 1966, 9, 49-52.

Sharma, M. A comparative study of organizational climate of governmental secondary schools of Churu district, Rajasthan. *Journal of Educational Research and Extension*, 1969, 5, 120-126.

Shaw, M.C., Edison, K., and Bell, H.M. The self concept of bright under-achieving high school students as revealed by an adjective check-list. *Personal and Guidance Journal*, 1960, 39, 193-196.

Sinha, D. Age, schooling and socio-economic factors in the development of certain perceptual skills. *Indian Journal of Psychology*, 1977, 52, 115-132.

Smith, A.C. The relationship of school organizational climate and student morale in selected schools. *Dissertation Abstracts International*, 1973, 34, 543.

Stern, G.G. Environments for learning. In N. Stanford (Ed.) *The American College*. New York : John Wiley & Sons, 1962.

Tripathi, L.B., and Misra, G. Cognitive activities as a function of prolonged deprivation. *Psychologlcal Studies*, 1975, 21, 54-61.

Tripathi, R.C., and Pande, N. *Motivational consequences of educational climate*. Paper presented to the 14th Annual conference of the Indian Academy of Applied Psychology, Indian Institute of Technology, Kharagpur, 1976.

Weiner, B. Frezier I. Kukla, A. Reed, L. Rest, S., and Rosenbaum, R.M. *Perceiving the causes of success and failure*. New York : General Learning Press, 1971.

Williams, R.L. Cognitive and affective components of Southern Negro students attitude towards academic integration. *Journal of Social Psychology*, 1968, **76**, 107-111.

Yee, A.H. Source and direction of causal influence in teacher-pupil relationships. *Journal of Educational Psychology*, 1968, **59**, 275-282.

Zigler, E., and Abelson, W.D., and Seitz, V. Motivational factors in the performance of economically disadvantaged children in the Peabody Picture Vocabulary Test. *Child Development*, 1973, **44**, 294-303.

SECTION THREE

INTERVENTION STRATEGIES

INTRODUCTION

THE PAPERS included in the earlier section show that psychosocial and economic deprivations have deleterious effects on cognitive skills and motivations of children because of which they perform poorly in school. Although various sociopsychological variables (such as, variety of stimulation, social support, etc.) are said to be the immediate or proximal causes of these negative effects, the fact remains that they result because a child belongs to a socially disadvantaged group in the first place. Any serious attempt to ameliorate the effects of deprivation, which ignores this basic fact of social inequality, is destined to remain at best a palliative. However, fundamental structural changes do not come about in a short-time, and social scientists certainly do not make revolutions. Nevertheless, social scientists do have an important role to play in this connection; they can act as advocates of social equality and justice. Through their work they may help in developing a social consciousness among people which initiates and fosters movements against social inequality. This apart, what can be done in the case of those children who have been victims of social disadvantage? Various intervention programmes have been suggested to remove these effects and minimize educational failure (e.g., the Headstart programme). Most of these programmes have been marginally successful, largely because they have focused only on remediation of symptoms rather than on the *total process* of intervention programmes.

Although research on socially disadvantaged children has not lagged behind in this country, not much attention has been paid to the development of strategies of intervention for improving cognitive skills and motivations of the socially disadvantaged children. The Psychology Department at the Utkal University has, however, carried out a number of such programmes. The paper by R. Rath in this section is based on the experiences gathered by him as a result of such intervention programmes. Rath emphasizes the need for developing structured teaching programmes for the benefit of the disadvantaged. He suggests that specific programmes may be developed (i) to remove learning deficiencies due to pre-school environment (ii) learning deficiencies in special subjects, and (iii) to satisfy basic needs of the socially disadvantaged children. The paper also discusses strategies for bringing about changes in the academic motivations of disadvantaged children.

FOURTEEN

Radhanath Rath

PROBLEMS OF INTEGRATION OF THE DISADVANTAGED TO THE MAIN STREAM

INTRODUCTION

AFTER a very extensive and intensive investigation relating to intellectual depression, achievement lag and personality aberrations of the culturally and economically disadvantaged, remedial measures for the all round development of their cognitive abilities have to be spelt out by the educationists and psychologists. Such a democratic commitment of educating all such children to their fullest social and intellectual potential is a national goal. In fact, this has been the socio-political goal of the entire world in the second half of the twentieth century. In addition to various social and economic measures taken in this direction, equalisation of educational opportunities for all sections of the society, the rich and poor, the urban and rural,the socially advantaged as well as disadvantaged has been envisaged as one of the major instruments for upward social mobility of the disadvantaged mass. But the problems and obstacles in bringing the disadvantaged on par with the national-cultural-mainstream is so stupendous that unless the educationists, social reformers, political leaders and administrators work jointly with a single minded socio-political dedication, it is not possible to achieve this goal inspite of colossal expenditure of money in this regard. Appointment of additional teachers, construction of more school rooms and supply of books would definitely go a long way in achieving this end but still the education of the disadvantaged section of people, particularly of the tribal children would remain as backward as ever unless the entire network of educational system is revised. The very subtle psychological and cultural problems of the tribals and scheduled caste people will stand in the way of their integration to the mainstream through educational process.

The problem is a multi-dimensional one and requires extended consideration in terms of careful planning of the instructional objectives and procedures for dealing with their intellectual and motivational problems effectively. The real break-through in educating the disadvantaged children will come if we concentrate upon the methodology of teaching than upon the causes of the disadvantaged conditions (Cohen, 1969). Middle class children are found to be better prepared with respect to reading at the beginning years of their education and in this they are very much supported and encouraged by their home environments and teacher expectations. Research data indicate that 'learning set' or 'learning readiness' can be learned and, therefore, it can also be taught (Cohen, 1969). Perceptual dysfunction and cognitive deficits add up to low IQs. Perception and cognition are learned behaviours and can therefore, be acquired. Hence, much of what is IQ is learned, and therefore, disadvantaged can be given programmes for increasing their IQ. Evidences for such argument is clear from the findings of Clarke and Clarke (1953) who demonstrated increase in IQ of children from adverse home conditions by eight points or more on the Wechsler Scale.

Havighurst (1964) maintains, "there is substantial doubt that socially disadvantaged children in our big cities have any positive qualities of potential value in urban society in which they are systematically better than children of families who participate more fully in mass culture". It appears that disadvantaged children living in their own culture may have more positive values than those in the urban area with middle and upper class children. Just placing them in an enriched environment may decrease their self confidence and create reservoirs of anxiety which according to Freud, when released would engulf them in great psychic upheaval. Thus, they should not be treated as passive agents merely standing to gain out of exposure to upper class values and standards. This is an erroneous practice, which accounts for the most part of the failure of the intervention programmes. Another erroneous practice results out of overemphasis in the child guidance movement upon protecting the child from emotional stress by creating a supportive environment and resolving some of the psychic conflicts of these children. Such orientations consider the child as somewhat like a patient, thus, suggesting a role of protecting the child in the same manner as a zookeeper arranges for the survival of his charges (DeCecco, 1968). Therefore, Deutsch (1964) suggests cognitive growth as the best therapy and best means of attaining meaningful standards of living. All the more, equal attention should be focused upon their cognitive and affective aspects of life, since motivational and personal style variables have been shown to exercise significant influences in their cognitive retardation. At their admission to the first grade, evidence should be obtained on each child with regard to many aspects of his cognitive growth such as perceptual development, language development, ability to attend and memorize, development of verbal mediation and motivation for learning (Bloom, Davis & Hess, 1965). These evidences would go a long way in assessing their true level of entering behaviour and in planning appropriate instructional procedures. Well structured programmes should be introduced in the pre-school years during age 4 to 5 to raise their level of entering behaviour necessary for learning at the first grade. Evidence for more acceleration in mental development comes from a number of comparisons of different studies at different age levels.

The reasons for early intervention programmes are mainly three :

(i) The child's method of learning concepts, habit patterns and interest areas are probably well established at a fairly early age (DeCecco, 1968).

(ii) After the child has developed one cognitive style, he may have difficulty in developing a more useful one (Fowler, 1962). In case of disadvantaged children his early impulsive response tendency, preference for concrete reinforcement and goal structure and physical behaviour may block his further attempts to develop a style consistent with abstract problem solving and verbal behaviour.

(iii) The pre-school years serve as a bridge between the two cultures—one of his own, and the other of the culture of the school and the city in which he is placed. Beyond this phase, intervention programmes may come as a cultural shock to him.

DeCecco (1968) suggests that programmes for the disadvantaged children should utilize motivation derived from curiosity and exploratory behaviour by using tangible incentives and allowing them to work under concrete goal structure, that low SES children learn better with material rewards than with symbolic rewards has been supported by many experimental findings (Terrel, Durkin, & Wiesley, 1959; Spence, 1971). Since improper sequencing of experiences on their part blocks their academic achievement, provisions should be made to provide them with a sequential and hierarchical arrangement of learning experiences. Van De Riet, Van De Riet and Springle (1968) have shown the effectiveness of a new sequential learning programme with five-year-old culturally disadvantaged pre-school children. The performance of children who were given an experimental sequential programme of planned and guided learning experiences, were significantly superior to the control group, who were exposed to a traditional programme. One time exposure to material is usually insufficient for the successful learning of the disadvantaged children. Sufficient time should be given to the students for reviewing, repeating and practising of what he has learned for consolidation of his learning experiences.

With a view to improving language skills such as auditory learning, meaning of auditory symbols, recognising relationships between concrete and symbolic concepts and objects, using words in a sequence and impressive language, Olson and Larson (1965) suggested the use of puppets to dramatize well known stories and to allow the children to project their speech without any personal exposure. Newton (1960) stressed the techniques of synonymity in teaching language to the disadvantaged children. Synonymity is the teacher's restating of the difficult words in various different and similar ways. Since they are weak in their abstracting ability, they have more trouble with mathematics because of the abstract nature of the subject. Frement (1964) suggests some concrete representations to be used in teaching of mathematics. One can use automated programmes, commercial aids, mathematical games and puzzles, manipulative devices, etc., for the purpose. Because disadvantaged children use restricted code, the use of elaborated code in public schools by teachers mainly coming from high SES retards whatever proficiency they have in their native language. Hence, according to Bernstein (1961) the teacher's job is to "preserve for the disadvantaged child the appeal and dignity of his accustomed code, while making available to him the possibilities of expression in the elaborated code".

Along with the well structured teaching programme the impact of the school environment requires extended consideration. Yee (1969) after critically reviewing the literature, suggests the importance of (a) teacher's and pupils' interpersonal behaviour, (b) attitudinal patterns characterizing pupils' perception of teachers and vice versa, (c) the predominant source of influence in teacher-pupil interaction, and (d) direction of influence in this interaction. Coleman (1966) summarizes the effects of school environment and achievement in the context of compensatory educational programme for the disadvantaged children in the following ways :

(i) Low quality school environment affects the achievement of the disadvantaged much more adversely as compared to the advantaged. Improvement in school quality will bring about most of the improvement in their scholastic ability.

(ii) Achievement is strongly related to the educational backgrounds and aspirations of the other students in the school. The report shows that the principal way in which the school environments of low and middle SES children differ is in the composition of the student bodies: the latter has a strong (80) correlation with the achievement of low-SES students.

(iii) The amount of variation in achievement that school characteristics account for depends much more on students and teachers than on facilities and curricula.

(iv) A pupil attitude factor which appears to have a stronger relationship to achievement than do all the school factors together is the extent to which an individual feels that he has some control over destiny. Low SES students have far less conviction than that of the middle SES ones that they can affect their own environment and future.

In a comparative study of Negro and White teachers employed in school, where most of the students were low SES Negroes, Gottlieb (1954) found that White teachers wanted more realistic professional training for the students, whereas, Negro teachers expected in them more knowledge in the school subjects. While White teachers are of opinion that their job dissatisfaction is due to lack of students' ability and motivation, the Negro teachers mentioned large classes, poor equipment, inadequate facilities and improper curriculum as factors contributing to their dissatisfaction. Negro teachers perceived these children as "happy, energetic and fun loving" but the same children appeared to the White teachers as "talkative, lazy and rebellious". On the whole, White teachers emphasized more the shortcomings of the pupils while Negro teachers tended to see much of their problems due to inadequate physical conditions in which they are allowed to work. Hence suggestions may be made that for teaching the disadvantaged children well-trained teachers from their own society should be appointed, because these teachers would be in a position to assess their pupils' problems better and establish proper rapport with them, both in and out of the class room situations. Another source of evidence comes from the findings of Becker (1952) who investigated the problem of social class conflict between the teacher and the pupil. He located three problem areas of the teachers from high social class employed to teach the poor children : (i) the students seemed to lack interest, ability and necessary persistence for class room learning, (ii) teachers gave rise to certain disciplinary problems when they tried to control unrestrained and physically aggressive children and (iii) the children offended the teachers' moral sensitivity by word, action and appearance and the teachers constantly failed to stand the strain of it. Hence, the necessity of appointment of well experienced and trained teachers from their society to teach them is heightened. They can deal with their pupils meaningfully and with proper training can also mediate effectively the cultural values of the upper class.

Basing upon the experimental evidences many programmes and projects have been taken up in the past in the western countries to bring the vast sections of the disadvantaged to their national level. The two comprehensive programmes which have received much publicity were Demonstration Guidance Project in 1956 and the Higher Horizons Programme in 1959. Demonstration Guidance Project specifically dealt with Negro students and provided among others such services as: a modified curriculum, small classes, remedial instruction, cultural activities, counselling, clinical services and relations with parents. Both the projects were quite effective in raising the motivational level and scholastic achievements of these groups of children.

In India, the need of the time is to put special emphasis on offering well structured teaching programmes to the vast disadvantaged mass with a view to bringing them on par with the advantaged sections of the society. In spite of well intentioned efforts of educators, the tribal children still remain in isolated islands of stagnation. The suggestions made here would go a long way in launching a massive revolutionary programme of education to loosen the bed rock of stagnation of these isolated islands and to swell them into the midst of the national mainsteam.

It is rather gratifying to note that now greater emphasis is being laid on primary education and attempts are being made to bring all children to the school. But putting all the children in the schools does not solve the problem of primary education. Free and compulsory primary education will create many more serious problems than the present schooling of free choice admission system. In our existing schools, we do not know all the reasons why about 40 per cent of the children drop out after Class I and only approximately one in five continues up to Class V. It is still more disturbing that proportionately more of the scheduled caste and scheduled tribe children drop out after Class I compared to the upper caste children. Systematic psychological and socio-economic studies have not been attempted to diagnose the causes of such large scale drop outs. Do they drop out because they are not able to cope with class work ? Do they drop out because their parents cannot afford to maintain them in the schools, as the children themselves have to earn their own living ? Do the scheduled caste and scheduled tribe children leave the schools in disproportionately large numbers because their cognitive development is hampered in the complex cross cultural academic interactions ? What compensatory teaching programmes have to be introduced to bring up the culturally disadvantaged children to the normal group level ? The educationists and psychologists in India have certainly not done much work in these areas of primary education, which is, psychologically, the basic foundation of cognitive and intellectual growth of children. Here is the vast uncharted educational field which offers great challenges as well as exciting opportunities to psychologists and educationists of the country. They can use their talents in solving these difficult problems of education. This challenge should stimulate multi-dimensional experimental and applied investigations. Since many of the problems are also global, a large number of research projects could be planned and designed at the national level with multi-disciplinary approach. This, of course, does not exclude specific and individual research projects with a view to bring out crucial experimental evidences to unravel the very complicated psychological processes involved in pupils' intellectual operations and manipulation of learning skills.

REMEDIAL PROGRAMMES FOR INTEGRATION

Problems relating to cognitive growth and pre-school training programme

By the time the socially disadvantaged child comes to primary school at the age of 5 or 6, his cognitive growth is already depressed. His home environment is devoid of any intellectually stimulating conditions. The uneducated parents can not possibly satisfy natural curiosities of the child about the environment. His innumerable questions remain unanswered. The parents, being very poor, remain absent from home most of the time and the child stays with other children or uninformed old adults. The language used by them is extremely poor in expression and their verbal underdevelopment is all pervasive. Moreover, whatever language he uses at home is also quite different from the standard language used in the primary schools. The text books used in the school are written by writers belonging to the culturally advantaged class. The concepts and images symbolised in the standard use of words are, therefore quite foreign to the socially disadvantaged child. So, when he comes to Class I and reads the first Reader written in the standard language, he starts with zero linguistic information and conceptualisation, whereas a child belonging to the advantaged class has quite a few familiar concepts and linguistic associations in common. Circles A and B, which are quite exclusive by nature, represent the existing linguistic background and new expected areas of acquisition, respectively, in the socially disadvantaged. In the case of advantaged children the two circles have a great deal of overlapping area.

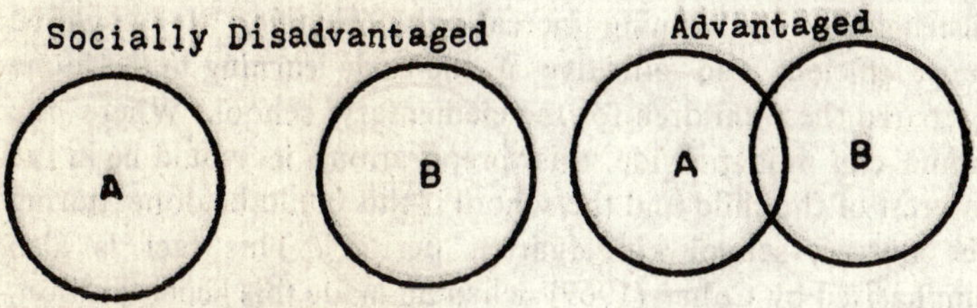

A—Linguistic background.
B—New area of acquisition required as per the text book.

In the case of the socially disadvantaged child, all the contents of circle B which is completely new to him are to be acquired whereas an advantaged child is required to acquire only a portion of area B. If they belong to the same class and are taught by the same teacher, the disadvantaged child is bound to develop certain amount of deficiency in linguistic and conceptual acquisition compared to the advantaged. Even if the disadvantaged child is taught in separate schools, still the deficiency would grow in a time bound linguistic curriculum. This deficiency acquired in Class I, will accumulate progressively as the child goes through other classes and his accumulated deficiency is ultimately responsible for his stagnation, dropping out and weaker motivation for higher education. Deficiency left unchecked at the earlier stage is likely to cause irreparable damage to intellectual as well as cognitive growth in the developing child. Deutsch (1965) calls this the "cumulative deficit phenomenon". Such deficits in Class I become more marked through the higher classes. In order to prevent this process of deterioration which may start in Class I of the primary school something has to be done before the child comes to school. Hence, there is a necessity of a preschool educational programme for these children.

There is experimental evidence to show that developmental processes before the age of 5 and 6 are extremely important for proper cognitive growth. Bloom (1964) states that about 50 per cent of development takes place between conception and age 4, about 30 per cent between ages 4 and 8 and about 20 per cent between ages 8 and 17. He further states that it is in the interest of the school to halt the cumulative deficits of these children as early as possible in order to make latter instruction and learning increasingly effective. "It would be most efficient and effective if the early learning in the home prepared these children for the elementary school. Where the home can not provide this preparation, it would be in the interest of the child and the school if this could be done during the nursery school kindergarten period". This fact is also emphasised by Cohen (1969) when he made this generalisation, "The earlier we apply compensatory, high intensity education, the better the results are likely to be. In an elementary school early intervention in the kindergarten or first grade, and, preferably in pre-kindergarten, is the best attack on the retardation in the culturally deprived child. The intermediate grades are dangerously late and junior high school compensatory education yields meagre results".

Then the next problem is to determine which behaviour can be taught and how they should be taught to influence children's general ability to learn. To help solve the problem of teaching learning at this stage Cohen (1969) suggests the following four models which are considered useful :

(1) The information processing model, including the processes of scanning, feedback and affective tone.
(2) The hierarchy of needs model to explain the psycho-dynamic factors of behaviour change.
(3) The syndrome model which establishes a scientific basis for considering the "whole child".
(4) The reading model which defines the reading act.

These models have to be worked out by the specialists depending upon the cognitive and other needs of the children at the pre-school stage.

Karnes (1958) has reported the efficacy of different educational programmes of intervention for pre-school children. Her work is based on five different kinds of intervention studies as stated below :

1. Traditional nursery school programme.
2. Montessori programme.
3. Community integrated programme in which several disadvantaged children were placed in a number of middle class nursery schools.
4. A highly structured direct verbal programme.
5. A programme designed to ameliorate learning deficits by Karnes.

The reported increase in Binet IQ for the five groups were as follows :

Community integrated	5.1
Montessori	5.5
Traditional nursery school	8.1
Amelioration of learning disabilities	14.3
Direct verbal approach	14.4

From the results it would appear that the newer programmes of amelioration of learning deficits and direct verbal approach are superior to other more common approaches to early childhood education (Kirk, 1968). It seems that the most effective approach would ultimately depend upon researches tried on our tribal children for whom the pre-school education is to be planned. But at the same time any meaningful and effective educational programming for the socially disadvantaged should clearly envisage the nature and type of deficiencies these children might have developed due to their socio-economic and cultural deprivation. It may be relevant to quote some of the major findings in this context.

Some of the components of basis cognitive deficiencies due

to impoverished home environments are enumerated as follows (DeCecco, 1968) :

(a) The environment lacks various types of objects to enrich visual perception (Deutsch, 1963).
(b) The non-verbal nature of environment leads to under development of auditory skills.
(e) As the adults are not in the habit of connecting the past and present meaningfully the children seem to have poor memory (Leshan, 1952).
(d) Adults are not capable of satisfying the curiosities of the children; so children do not depend on the adults for information.
(e) Language development is poor due to inadequate labelling of the environment at home.
(f) Speech sequences are poor and defective.

Thus the major deficiencies are in perceptual and verbal learning which have to be removed in pre-school learning situation before the children enter the regular school. With the help of various processes of reinforcement, perceptual training, behaviour modification, discriminatory form of recognition, etc., a child's verbal skills can be considerably developed. This, in turn, would stimulate his intellectual growth. In short, stimulus deprivation being one of the important causes of socio-cultural deprivation, and, as it is not possible to provide enrichment at home, all possible measures have to be taken to provide rich and complex stimulating environment in the pre-school situation for these children long before any formal education is imparted in the existing primary schools. Attempts should be made in such a way that the disadvantaged child develops a cognitive background with deep impressions of various concepts and their complex perceptual associations comparable to that of the advantaged child, so that the two circles representing cognitive background and the contents of the new education mentioned earlier do not exclude each other but rather overlap to a considerable extent. In other words, the pre-school compensatory education should be programmed for internalising this basic minimum in the disadvantaged.

In addition to the suggestions made above certain other basic characteristics about the nature of the disadvantaged children have to be kept in view in preparing the pre-school programme. Newton (1960) made the following observations to highlight the kind of difficulties the disadvantaged children and their teachers experience in a pre-school programme :

1. Culturally disadvantaged children seem generally unaware of the "ground rules" for success in school settings.
2. Culturally disadvantaged children are less able to learn from being told than are the middle class children.
3. Culturally disadvantaged children are often unable to make simple symbolic interpretations.
4. Culturally disadvantaged children tend to have short attention span and consequently have difficulty in following direction.
5. Culturally disadvantaged children are unable to use language in a flexible way.
6. Culturally disadvantaged children tend to have little concept of relative size.
7. Culturally disadvantaged children are less likely to perceive adults as people to whom they can turn for help.
8. Culturally disadvantaged children seem to have low level of curiosity about things.

Special compensatory programmes

The objective of pre-school education is to equip the disadvantaged children with an enriched cognitive background comparable to that of other advantaged children. This will enable them to come to the school with a marked self confidence. But when they go through the teaching-learning processes in the class room interaction due to various other reasons some of the disadvantaged children may not be able to cope with the ongoing progress of the class room teaching. Such children have to be picked up along with other advantaged children who may also be in the same position like the disadvantaged and all of them have to be given additional coaching in the subjects in which they fall behind in the class.

Teachers with specialised training to tackle the subject-wise backward children should take up the responsibilities of making them up-to-date in their weak subjects, Disadvantaged children need greater help, especially, in subjects like language and arithmetic. They need the maximum help in language training. Not only they do not use the book language at home but due to restricted and limited verbal use in the disadvantaged homes they are not accustomed to use complex sentences and symbolised concepts. Such cases are tackled very effectively in the schools of the U.S.A. by specially trained teachers. At this stage the teacher has to examine the deficiency on multi-dimensional considerations. It has to be specifically diagnosed as to whether the deficiency is related to intra-sensory or inter-sensory disabilities or whether it is verbal or non-verbal or it relates to the effects of the disability to types of educational achievement or to the effect of learning disability on total social maturity (Jensen, 1971).

Compensatory training based on such specific diagnosis is very effective in the earlier classes. At the secondary school stage it becomes extremely difficult to tackle this problem with considerable success. Many successful experiments have been tried in the advanced countries in this respect. There is no reason why the disadvantaged children of our country also cannot be brought up to the normal class room standard in course of time unless some of them are intellectually retarded to a level of uneducability.

Jensen (1971) and others suggest differentiated education depending on individual differences of the children. If the tribal child is good at drawing and some other kind of skills involving finger dexterity and muscular manipulation, etc., he should be given that kind of training more and more along with the basic minimum achievement in language and arithmetic. There should not be a standardised curriculum for all children even at the elementary school stage. For such children there could be greater emphasis on work-study plans in which they can learn in relation to work experience. This is certainly important for all but it is especially useful for the tribal and other disadvantaged children.

Satisfaction of basic needs of the disadvantaged children

The disadvantaged children come from very poor families. All the members of the family, adults as well as children go out for work to sustain their livelihood. So the adults are not interested in allowing their children to go to school. Even if some of them do come to school, these starving children are not likely to go through any kind of meaningful education in the pre-school or regular school situations. In one of our studies (Roy & Rath, 1972) it was found that the tribal children could be attracted to schools if mid-day meals were provided. Enrolment of tribal children in Class I was considerably increased in the schools supplying mid-day meals. But as the meals were found to be of poor quality and were provided irregularly during the year the children started dropping out from Class II onwards. Thus, no education of any kind is possible unless full meals are supplied to these children at least during the day and throughout the year. When meals are discontinued, the children go back to their earlier ways of behaviour to collect food. Since, this habit is very strongly embedded in them from early childhood it is easier for them to revert to the older habits once the meals are discontinued. The older habits, by no means should be reinforced in them even for a temporary period. Once the basic biological need is satisfied a positive motivation for education could be initiated in these children. They should not only be fed but also affectionately looked after by the teacher in-charge of pre-school education.

In addition to this biological need, the tribal child has another very important need—his need for affiliation to the other group which is supposed to represent another culture. The teaching agencies are absolutely new to him and his social group. He is likely to have a sense of hostility and dissatisfaction towards school. This is an important psycho-social barrier between the teacher and the taught in such schools. If the teacher belongs to his own community this hostility may be less, but the very fact that he is required to enter into a new area of psycho-social interaction with the child the feeling of hostilily and suspicion would remain in the child. This barrier has to be broken by the teacher by creating an atmosphere of sympathy and affection and fostering a sense of confidence in the child. By this process, the need for affiliation is taken care of.

With the satisfaction of these two basic needs of the tribal child, a stronger and lasting motivating base can be built in him and he will gradually become an active member of the other group—the group representing new culture and education.

Problems relating to personality adjustment

School as a social institution provides a completely new environment for the tribal and disadvantaged children. They are expected to become active participants in this new culture. To start with, they face problems of adjustment to this new social situation imposed on them. The adjustment problem is also linked with personality deficiencies which they are likely to develop in the context of educational process. In the atmosphere of new sub-culture the disadvantaged children may develop low self esteem and inferiority in comparison with others. There are enough evidences to indicate that, children with low level of aspiration and almost zero educational background have low self-esteem and possess a strong sense of inferiority. This itself may be the single major cause of early drop out. This problem has to be tackled by specially trained staff including the subject teachers. This is not only true of scheduled tribe children but it is characteristic of any group of culturally deprived and socially disadvantaged. Here, due to social isolation and cultural segregation the scheduled caste communities are found to have more personality aberrations compared to upper caste communities.

Creation of a new set of goals and social reinforcement

As mentioned earlier tribal children have lower levels of aspiration in every sphere of life. Their goal orientations are nothing but the internalised low aspirations of their parents. The upper class children as well as their parents have much higher levels of goal aspirations. The former are likely to respond more to tangible and immediate rewards compared to the latter who have learned to look for more symbolised, more distant and more deferred goals which have greater social value. The disadvantaged children will have greater difficulties in visualising any future rewards. So the teacher should be more conscious of this fact and arrange a set of social reinforements accordingly. But it is not always an easy thing to do so, unless the need system of these children is radically altered. This reorientation is possible through a series of non-formal educational programme. Short films and special story books and other forms of non-formal teaching aids prepared for them with a view to emphasising new goals and orientations of social values have to be presented to them constantly in the schools. This is likely to reinforce their aspirations in different directions. Mobile vans with appropriate equipment fitted inside and the television, which is being introduced in India now, would go a long way in strengthening this reorientation programme.

Problems relating to aspirational level

From our studies it is clearly seen that levels of educational and income aspirations as well as job requirements are extremely low in the scheduled caste and scheduled tribe children as well as their fathers. This is really a very serious matter in the context of equalising educational opportunities for children. With such low levels of aspiration it is difficult to retain these children in the school for long. If the parental aspirations which normally force the children to come to the school and continue their education for a longer period is also low, then it is almost impossible to keep them in school for long. If the parents of low caste groups do not want education for their children no amount of slogans and verbal persuasion is likely to succeed in creating stronger motivation in their children. So such children who come to school under extraneous pressure with no stable aspirations or motivations are not likely to go very far. When the teaching and learning situation is dull and it becomes increasingly difficult for these children to cope with it, they drop out of school as quickly as possible. As there is no push from home and no pull from the school the children adopt the normal behaviours of escape from such a painful and constrained situation.

The author had an occasion to discuss this in a seminar attended by a group of educationists belonging to the top elite class. Some prominent participants raised the question as to why people were so worried about the low level of aspiration of the scheduled caste and scheduled tribe people. Their argument was, when the country today is unable to provide jobs to the existing educated unemployed, why should we try to raise the level of aspiration of the tribals who, according to them were quite happy with their low level of aspiration. Unfortunately attitude of the upper class educated is at the care of those who count in shaping the national policy of education of this country. This may explain the fact that 15 per cent of the tribal college going children in one study were not even aware of the special reservations of jobs, etc. (Rath & Misra, 1973). This pernicious social philosophy and attitude of mind of the elite has to be fought tooth and nail; otherwise, a section of the Indian population will remain backward for all time to come. It is absolutely desirable that all possible efforts should be made through mass-media to raise their level of aspiration.

Teacher-parent training

It is found that due to poor educational family background of the disadvantaged children the teachers have a low estimation of their intelligence and educational abilities compared to other children. They may think that they cannot learn as well as other class children. This discouraging attitude of the teachers is imperceptibly transmitted to these children in the class room situation. This inevitably creates a negative study atmosphere for the already disadvantaged children. Moreover, the specialised pre-school and co-curricular compensatory, education would never be a success unless the teachers are warm, flexible, affectionate and have patience and a sense of humour. Such teachers have to be especially recruited and trained by specialists like psychologists, linguists, and language therapists and other educational professionals. In other words, any teacher can not impart special education either at the pre-school or at the co-curricular stages without specialised training for the purpose.

Moreover, as this programme has to be concerned with the whole child and not just with his class room achievement, close cooperation with the parents as well as the other educational, health and welfare agencies available in the locality is considered essential. This programme should also include a lot of outside activities including, summer camps, sports and other interesting recreational activities.

It may not be difficult to train teachers to take up this responsibility of educating these children but it may be extremely difficult to involve their parents in the process of education. But at the same time it is very much necessary to inculcate a new attitude in the parents towards the education of their children. Their low motivation and level of aspiration for education is internalised by their children. So they have to be involved in the educational process. As they they have no idea about the utility and social implications of education, they have to be given a new ideological orientation, however weak and ineffective it might be in the beginning. If some homes are extremely pathological and reactionary the school should provide dormitory facilities for these children who may be kept away from homes exerting negative influences on their newly formed attitudes and their emotional and social adjustments.

In addition to special educational programmes meant for the children of the disadvantaged all kinds of non-formal educational programmes may be introduced for the adults. The new educational processes should be so linked up with the day-to-day work of people that it would be easier for them to accept it. Education must not only be theoretical. It must work and must be made an integral part of the processes. The up-to-date methods of educational technology and audio-visual aids could be utilised for the purpose. In other words, the society should be involved in a gigantic mass movement to facilitate the processes of change.

REFERENCES

Becker, H.S. Social-class variations in the teacher-pupil relationship. *Journal of Educational Sociology*, 1952, **25**, 451-65.

Bernstein, B. Social structure, language and learning. *Educational Research*, 1961, **3**, 163-176.

Bloom, B. *Stability and change in human characteristics*. New York; John Wiley and Sons, 1964.

Bloom, B., Davis, A., and Hess, R. *Compensatory education for cultural deprivation*. New York : Holt, Rinehart and Winston, 1965.

Clarke, A.D.B., and Clarke, A.M. How constant is the I.Q. *Lancet*, 1953, 2, 877-880.

Cohen, A S. *Teach them all to read.* New York : Random House, 1969.

Coleman, J.S. *Equality of educational opportunity.* Washington, D.C. : U.S. Department of Health, Education and Welfare, 1960.

DeCecco, J.P. *The psychology of learning and instruction.* New York : Prentice-Hall, 1968.

Deutsch, M. Nursery education : The influence of social programming on early development. *Journal of Nursery Education*, 1963, **19**, 191-97.

Deutsch, M. Facilitating development in the pre-school child : Social psychological perspectives *Merril-Palmer Quarterly*, 1964, **10**, 249-63

Deutsch, M. The role of social class in language development and cognition. *American Journal of Orthopsychiatry*, 1965, **35**, 77-78.

Fowler. W. Cognitive learning in infancy and early childhood. *Psychological Bulletin*, 1962, **59**, 116-152.

Frement, H. Some thoughts on teaching mathematics to disadvantaged groups. *Arithmetic Teacher*, 1964, **11**, 319-322.

Gottlieb, D. Teaching and students : The views of Negro and White teachers. *Sociology of Education*, 1964, 37, 345-353.

Havighurst, R.J. Who are the socially disadvantaged ? *Journal of Negro Education*, 1964, **33**, 210-217.

Karnes, M.B. *The effects of various pre-school intervention programmes.* Paper presented at the AREA Convention, Chicago, February 10, 1958.

Kirk, S A. *Cultural deprivation and its modification : Effects of intervention.* Paper presented at the International Conference on socio-cultural aspects of mental retardation, Nashville, 1968.

Leshan, L L. Time orientation and social class. *Journal of Abnormal and Social Psychology*, 1952, **48**, 589-592.

Newton, E.S. Verbal destitution : The pivotal barrier to learning. *Journal of Negro Education* 1960 , **29**, 111-113.

Olson, J.L. and Larson. R.G. An experimental curriculum for culturally deprived kindergarten children. *Educational Leadership*, 1965. (May).

Rath, R. From social isolation to stagnation : A study of scheduled caste students. *Social Action*, 1974, 24, 101-116 (a).

Rath, R., and Misra, S.K. *The study of scheduled caste and scheduled tribe college students in Orissa.* Project Report, Indian Council of Social Science Research, New Delhi, 1973.

Roy, P., and Rath, R. *School lunch in Orissa.* Delhi : Council for Social Development, 1972.

Spence, J.T. Do material rewards enhance the performance of lower class children. *Child Development*, 1971, 42, 1461-70.

Terrel, G. Jr., Durkin, K., and Wiesley, M. Social class and the nature of the incentive in discrimination learning, *Journal of Abnormal and Social Psychology*, 1959, **59**, 270-272.

Van De Riet, V., Van De Riet, H., and Springle, H. The effectiveness of a new sequential learning program with culturally disadvantaged pre-school children. *Journal of School Psychology*, 1968, **69**, 5-15.

Yee, A.H. Social interaction in class rooms : Implications for the education of disadvantaged pupils. *Urban Education*, 1969, 203-219.

INDEX